Past, Present, and Future Research on Teacher Induction

Past, Present, and Future Research on Teacher Induction

An Anthology for Researchers, Policy Makers, and Practitioners

Jian Wang, Sandra J. Odell, and Renée T. Clift

Published in partnership with the
Association of Teacher Educators

ROWMAN & LITTLEFIELD PUBLISHERS, INC.
Lanham, Maryland • *New York* • *Toronto* • *Plymouth, UK*
2010

Published in partnership with the Association of Teacher Educators

Published in the United States of America
by Rowman & Littlefield Education
A division of Rowman & Littlefield Publishers, Inc.
A wholly owned subsidary of The Rowman & Littlefield Publishing Group, Inc.
4501 Forbes Boulevard, Suite 200, Lanham, Maryland 20706
http://www.rowmaneducation.com

Estover Road, Plymouth PL6 7PY, United Kingdom

British Library Cataloguing in Publication Information Available

Library of Congress Cataloging-in-Publication Data

Past, present, and future research on teacher induction : an anthology for
researchers, policy makers, and practitioners : a collaborative work of the
Commission on Teacher Induction and Mentoring, Association of Teacher
Educators / edited by Jian Wang, Sandra J. Odell, and Renée T. Clift.
    p. cm.
  Includes bibliographical references.
  ISBN 978-1-60709-762-4 (cloth : alk. paper) — ISBN 978-1-60709-763-1 (pbk. :
alk. paper) — ISBN 978-1-60709-764-8 (electronic)
  1. Teacher orientation—Research. I. Wang, Jian, 1960. II. Odell, Sandra J. III.
Clift, Renée Tipton. IV. Association of Teacher Educator. Commission on Teacher
Induction and Mentoring.
  LB1729.P37 2010
  371.1—dc22

                                                                    2010006264

©™ The paper used in this publication meets the minimum requirements of
American National Standard for Information Sciences—Permanence of Paper
for Printed Library Materials, ANSI/NISO Z39.48-1992.
Manufactured in the United States of America.

Contents

Introduction

Jian Wang, University of Nevada, Las Vegas
Renée T. Clift, University of Arizona
Sandra J. Odell, University of Nevada, Las Vegas with
 Pearl Mack, Harvey, IL, Public School, District No. 152
Sharon A. Schwille, Michigan State University and
 Michael Strong, Center for Research on the Teaching
 Profession, University of California, Santa Cruz

In 2004 Ed Pultorak, then the president of the Association of Teacher Educators (ATE), created the Commission on Teacher Induction and Mentoring and charged it with providing the association and the profession with a synthesis of the most current knowledge of the scope and impact of teacher induction. The members of the commission, which included experienced teacher educators, researchers, program developers, and practitioners working in the field of teacher induction, identified the important issues and surveyed the existing research on teacher induction to get a general sense of the field. Over the duration of the Commission, members included Sandra J. Odell (Commission Chair), Renée Tipton Clift, Katherine Cummings, Richard Lange, Pearl Mack, Ed Pultorak, Virginia Resta, Sharon Schwille, Randi N. Stanulis, Michael Strong, Jian Wang, Elizabeth A. Wilkins, and Ann Wood.

This volume is the result of five years of the Commission's attention to current and past practices in the implementation and study of mentoring and induction programs for novice teachers. The editors of this volume, Commission Chair Sandra J. Odell and members Jian Wang and Renée Clift, agreed to compile the work of the Commission and that of others who are dedicated to studying induction and mentoring.

Induction and mentoring crosses three professional education communities—district-level and classroom-level teaching, teacher education practice, and scholarly practice. Three Commission members, Pearl Mack, Sharon Schwille, and Michael Strong, agreed to provide their individual commentaries on what they see as the role of research on induction and mentoring.

Their comments are interspersed with our description of the content and scope of this volume.

OVERVIEW

The first part of the book, containing the first five chapters, provides a scholarly assessment of the conceptual and practical background related to induction and mentoring. Feiman-Nemser's chapter analyzes the discourse concerning induction and mentoring and identifies the possible relationships among three meanings of induction and subsequent policy and practice.

Paine and Schwille provide a cross-national analysis of induction and mentoring as they document the ways in which the transition of teacher candidates into the teaching profession is enabled outside of the United States. Flores also provides an international perspective of the ways in which school cultures directly and indirectly do and do not provide support for beginning teachers. Youngs, Qian, and Holdgreve-Resendez review the literature on urban diverse contexts and their influences on teacher induction in U.S. school settings. Finally, Pultorak and Lange describe how different states within the United States have adopted polices and practices to assist new teachers.

The six chapters that constitute the second part of the book review recent empirical studies on the components of induction and mentoring, the methods of inquiry, and the impact (or lack of impact) of individual components or entire induction programs. Reiman, Corbell, Horne, and Walker-DeVose conceptualize beginning teaching as learning to take on new roles as they analyze the implications of research on role quality for supporting and retaining new teachers. Smith and Finch describe the research on retention from a different, but complementary, perspective in their critique of research designs and methodologies. Hanson documents the research on how induction impacts mentors and highlights how little research there is on this important topic.

Wood and Stanulis consider what we have learned about effective program components based on the development of induction and mentoring in the United States. Clift, Hebert, Cheng, Moore, and Clouse analyze the emerging, and understudied, use of the Internet to support beginning teachers. In the final chapter of this part, Carver traces university-based teacher preparation program attempts to support beginning teachers from preservice preparation through the beginning years of teaching.

The last part of the book provides concrete examples of current research on teacher induction. Each of the four empirical studies uses a different research design and methodology. Achinstein and Athanases's mixed-methods study investigates mentors' abilities to engage novice teachers in teaching second-language learners in ways that promote social justice. Luft, Neakrase, Adams, Firestone, and Bang provide qualitative and quantitative data on the importance of subject-matter-specific induction for beginning science teachers.

Isenberg, Glazerman, Johnson, Dolfin, and Bleeker report on a large-scale, quantitative study of student achievement by comparing two nationally recognized induction programs with local, district-based programs. Huling and Resta also examine student achievement by offering a new methodological approach to ascertaining induction program impact.

WHY IS CONDUCTING AND EXAMINING RESEARCH IMPORTANT?

To answer this question we now turn to our commentators—three Commission members whose active participation in debates, wonderings, and affirmations offers three overlapping answers concerning the important role of research in informing practice, policy, and induction and mentoring program design.

Pearl Mack: An Experienced Teacher Mentor from Harvey Public School, District No. 152

School administrators and committed teachers have always viewed mentoring as one of the more important endeavors to effective teaching that positively impact student learning. As a result, the public school district in Illinois where I taught for thirty-eight years ventured onto rocky ground and sought money to implement induction programs during the early 1990s with little to no documented research as a guiding base. Each district had its separate and unique set of criteria for commencing to deliver, change, or eliminate its respective mentoring and induction program. Almost everyone worked independently. Progress and/or problems were shared and discussed primarily at conferences or periodic professional meetings.

Teacher Involvement

Oftentimes, teachers' voices were not included in program design or in setting program goals. Nor were teachers among those attending the state level and national professional conferences. As a collective group, teachers had little concrete knowledge of mentoring programs that were being designed, monitored, or changed. They had little comprehension of what the objectives were for all the facets of the mentoring program, including what had been achieved and what was expected of future mentors. Important lessons learned from this experience included what not to do and the pitfalls to avoid in program development.

Teachers want the best practitioners with verifiable qualifications and inclusive attitudes to be mentors. Criteria for evaluating individual mentors and the results they achieve at specified times throughout the program should be essential data. Mentors should be able to embrace and demonstrate the best teaching strategies; they should exemplify appropriate professional dispositions. They should also be inclusive. It is not the total responsibility of any one person or group in the education field to act as the only contact with the community. The collective *we* must continue to maintain close connection with the community. All of us are accountable for keeping everyone informed of progress in meeting the needs of the students, the community, and society.

Administrator Involvement

District superintendents and other district administrators must function as collaborative partners—seeking, incorporating, supporting, and respecting new teachers and mentors. This is essential in building a foundation for educators to analyze, engage in purposeful discussion, and exchange ideas as well as opinions. All of these activities should be able to utilize reliable data to modify and improve induction and mentoring programs. Both data and the ability to work together will help eliminate any barriers that may be raised by strong-willed and/or highly opinionated educators and noneducators. Administrators and teachers should be able to look to researchers to collect, analyze, and share the data. These data will be useful for those who want to continue, to expand, and to improve mentoring and induction programs.

The Importance of Data and Decision Making

In my experience, each year that we gathered more information enabled us to see the program more clearly and to reassess where we were and what plans we needed to make to get us where we needed to be. Establishing benchmarks and using them as tools to help make accurate predictions and decisions regarding the elimination of parts of the program that were not working was not only beneficial but also put everyone on the same page. It created conditions for reaching agreements and resolving problems. Recognizing progress on many levels also reveals and permits us to assert that further tweaking in some areas relative to matching personnel must occur.

During those years of early trial and error, the districts' goals were seldom met. I fully expect that future mentoring and induction programs will be designed to enable practitioners to improve their ability to ensure that our students' social, emotional, environmental, physical, and mental needs are being met. My belief as a practitioner is that all of us who work in educational settings must collectively perfect our skills to create diverse learning opportunities for all students. We go without debate, and needless to say at warp speed, hoping we are ahead or at least abreast of our students in using and incorporating technology in our daily lives. This may also hold true for those who teach teachers. We have, without question, entered that zone of needing to rapidly adapt to this Age of Information and to work with one another.

Working Together

Practitioners expect that when states, special interest groups, or foundations cease to fund mentoring and induction programs, public school districts will. When the district commits the financial resources necessary for continuation of the program, they will enable school staff, colleagues, and university faculty members to work collaboratively. Some districts are truly getting it right. More districts have released-time or full-time coordinators for their mentoring programs. These districts are fully committed, and it is reflected in their budgets. We are in a better place than we were in the early 1990s. We haven't arrived at where we want to be, but it is doable.

Progress will occur faster when more districts sign on, when more colleges and universities link to their respective districts, and community leaders and activists make sure state and national legislators hear our collective voice. Research can contribute much to helping the education community and our country understand the importance of teachers. With the documentation of findings being discussed in a variety of forums across the United States, legislators and their aides can see what roles they need to play if our nation is to move beyond surviving and take actions for thriving.

I wholeheartedly believe mentors working with mentees elevate the level of teaching that happens in classrooms every day. These talented practitioners do more than guide learners toward successful completion at different educational levels to pick up certificates, diplomas, or degrees. They help students master new knowledge and acquire skills and strategies for lifelong learning. I also hold in my own core values the belief that to remain a world-class nation, our schools, our students, and our teachers must not be isolated, separated, or allowed to fail.

Sharon A. Schwille: A Preservice Teacher Education Program Director at Michigan State University

As a teacher preparation program director, I have much at stake in research on effective induction programs that include a strong mentoring component. Preservice teacher preparation programs can only go so far toward preparing a beginner to teach effectively and to use methods that promote sophisticated student learning. Although preservice teachers have field experiences, typically in an experienced teacher's classroom, the classroom teacher and a university supervisor can only help the prospective teacher begin to learn to teach.

This preservice experience prepares a novice teacher to move along a developmental continuum, and well-designed induction programs continue a beginning teacher's learning and intellectual growth. Teacher preparation program directors can design better transition experiences for novice teachers if they know what kinds of mentoring are effective in relation to subject-matter content and pedagogy and in relation to teaching context.

Context Matters

Each induction program is nested in a school and district context; in most programs a mentoring component is nested within the induction program. Each of these "nests" has some influence on what and how the novice teacher both should learn and can learn. Research into the influence these contexts have on beginning teachers' learning helps us understand characteristics of supportive contexts and how that support affects novices' learning, teaching, and retention in the profession. It also helps us better prepare mentors and cooperating teachers in the preservice programs.

As Feiman-Nemser, Schwille, Carver, and Yusko (1999) pointed out, mentoring aimed at educating rather than simply providing social and/or emotional support requires mentors to learn an approach for teaching novices that differs from classroom teaching. Research into contextual characteristics and learning opportunities that foster such learning can inform teacher preparation program directors' work and the preservice preparation curriculum. More research on how electronic contexts can enhance a novice's learning to teach and a mentor's learning to mentor will also be valuable.

With the use of technology, teaching is becoming less dependent on face-to-face instruction. Electronic platforms provide contexts that can facilitate professional development for mentors to learn the practice of mentoring as well as offer a means for mentors to communicate with beginning teachers without always having to be physically present in the novice's classroom (Bierema and Merriam, 2002; Klecka, Cheng, and Clift, 2004). Research on the differences between, and the effects of, electronic mentoring and face-to-face mentoring can help all participants, including program developers, make wise choices in delivery systems.

Assessing Impact Matters

The more we can learn about how effective mentors enable beginning teachers to enhance students' learning, the more able we are to teach effective mentoring practices to those who work with both preservice and in-service novices.

For example, the Launch into Teaching team at Michigan State University is concentrating on mentoring beginning teachers to learn and use certain targeted teaching practices, such as accountable talk, academic rigor, and clear expectations, within specific subjects. The team's early findings indicate that what they term *intensive mentoring* is resulting in beginning teachers shifting toward the targeted teaching practices (Stanulis, Wibbens, and Little, in review). This kind of focused research on mentor development, teaching practices, and student learning will do much to help us understand the complexities of mentoring and learning to teach and thereby help program developers construct either a preservice or induction program with clearer and more precise goals for beginning teacher learning.

We need to learn more about the intricacies and nuances of effective mentoring. Most mentoring occurs through talk, so it is important to learn what effective mentors talk about and how they do that talk. Research such as Wang, Strong, and Odell (2004) and Strong and Baron (2004) give us insights into mentoring conversations. We need to build on such studies to learn what is important to talk about and how that talk should occur to best move a beginning teacher's thinking and practice to a deeper or more sophisticated level.

We need to learn more about other approaches to mentoring (other than conferencing) that result in beginning teacher learning. For example, Feiman-Nemser (2001) gives us a vivid portrait of a mentor that she identifies as exemplary, one who not only talks with his beginning teacher but also models teaching practice for him. More case studies of exemplary mentors would help us understand the common characteristics as well as the differences in their mentoring practices.

Improved student learning is the ultimate goal of teaching and, therefore, an important component of an effective induction program. In spite of the difficulties in connecting student learning to beginning teacher support through induction programs and especially mentoring, recent studies are attempting to examine this link, many of which are discussed later in this book. Strong (2009) laid out the multiple challenges in designing and implementing a study that would provide evidence that an induction program, and more specifically intensive mentoring, results in improved student achievement as measured by standardized test scores. With more research on the relationship among induction programs, intensive mentoring, teachers' practices, and student learning, we can determine how to improve programs and delivery systems.

Conclusion

Empirical research that clarifies the complexities and intricacies of the roles of induction and mentoring on learning to teach will help teacher preparation program directors and developers design| educative, cost-effective opportunities for mentors and mentees that are rich learning experiences for all participants. It will also help us understand the university's role in designing and offering induction support for beginning teachers.

For example, at this point we do not know if university faculty members offer resources and areas of expertise that cannot be duplicated by school districts. We cannot say what enables partnerships between school districts and universities in their efforts to help support teachers. Research can bring us closer to answering these questions in more definitive ways and can then help program developers design appropriate structures to provide optimal learning for preservice and in-service beginning teachers and their mentors.

Michael Strong: A Researcher at the Center for Research on the Teaching Profession, University of California, Santa Cruz (former director of Research, New Teacher Center)

New teacher induction and mentoring programs have been prominent in schools across many parts of the world for long enough that we should, by now, have a good idea of the effects they have on teachers, students, and the education process. One of the most common questions that educators and policy makers are asking about teacher induction (and indeed about most educational interventions) is whether it has a positive effect on student learning. This question is one of the most difficult to address because of all the variables that might influence changes in student learning. Other common questions concern the effects on teacher retention and new teachers' practices and about which kinds of induction support are likely to have the more positive outcomes.

The call for induction research is tempered by the difficulty in accessing relevant data and the scarcity of research funding. Furthermore, the complexities of designing studies that enable us to draw causal conclusions lead us to conduct nonexperimental or quasi-experimental research in natural-istic settings where important design elements, such as random assignment of students to classes or of professional development interventions to teachers, are typically not possible.

In 2005 Mathematica Policy Research was funded by the Institute of Education Sciences to study induction treatment to new teachers in several large school districts using a randomized controlled trial (RCT) design (Glazerman, Senesky, Seftor, and Johnson, 2006; Isenberg, Glazerman, Bleeker, Johnson, Lugo-Gil, et al., 2009). This study is described elsewhere in this volume, so I will not describe it in detail here.

Suffice it to say that there were challenging methodological and definitional issues that impacted the research and the conclusions that could be drawn. For example, all mentors in the treatment group were using a new approach to mentoring for the first time. Furthermore, not all teachers attended all of the required professional development sessions that were offered. For the implementation to be successful and if comparisons are to be made, it is important that people actually participate in the treatment.

In an attempt to assess impact, Mathematica looked for differences between the two groups with regard to intensity of support, classroom practice, student achievement, teacher retention, and the composition of the district's teaching workforce. Intensity was significantly higher for the treatment group, although differences were a lot smaller than might have been expected (average time with mentor over one week was ninety-five versus seventy-four minutes; average time the mentor modeled a lesson was eleven versus seven minutes; average time in one-on-one meetings with a mentor was thirty-four versus twenty-one minutes). Given the small relative differences in intensity between the two groups, one might argue that the study failed to identify treatment and control groups that were sufficiently distinct.

RCT studies are considered by some to be the gold standard for research. The main disadvantage of randomized controlled studies lies in the threat to external validity posed by the artificiality of the experimental treatment. It may be argued that this was indeed a problem for the Mathematica study. If we cannot get satisfaction from such a well-funded, large-scale study conducted by experts in this kind of research, what then should we be seeking in induction research? I propose two areas of study that would be useful to program designers and policy makers.

Investigations on the Components of Induction Support

We need to discover which components (such as orientation, new teacher learning communities, mentoring, release time to observe veterans, etc.) and in what forms they are most likely to produce the outcomes of interest. Mentoring, for example, can be provided in many ways. Teachers may be assigned a full-time mentor, a part-time mentor, or a colleague who has no formal release time for mentoring. What is the relative effectiveness of these kinds of mentoring? What is the ideal caseload for a full-time mentor? Is it more beneficial to have a mentor readily accessible in the same school or an itinerant mentor who is independent of the school politics? How much time should be devoted to mentoring and observation? What kinds of training should mentors receive? How should mentors be matched with teachers?

Research studies in different program settings can help answer these and countless other questions related to program components. They can be qualitative to describe the components, and then quasi-experimental to compare groups of teachers receiving different program variations, with randomization when possible. We can often learn as much from several smaller studies that show a pattern as from one large-scale study that attempts to do it all at once.

Studies Showing How Induction Support Affects Teaching Practice

There are several difficulties that arise when attempting to document how teaching practice changes as a result of mentoring and induction. Most of the complexities revolve around the observation and measurement of teaching practice—what to observe, when to observe, how to observe, how long to observe. Teacher observation is difficult, time-consuming, and expensive.

Additionally, there are so many individual differences among beginning teachers that it is difficult to construct a sample where one can be confident that observed differences in practice are due to induction and mentoring as opposed to variations in teacher preparation, personality, student characteristics, school setting, principal support, subject matter differences, grade level, and so on. Some researchers choose to interview teachers about their classroom practice rather than observe them in action, losing in reliability what they gain in efficiency. Good research on the effects of induction and mentoring on teacher practice requires a clear idea of which practices are to be measured, a valid and reliable measurement instrument, and a design that allows for comparison between groups of teachers with and without the target induction intervention.

Although the common call is for research that shows effects on student achievement, I would advocate more strongly for research that demonstrates how induction and mentoring improve teacher practice. Since we have robust evidence that good teaching is the most powerful influence on student learning, if researchers can show that induction programs result in the accelerated development of a teacher's skills, then we can deduce that induction is also positively influencing student learning.

THIS VOLUME AS A COLLECTIVE
RESPONSE TO THE NEEDS OF THE FIELD

Our three commentaries inspire us to address several issues. First, the research community must address the differing needs of different types of practitioners by providing useful research on how to collaborate with each other in selecting mentor teachers, establishing mentor-novice relationships, promoting effective mentoring process, and providing necessary resources for teacher induction. The research must also enable practitioners to generate and disseminate the data-based information themselves.

Second, research and practitioners working together must examine the ways various contexts for teacher induction can shape and influence both the components and processes of teacher induction programs. It is important for the community to help the induction program developers to understand the effects of various programs sponsored by the school districts, individual schools, regional consortia, and universities. In this way, programs and communities can work together to allocate limited resources efficiently in designing and creating educative and cost-effective opportunities for mentors and novices that ultimately will benefit the students with rich learning experiences.

Third, the complex relationships among the different contexts, components, processes of teacher induction, and their effects on beginning teaching do not lend themselves a single methodology. Researchers will need to adopt multidimensional designs that combine qualitative and quantitative evidence and that do not rush to impose a simple answer to a complicated problem. They will need to learn how to inspire, work with, and learn from practitioners, the community, and each other in exploring the solutions and the questions raised by adopting those solutions.

This book informs both practitioners and researchers by describing what we know and do not know about topics such as: (a) effective ways to select, to support, and to evaluate mentor teachers; (b) issues concerning the design, implementation, and impact of general as opposed to content-specific induction and mentoring programs; (c) methods of conceptualizing and studying impact; and (d) the efficacy of differing levels of support within different induction and mentoring contexts. Each chapter pays special attention to the needs for research in teacher induction from the perspectives of practitioners, policy makers, and researchers. As a collective the chapters demonstrate how far we have come conceptually and methodologically—and how far we need to go in order to address many of the issues raised by the commentators.

Editing this book has made us keenly aware of all of the dedicated professionals who occupy different, but vital, roles in encouraging talented professionals to enter and thrive in schools and classrooms. It has been a lengthy, complex, challenging, and intensely rewarding process for each of us. We should like to acknowledge the support from our families, colleagues, and the ATE throughout this process. These include Weiling Yang, who sadly left us forever during the process, Lily Wang, Yang Wang, Douglas Ferraro, Richard Clift, JoAnn Hurley, and Hilarie Welsh. We especially want to acknowledge David Ritchey and the ATE Public Communication Committee for endorsing the book project and Roman and Littlefield Publishers for their trust and patience.

REFERENCES

Bierema, L. L., and S. B. Merriam. 2002. E-mentoring: Using computer mediated communication to enhance the mentoring process. *Innovative Higher Education* 26(2):211–27.

Feiman-Nemser, S. 2001. Helping novices learn to teach: Lessons from an exemplary support teacher. *Journal of Teacher Education* 52(1):17–30.

Feiman-Nemser, S., S. Schwille, C. Carver, and B. Yusko. 1999. *A conceptual review of the literature on new teacher induction* (NPEAT Report). East Lansing: Michigan State University.

Glazerman, S., S. Senesky, N. Seftor, and A. Johnson. 2006. *Design of an impact evaluation of teacher induction programs* (Final Report No. 6137–070). Washington, DC: Mathematica Policy Research.

Isenberg, E., S. Glazerman, M. Bleeker, A. Johnson, J. Lugo-Gil, M. Grider, S. Dolfin, E. Britton, and M. Ali. 2009. *Impacts of comprehensive teacher induction: Results from the second year of a randomized controlled study* (NCEE 2009–4072). Washington, DC: National Center for Education Evaluation and Regional Assistance.

Klecka, C. L., Y. Cheng, and R. T. Clift. 2004. Exploring the potential of electronic mentoring. *Action in Teacher Education* 26(3):2–9.

Stanulis, R., E. Wibbens, and S. Little. In review. Intensive mentoring that contributes to change in beginning elementary teachers' instructional in literacy.

Strong, M. 2009. *Effective teacher induction and mentoring: Assessing the evidence.* New York: Teachers College Press.

Strong, M., and W. Baron. 2004. An analysis of mentoring conversations with beginning teachers: Suggestions and responses. *Teaching and Teacher Education* 20(1):47–57.

Wang, J., M. Strong, and S. J. Odell. 2004. Mentor-novice conversations about teaching: A comparison of two U.S. and two Chinese cases. *Teachers College Record* 106(4):775–813.

I

CONCEPTIONS AND CONTEXTS OF TEACHER INDUCTION

1

Multiple Meanings of New Teacher Induction

Sharon Feiman-Nemser, Brandeis University

Interest in supporting and assisting beginning teachers is currently on the upswing, motivated by concerns about teacher retention and teacher quality. The 2000 Schools and Staffing Survey revealed that 83 percent of new teachers participated in some form of induction, up from 51 percent in 1990 (Smith and Ingersoll, 2004). Whether this leads to comprehensive systems of new teacher induction depends in part on whether educational leaders and policy makers embrace the fact that beginning teachers are novices to teaching and newcomers to their schools and, then, consider what these facts imply for induction programs, policy, and research.

This chapter examines these realities and their implications by analyzing three meanings of induction that appear in the discourse of researchers, educators, and policy makers. Each meaning highlights enduring issues of induction policy and practice. Each meaning also points to tensions that must be confronted if induction is to realize its potential as a lever for educational change. The high cost of teacher attrition and the persistent achievement gap among diverse groups of students underscore the importance of seeing induction as part of a larger effort to strengthen the quality of teaching and learning in our nation's schools.

Sometimes the term *induction* is used to label a unique *phase in learning to teach*. Stories by beginning teachers and studies of beginning teaching concur that the early years of teaching are a special time in a teacher's career, different from what has gone before and what comes after. The literature on new teacher induction tends to privilege teachers' immediate concerns, but a serious approach to induction must ultimately reconcile the tension between teachers' self-defined needs and the requirements of effective teaching and learning (Buchmann, 1993; Feiman-Nemser, 2001).

The term *induction* also refers to a *process of socialization.* This meaning highlights the institutional contexts and professional cultures that surround new teachers; the messages they send about what it means to teach in a particular school; and their impact on new teachers' identity, practice, and career trajectory. Thinking of induction as a process of socialization highlights the tension between helping new teachers fit into schools as they are and helping them participate in transforming schools into more effective sites for teacher and student learning (Little, 1990a).

Conceptions of induction as a phase in teacher learning or a process of teacher socialization remind us that, for better or worse, induction happens with or without a formal program. Still, in contemporary discussions of education practice and policy, induction most often refers to a formal *program for beginning teachers.* What counts as an induction program ranges from a statewide system of support and assessment to a district-sponsored orientation for new teachers. Most often it is equated with mentoring. Thinking about induction as a formal program for beginning teachers highlights the tension between the short-term, instrumental purpose of eased entry and the long-term, educative purpose of new teacher development (Odell and Huling, 2000; Wang and Odell, 2002).

This chapter is organized around these three meanings and their associated tensions or dilemmas. Drawing on relevant literature, I examine induction as a phase in learning to teach, a process of enculturation, and a program of support and development and show how each meaning points to critical issues and dilemmas. I also argue that more effective induction programs and policies depend on an understanding of all three meanings and what they imply for teacher education, professional development, school leadership, school reform, and educational policies at all levels.

INDUCTION AS A PHASE IN LEARNING TO TEACH

The notion of induction as a unique phase in the life of a teacher encompasses two related ideas. First, it underscores the special character of the new teacher's first encounter with the reality of being completely in charge of a classroom, as opposed to supervised practice teaching. Second, it highlights the place of induction as part of a comprehensive approach to ongoing, job-embedded teacher development. In that sense, induction is like Janus, the two-faced Roman god, looking backward to teacher preparation and forward to professional development.

A Unique Learning Agenda

The first year of teaching is a time of survival and discovery when the learning curve is steep and emotions run high (Huberman, 1989). Charged with the same responsibilities as their more experienced colleagues, beginning teachers are expected to perform and to be effective. Yet most aspects of the situation are unfamiliar. Moreover, the complexities of teaching confront the novice with daily dilemmas and uncertainties (Jackson, 1963; McDonald, 1980; Ryan, 1970). Having limited experience or little practical knowledge increases beginning teachers' uncertainty and frustration.

Some of the most important things new teachers need to know can only be learned on the job. As Judith Warren Little (1999) put it, "The learning demands that inhere in the work [of teaching] cannot be fully anticipated or met by preservice preparation, even when that experience is stellar" (234). A good preservice program can lay a strong foundation and help new teachers understand what they need to learn and how to go about it, but new teachers face a learning agenda that goes beyond what we typically assume.

The daily realities of teaching challenge all beginning teachers, even those with extensive preparation. Beyond maintaining order, generally viewed as the primary concern of new teachers (Veenman, 1984), the learning needs of novice teachers include issues of curriculum, instruction, assessment, management, school culture, and the larger community. As more and more teachers enter teaching with reduced preparation and face increasingly diverse students, the idea of induction as a critical phase in learning to teach takes on increased urgency (Grossman and Loeb, 2008).

Expert/novice comparisons reinforce the idea of induction as a distinct phase in learning to teach by uncovering qualitative differences in the thinking and performance of teachers at different stages in their careers. Berliner (1986) identified six dimensions on which novices and expert teachers differ. These include their abilities to interpret classroom phenomena, discern important events, use routines, make predictions, judge typical and atypical events, and evaluate performance. "What looks easy for the expert and so clumsy for the novice is the result of thousands of hours of experience and reflection" (15). In this heuristic model of skill development in teaching, novices and advanced beginners achieve competence by the third or fourth year. Proficiency may come to some teachers by the fifth year of teaching, but only a few attain the highest stage of expertise, which is characterized by fluid and efficient performance.

Novice/expert comparisons underscore the point that competence, proficiency, and expertise take time to develop and do not automatically flow from experience. They do not, however, tell us how novices gain skill and develop competence over time. That requires longitudinal research that takes into account the interaction of teachers' background, preparation, and school context.

In one longitudinal study, for example, researchers followed a group of beginning elementary and secondary teachers from their last year of teacher education through their first three years of teaching (Grossman, Smagorinsky, and Valencia, 1999). They found that the teachers used the reflective stance they had developed during their teacher education program to make sense of their teaching situation. Although some struggled as first-year teachers, by the second year most were able to use specific pedagogical tools (e.g., Writers' Workshop) they had learned about in their teacher preparation. The research team also identified particular aspects of the school and district context, including access to curricular materials and professional development opportunities, which dramatically affected teachers' on-the-job learning and their ability to use ideas and strategies introduced in teacher education. (These aspects of school context come to the fore in discussing the second meaning of induction.)

Part of a Professional Learning Continuum

The flip side of understanding induction as a distinct phase in learning to teach is seeing its place in a professional learning continuum (Feiman-Nemser, 2001). This means looking at induction as both an extension of initial preparation and a bridge to professional development. From this perspective, induction is justified not because it eases the new teacher's entry into teaching or compensates for inadequate preparation but because it contributes to the ongoing study and improvement of teaching.

The beginning years of teaching offer a natural opportunity to situate novices' learning in the central tasks of teaching—planning, instruction, assessment of student learning, and reflection on teaching. Unfortunately the induction literature rarely asks what kind of teaching new teachers should be learning and how they can be helped to learn new concepts (Ball and Cohen, 1999; Borko and Putnam, 1996; Feiman-Nemser and Remillard, 1995). Making beginning teaching a time of intentional, rather than incidental, learning is especially important if we want new teachers to practice the kind of standards-based teaching advocated by reformers (National Commission on Teaching and America's Future, 2006; Wang and Odell, 2002).

If preservice preparation has been successful, beginning teachers will have a compelling vision of good teaching; a beginning repertoire of approaches to curriculum, instruction, and assessment; and the tools to learn in and from their practice (Darling-Hammond and Bransford, 2005). A major task of induction is helping new teachers adapt and enact what they bring to teaching in ways that fit their students and local context. Sometimes the challenges of teaching alone for the first time lead novices to abandon pedagogies they learned in their preservice preparation.

In cases where induction support is continuous with initial preparation, it may keep novices from giving up on more demanding approaches in favor of what may seem like safer, less complex activities. This presumes a level of continuity between the principles and pedagogies studied during teacher preparation and the kind of teaching and learning required by the school or mandated by the district (Clift and Brady, 2005).

Besides conceptualizing induction as an extension of preservice instruction, the induction phase has been viewed as an "entry piece to a career-long professional development program for teachers" (Huling-Austin, 1990, 545). This highlights the necessary connection between induction and in-service education. Because of the patchwork nature of professional development, most induction programs, like most in-service programs, operate as discrete, isolated entities (Wilson and Berne, 1999). Thinking about induction as a form of professional development pushes us to consider how principles of effective professional development apply to learning opportunities for new teachers and move induction from short-term assistance for first-year teachers to the beginning of ongoing, job-embedded professional development (Hawley and Valli, 1999).

INDUCTION AS A SOCIALIZATION PROCESS

In the literature on the professions, induction traditionally refers to influences exerted by systems of recruitment, professional education, and work initiation as novices move along a path toward full membership in a professional community. Through a process of interaction and learning, recruits are "induced" to take on the dominant language, values, norms, and knowledge of their field. Looking at teacher induction through a socialization lens means looking at how new teachers are incorporated into the profession of teaching and into a particular work setting. It also highlights the tension of helping new teachers fit into schools as they are and expecting them to become change agents.

Traditional models of induction, like traditional theories of teacher socialization, stressed the one-way fitting of rookies into the existing system (Waller, 1932). Both have been criticized for portraying teachers as passively taking on the coloration of their surroundings (Lawson, 1992). Zeichner and Gore (1990) argued that teachers are not only shaped by institutional and cultural forces but also shape them as well, a process that contemporary studies of teacher socialization uncovered (Lacey, 1977).

This section focuses on the socialization that occurs as new teachers are inducted into a particular school community. If the process helps new teachers fit into schools as they are, it serves as a force for continuity. If it connects new teachers to educators who are working to transform existing norms and practices, induction can serve as a force for change. Viewing induction through a socialization lens highlights this tension between adaptation and transformation.

The Dominant Narrative

Many studies of teacher socialization have documented the tendency of new teachers to abandon their ideals and lower their expectations in order to conform to occupational or organizational realities (Richardson and Placier, 2005). From personal accounts by beginning teachers and studies by academic researchers, the story line is remarkably consistent (Codell, 1999; Grossman, 1990; Herndon, 1965; Ryan, 1980; Sentilles, 2005). New teachers struggle to succeed in an uncertain environment that demands much but offers little in the way of support. The main themes are reality shock, loneliness, and loss of idealism. Reviewing seven longitudinal studies of first-year teachers, Wideen, Mayer-Smith, and Moon (1998) concluded that the first year of teaching was one of dashed expectations.

This story line underscores how the practice and conditions of teaching shape the experience and outlook of beginning teachers. The primary mechanism of induction as socialization is everyday experience. By doing the work of teaching and interacting with colleagues, new teachers learn what is expected of them. They also form dispositions toward their work and their own learning. If we want to understand the induction process and direct it toward desired ends, we must attend to the socializing influence of school culture and structures.

Workplace Conditions

Since the 1980s, numerous studies have confirmed the power of school contexts to shape what teachers do and what they learn (Johnson, 2004; Little, 1982, 1999; McLaughlin, 1993; Rosenholtz, 1989). Three aspects of school life are especially salient for beginning teachers—teaching assignment, access to curricular resources, and relationships with colleagues. These factors shape the experience of beginning teaching and mediate its impact.

Teaching Assignment

It is not unusual for new teachers to find themselves teaching outside their areas of training, coping with more classes than usual, or dealing with known behavioral problems (Fideler and Haselkorn, 1999; Johnson and

Liu, 2004). Such inappropriate assignments are a "poor fit" with new teachers' background and interests. They jeopardize pupils' learning, devalue the expertise of veteran teachers, and discourage deliberative planning and reflection (Little, 1999). As Johnson and Birkeland (2003) learned from a study of participants in thirteen alternative certification programs in four states: "No amount of commitment to teaching, love of young people, subject matter knowledge, or just-in-time training could compensate for an unreasonable and unmanageable teaching assignment" (121).

Access to Curriculum

The responsibility of planning and teaching lessons in multiple subjects or classes can be daunting for new teachers who do not yet know what students of different age groups should be learning and do not yet have an extensive pedagogical repertoire. Yet, in a study of fifty new teachers in Massachusetts, researchers found that nearly all wanted more curricular guidance than they got (Johnson, 2004).

Some new teachers face a "curriculum void," and others receive highly prescriptive instructional materials. This occurs most often in "underperforming" districts serving students from low-income and minority backgrounds where such materials are supposed to raise achievement test scores. Critics of such "teacher-proof" curricula argue that they deskill teachers by ignoring their judgment about what their students need. Advocates counter that such materials ensure greater equity across districts and mediate the unevenness in teachers' backgrounds.

In a provocative study, Achinstein, Ogawa, and Speiglman (2004) contrasted the experiences of Liz, an uncredentialed beginning teacher in a low-income district, with those of Sam, a graduate of a teacher credential program teaching in a progressive public school. Liz appreciated the highly prescriptive reading curriculum mandated by her district because she did not know how to teach reading to her students. Sam welcomed the opportunity to figure out what his students needed and created a literacy program to support their learning. Based on these cases, the researchers argue that school and district responses to accountability pressures not only influence teacher socialization but also they may create a system of teacher tracking that reproduces inequities related to achievement.

Relations with Colleagues

The typical school organization, which Little (1999) wryly referrred to as "individual classrooms linked by a common parking lot" (256), maintains teachers' independence and isolation from one another. This limits the possibility of serious collaboration and problem solving. One result is that teachers may feel reluctant to ask for help or share problems, believing that good teachers figure things out for themselves. Even if teachers do get together, they may not know how to talk about teaching and learning in productive ways. Too often the need to maintain comfort and harmony take precedence over asking for evidence or offering a different perspective (Ball and Cohen, 1999; Lord, 1994).

In the study of fifty beginning teachers mentioned above, researchers learned how professional cultures in schools do and do not support new teachers (Johnson, 2004). Some new teachers found themselves in schools with a *veteran-oriented culture*, where experienced teachers protected their autonomy at the expense of collegial interaction and new teachers felt alone and unsupported. Other beginning teachers found themselves in schools with a *novice-oriented culture*, where enthusiasm and idealism were high but there was no one to provide expert guidance. The most fortunate beginning teachers found themselves in schools with integrated *professional cultures*, where all teachers participated in ongoing professional development, and professional exchanges across experience levels were the norm.

Thinking about induction as a process of socialization focuses attention on the school site where key factors that influence new teacher induction converge. Unfortunately, most schools are not organized to support new teacher development, and it may not always be in the interests of new teachers to rely on colleagues as dependable sources of knowledge about students, subject matter, or pedagogy. Too often the dominant teacher socialization narrative results from "sink-or-swim" induction in a bureaucratic school context. If we want to rewrite this socialization narrative, we need to change the working conditions and professional cultures in schools.

INDUCTION AS A FORMAL PROGRAM

Most educators regard induction as a formal program of support for beginning teachers. Huling-Austin (1990) endorsed this meaning in an early review of the literature where she defined induction as "a planned *program* intended to provide some systematic and sustained assistance to beginning teachers for at least one school year" (536). More expansive definitions broaden the purposes of induction programs to include new teacher development and assessment, although the relationship between assistance and assessment remains contested (Yusko and Feiman-Nemser, 2008).

Thinking about induction as a formal program fixes attention on the needs of beginning teachers that may reinforce an individualistic orientation to teaching and weaken collaboration and a sense of collective responsibility among teachers. Thinking about induction as a formal program surfaces a second tension as well, a tension between the goals of teacher retention and teacher quality. As researchers redefine teacher shortages as a problem of retention and not as a matter of insufficient supply, induction programs become a strategy for keeping people in teaching. But increased rates of retention do not tell us anything about the quality of new teachers' practices or the learning of their students. Linking induction programs to such outcomes is a serious challenge for research (Strong, 2009).

Comprehensive Induction

Recent calls for comprehensive induction expanded our understanding of elements other than strong mentoring that make an effective induction program. For example, the Alliance for Excellent Education (2004) defined comprehensive induction as "a package of supports, development and standards-based assessments provided to beginning teachers during at least their first two years of full-time professional teaching" (11). The package includes (a) structured mentoring from a carefully selected and trained mentor, (b) common planning time to collaborate with mentors and other teachers, (c) ongoing professional development, (d) participation in an external network of teachers, and (e) standards-based assessment and evaluation. Comprehensive induction involves both formal and informal learning opportunities inside and outside the school.

The Alliance for Excellent Education (2004) also stipulated the conditions that enable induction programs to succeed, including (a) strong principal leadership; (b) high-quality support providers; (c) additional support for teachers with little preparation; (d) incentives to participate in induction activities; (e) adequate and stable funding; (f) alignment between induction, classroom needs, and professional standards. These conditions tie induction to professional standards, differentiate the kind and amount of support available to new teachers based on their preparation and experience, accord the principal a critical role in making induction an integral part of school culture, recognize the need for adequate fiscal resources, and acknowledge that "support providers" require training.

Inherent Tensions

Thinking about induction as a formal program highlights certain tensions. One concerns the pull between an individual versus a collective orientation toward teaching and teacher learning. A second concerns the potential incompatibility between the goals of teacher retention and teacher quality. A third turns on the question of whether it is productive to think of induction as a stand-alone program or part of a school improvement initiative.

Individual versus Collective Orientation

It is easy to see how induction programs might promote an individual rather than a collective stance toward teaching and teacher learning. Focusing on the needs and concerns of beginning teachers invites an individual as opposed to a sociocultural model of learning. Moreover, the culture of teaching itself favors an individualistic orientation, which the practice of mentoring may inadvertantly reinforce.

Most teachers work alone in the privacy of their classrooms, out of the sight of colleagues and protected by a culture of autonomy and noninterference (Little, 1990a). Many teachers are reluctant to share problems with colleagues or ask for help, believing that good teachers figure things out on their own. Making independent decisions on behalf of their students is a valued aspect of teaching (Lortie, 1975). Yet these norms and patterns of interaction can limit collegial influence and work against shared professional standards.

In such a context, mentoring can easily promote an individualistic orientation toward teaching and learning to teach. If mentors pull back as soon as novices begin to feel comfortable, they may send the message that learning to teach is something you do on your own with a little advice on the side. If mentors do not model a sense of shared responsibility for student learning, new teachers may not come to see themselves as part of a broader collectivity working toward improved teaching and learning for all students. Some mentors feel uneasy about the expectation that they are supposed to influence or direct new teachers' practice, which may also encourage a reliance on individual preference rather than shared standards of good teaching (Feiman-Nemser and Parker, 1993; Little, 1990b; Smylie and Denny, 1989; Strong and Baron, 2004).

Retention or Quality

Of all the outcomes associated with new teacher induction, improved retention has the most solid support from research (Strong, 2009). Still we should not mistake increased teacher retention with enhanced teaching quality. We have to discern whether the right teachers are being retained and whether induction improves their practice.

Teacher shortages place pressure on states and districts to grant emergency certificates and create fast-track pathways into teaching. Some believe these moves undermine efforts to professionalize teaching; others view new sources of teachers as a way to enrich the teaching population. In any case, we need to adjust the induction curriculum to fit the backgrounds of different teachers and document the impact on teachers' practice, their retention patterns, and their students' learning.

Discrete Program or Schoolwide Initiative

Defining induction as a formal program might suggest something discrete and freestanding, but a view of induction as a process of socialization and the idea of comprehensive induction both challenge this conception. Both highlight the ways in which formal and informal induction processes can strengthen beginning teaching and contribute to a more collaborative and accountable professional culture in schools.

When teachers across experience levels have regular opportunities to develop curriculum, analyze student work, discuss classroom problems, or participate in peer observation, new teachers can learn from the practical knowledge of their more experienced colleagues. Such exchanges can also build professional community and strengthen teaching and learning across the board. These activities are commonplace in schools with an integrated professional culture wherein teaching is regarded as a public practice and teachers share the responsibility for new teacher development.

The notion of comprehensive induction highlights the workplace conditions that enable effective support for beginning teachers, including strong administrative leadership and teacher collaboration. In a real sense, creating the structures and professional culture that support new teacher learning builds the schools' organizational capacity to support teacher learning more generally. From this perspective, induction becomes less a discrete program for new teachers and more of a lever for fostering professional community and promoting a continuum of teacher development across experience levels.

CONCLUSION

This chapter explored three interconnected meanings of the term *induction* as it applies to new teachers and their early years on the job. Each meaning highlights a different aspect of beginning teaching, but together they offer a rounded understanding of new teacher learning in context. If we took beginning teaching seriously as a time for professional learning and socialization and not just for short-term support, we would think differently about what constitutes an effective induction program.

Defining induction as a distinct phase in learning to teach reminds us that new teachers have two jobs. They have to teach and they have to learn to teach in a particular school context. If we want new teachers to learn well from experience, we must provide them with curricular resources, guidance, models, and feedback rather than leave their learning to chance. We must also be clear about the kind of teaching we want new teachers to learn and to practice.

As more teachers enter the field with limited formal preparation, the need to treat the early years of teaching as a critical time for learning to teach gains increased urgency. Some alternate route programs require beginning teachers to work toward a master's degree and certification by taking the same courses at night that are offered to preservice teachers. This may not be the best model for integrating teacher preparation and induction if it ignores the pressing questions and problems that arise during the school day. Such a situation calls for new models that honor the emergent needs of new teachers while integrating professional knowledge and skills needed to help all students learn. Urban teacher residency programs such as those in Boston, New York, and Philadelphia offer one such model.

Viewing induction as a process of socialization reminds us that school structures and cultures mediate new teachers' learning and influence their teaching and their decision to stay, move, or leave. If we want novices to stay in teaching long enough to become accomplished practitioners, then we must induct them into a professional culture of collaboration, high standards, and collective accountability. Because such a culture does not exist in most schools, induction must become part of an overall school change effort.

Assigning mentor teachers to work with beginning teachers can be a step in the right direction, especially when mentors are prepared for this new role and have time to carry it out. But placing the whole responsibility for induction in the hands of a mentor ignores the limits of mentoring (Carver and Katz, 2004; Kapadia, Coca, and Easton, 2007; Katz and Feiman-Nemser, 2003) and the impact of working conditions on new teachers' satisfaction, success, and retention. When school leaders provide new teachers with clear curricular guidelines, a transparent teacher evaluation process, opportunities to observe and be observed, and easy access to colleagues' guidance, they not only help new teachers succeed but also they make induction a schoolwide responsibility.

As the linchpin between initial preparation and continuing professional development, induction has the potential to connect teacher learning and school reform. Development-oriented induction (as distinguished from short-term, personally affirming support) blurs the boundary between induction programming for new teachers and ongoing learning for all teachers. When this happens, professional communities are strengthened as teachers across experience levels work together to improve their teaching and their students' learning.

Finally, policy makers can influence the quality of induction by the way they define the problem of beginning teaching, the time frame they stipulate for induction support, and the programmatic tools and financial resources they provide (Carver and Feiman-Nemser, 2009; Grossman, Thompson, and Valencia, 2002; Youngs, 2007). For instance, California and Connecticut mandate two years of induction support organized around standards and linked to state licensure, and both states have dedicated funds for local induction activities, although the amounts differ significantly. Still, the impact of induction policy will always be limited by the local context in which it occurs.

If we want more effective induction programs and policies, we need a richer understanding of the meanings of new teacher induction. When teacher educators, school leaders, state policy makers, and classroom teachers understand that induction is a formative phase in learning to teach and a powerful process of occupational socialization and appreciate what those meanings entail, they are more likely to create purposeful and effective induction programs and policies.

REFERENCES

Achinstein, B., R. T. Ogawa, and A. Speiglman. 2004. Are we creating separate and unequal tracks of teachers? The effects of state policy, local conditions, and teacher characteristics on new teacher socialization. *American Educational Research Journal* 41(3):557–603.

Alliance for Excellent Education. 2004. *Tapping the potential: Retaining and developing high-quality new teachers.* Washington, DC: Author.

Ball, D. L., and D. K. Cohen. 1999. Developing practice, developing practitioners: Toward a practice-based theory of professional education. In *Teaching as the learning profession: Handbook of policy and practice*, eds. L. Darling-Hammond and G. Sykes, 3–32. San Francisco: Jossey-Bass.

Berliner, D. C. 1986. In pursuit of the expert pedagogue. *Educational Researcher* 15(7):5–13.

Borko, H., and R. T. Putnam. 1996. Learning to teach. In *Handbook of educational psychology*, eds. D. C. Berliner and R. C. Calfee, 673–708. New York: Simon & Schuster Macmillan.

Buchmann, M. 1993. Role over person: Morality and authenticity in teaching. In *Detachment and concern: Conversation in the philosophy of teaching and teacher education*, eds. M. Buchmann and R. Floden, 145–57. New York: Teachers College Press.

Carver, C., and S. Feiman-Nemser. 2009. Using policy to improve teacher induction: Critical elements and missing pieces. *Educational Policy* 23(2):295–328.

Carver, C., and D. Katz. 2004. Teaching at the boundary of acceptable practice. *Journal of Teacher Education* 55(5):449–62.

Clift, R., and P. Brady. 2005. Research on methods courses and field experiences. In *Studying teacher education: The report of the AERA panel on research and teacher education*, eds. M. Cochran-Smith and K. M. Zeichner, 309–424. Hillsdale, NJ: Lawrence Erlbaum Publishers.

Codell, E. R. 1999. *Educating Esmé: Diary of a teacher's first year.* Chapel Hill, NC: Algonquin.

Darling-Hammond, L., and J. Bransford. 2005. *Preparing teachers for a changing world. Report of the committee on teacher education of the national academy of education.* San Francisco: Jossey-Bass.

Feiman-Nemser, S. 2001. From preparation to practice: Designing a continuum to strengthen and sustain teaching. *Teachers College Record* 103(6):1013–55.

Feiman-Nemser, S., and M. Parker. 1993. Mentoring in context: A comparison of two U.S. programs for beginning teachers. *International Journal of Educational Research* 19(8):699–718.

Feiman-Nemser, S., and J. Remillard. 1995. Perspectives on learning to teach. In *The teacher educator's handbook: Building a knowledge base for the preparation of teachers,* ed. F. Murray, 61–91. San Francisco: Jossey-Bass.

Fideler, E., and D. Haselkorn. 1999. *Learning the ropes: Urban teacher induction practices in the United States.* Belmont, MA: Recruiting New Teachers.

Grossman, P. 1990. *The making of a teacher: Teacher knowledge and teacher education.* New York: Teachers College Press.

Grossman, P., and S. Loeb. 2008. *Alternate routes to teaching.* Cambridge, MA: Harvard Education Press.

Grossman, P. L., P. Smagorinsky, and S. Valencia. 1999. Appropriating tools for teaching English: A theoretical framework for research on learning to teach. *American Journal of Education* 108(1):1–29.

Grossman, P., C. Thompson, and S. Valencia. 2002. Focusing the concerns of new teachers: The district as teacher educator. In *School districts and instructional renewal,* eds. A. M. Hightower, M. S. Knapp, J. A. March, and M. W. McLaughlin, 129–42. New York: Teachers College Press.

Hawley, W. D., and L. Valli. 1999. The essentials of effective professional development: A new consensus. In *Teaching as the learning profession: Handbook of policy and practice,* eds. L. Darling-Hammond and G. Sykes, 127–50. San Francisco: Jossey-Bass.

Herndon, J. 1965. *The way it spozed to be.* New York: Bantam Books.

Huberman, M. 1989. On teachers' careers: Once over lightly, with a broad brush. *International Journal of Educational Research* 13(4):347–61.

Huling-Austin, L. 1990. Teacher induction programs and internships. In *The handbook of research on teacher education,* ed. W. R. Houston, 535–48. New York: Macmillan.

Jackson, P. 1963. *Life in classrooms.* New York: Holt.

Johnson, S. M. 2004. *Finders and keepers: Helping new teachers survive and thrive in our schools,* 167–92. San Francisco: Jossey Bass.

Johnson, S. M., and S. Birkeland. 2003. Pursuing a "sense of success": New teachers explain their career decisions. *American Educational Research Journal* 40(3):581–617.

Johnson, S. M., and E. Liu. 2004. Making better matches in hiring. In *Finders and keepers,* ed. S. M. Johnson, 167–92. San Francisco: Jossey-Bass.

Kapadia, K., V. Coca, and J. Q. Easton. 2007. *Keeping new teachers: A first look at the influences of induction in the Chicago public schools.* Chicago: Consortium on Chicago School Research, University of Chicago.

Katz, D., and S. Feiman-Nemser. 2003. New teacher induction in a culture of professional development. In *The teaching career*, ed. J. Goodlad, 96–116. San Francisco: Jossey-Bass.

Lacey, C. 1977. *The socialization of teachers*. London: Methuen.

Lawson, H. A. 1992. Beyond the new conception of teacher induction. *Journal of Teacher Education* 43(3):163–72.

Little, J. W. 1999. Organizing schools for teacher learning. In *Teaching as the learning profession: Handbook of policy and practice*, eds. L. Darling-Hammond and G. Sykes, 233–62. San Francisco: Jossey-Bass.

———. 1990a. The mentor phenomenon and the social organization of teaching. In *Review of research in education*, ed. C. B. Cazden, 297–351. Washington, DC: American Educational Research Association.

———. 1990b. The persistence of privacy: Autonomy and initiative in teachers' professional relations. *Teachers College Record* 91(4):509–36.

———. 1982. Norms of collegiality and experimentation: Workplace conditions of school success. *American Educational Research Journal* 19(3):325–40.

Lord, B. 1994. Teachers' professional development: Critical colleagueship and the role of professional communities. In *The future of education: Perspectives on national standards in America*, ed. N. Cobb, 175–204. New York: College Board Publications.

Lortie, D. C. 1975. *Schoolteacher: A sociological study of teaching*. Chicago: University of Chicago Press.

McDonald, F. 1980. *The problems of beginning teachers: A crisis in training*, vol. 1. Princeton, NJ: Educational Testing Service.

McLaughlin, M. W. 1993. What matters most in teachers' workplace context? In *Teachers' work: Individuals, colleagues, and contexts*, eds. J. W. Little and M. W. McLaughlin, 79–103. New York: Teachers College Press.

National Commission on Teaching and America's Future. 2006, January. *New initiatives from NCTAF: Teacher induction*. Paper presented at the AACTE/CADREI, San Diego, CA.

Odell, S. J., and L. Huling, eds. 2000. *Quality mentoring for novice teachers*. Indianapolis, IN: Kappa Delta Pi.

Richardson, V., and P. Placier. 2005. Teacher change. In *Handbook of research on teaching*, 4th ed., ed. V. Richardson, 905–47. Washington, DC: American Educational Research Association.

Rosenholtz, S. 1989. *Teachers' workplace: The social organization of schools*. New York: Longman.

Ryan, K. 1980. *Biting the apple: Accounts of first year teachers*. New York: Longman.

———. 1970. *Don't smile until Christmas: Accounts of the first year of teaching*. Chicago: University of Chicago Press.

Sentilles, S. 2005. *Taught by America: A story of struggle and hope in Compton*. Boston: Beacon Press.

Smith, T., and R. Ingersoll. 2004. What are the effects of induction and mentoring on beginning teacher turnover? *American Educational Research Journal* 4(2):681–714.

Smylie, M., and J. Denny. 1989, March. *Teacher leadership: Tensions and ambiguities in organizational perspective.* Paper presented at the annual meeting of the American Educational Research Association, San Francisco, CA.

Strong, M. 2009. *Assessing the evidence: How effective is teacher induction?* New York: Teachers College Press.

Strong, M., and W. Baron. 2004. Analysis of mentoring conversations with beginning teachers: Suggestions and responses. *Teaching and Teacher Education* 20(1):47–57.

Veenman, S. 1984. Perceived problems of beginning teachers. *Review of Educational Research* 54(2):143–78.

Waller, W. 1932. *The sociology of teaching.* New York: Wiley.

Wang, J., and S. J. Odell. 2002. Mentored learning to teach and standards-based teaching reform: A critical review. *Review of Educational Research* 72(3):481–546.

Wideen, M., J. Mayer-Smith, and B. Moon. 1998. A critical analysis of the research on learning to teach: Making the case for an ecological perspective on inquiry. *Review of Educational Research* 68(2):130–78.

Wilson, S., and J. Berne. 1999. Teacher learning and acquisition of professional knowledge: An examination of research on contemporary professional development. In *Review of research in education,* eds. A. Iran-Nejad and P. D. Pearson, 173–209. Washington, DC: American Educational Research Association.

Youngs, P. 2007. District induction policy and new teachers' experiences: An examination of local policy implementation in Connecticut. *Teachers College Record* 109(3):797–837.

Yusko, B., and S. Feiman-Nemser. 2008. Embracing contraries: Assistance and assessment in new teacher induction. *Teachers College Record* 110(5):923–53.

Zeichner, K. M., and J. M. Gore. 1990. Teacher socialization. In *Handbook of research on teacher education,* ed. W. R. Houston, 329–48. New York: Macmillan.

2

Teacher Induction in International Contexts

Lynn W. Paine and John R. Schwille,[1] *Michigan State University*

WHAT IS INDUCTION?

While induction has become familiar territory in U.S. scholarship, there is much variation and discussion in terms of whether programs are mandated or voluntary, whether and how they are funded, how long a novice teacher participates, whether mentors are full-time or part-time mentors, whether mentors are released from their own classrooms or are currently not teaching, and so on (Breaux and Wong, 2003; Fideler and Haselkorn, 1999; Smith and Ingersoll, 2004; Villani, 2002). Therefore, much needs to be learned about induction as well outside the familiar borders. An international perspective broadens our understanding of what induction is and might be. International experience can offer possibilities and a natural laboratory to examine the conditions for and consequences of various approaches that U.S. educators have not imagined.

We recognize that there is no common term that, when translated, means "induction" in each country. This is indicative not just of linguistic but also of conceptual issues that need to be addressed when considering variation in induction across the world. While we do not suggest that induction practice is readily transferable from one country to another, we do think that exploring these contrasts can encourage knowledgeable innovation and lead us to question what we have been taking for granted.

Induction itself is not an innovation. It is a necessary and universal phase in learning to teach that follows the point at which beginning teachers first take full responsibility for one or more regular classes of elementary or

31

secondary students. The experience of being a novice and learning how to teach within an established community of practice may be very different from school system to school system and be labeled and understood very differently, but it is all induction. Taking this definition as our point of departure, we can see that induction is not new and that it existed long before the term *induction* began to be widely used. Induction in Germany is a case in point, as explained by our German colleague Sigrid Blömeke:

> German teacher education consists of two steps. The second one is highly practical and it takes place at small state institutions as well as at schools. At the beginning of this second step, there is an introductory phase of a couple of weeks. Future teachers learn about how schools are organized, how to plan lessons in a practical sense and they observe teachers in schools. After this they are assigned to their training school [i.e. a regular German elementary or secondary school] in which they are required to take full responsibility for several classes. They receive half of the salary of a practicing teacher. So in many respects you could say that this is a formally organized induction (Blömeke, personal communication).

Such a system has existed in nearly its present form since the late 1800s for secondary teachers and since the 1960s for primary teachers. Therefore, it is a well-rooted form of teacher education, not an organizational innovation of the late twentieth, early twenty-first centuries (Blömeke, personal communication).

SURVEYING INDUCTION INTERNATIONALLY

This review draws on the past ten years of empirical work, some by us, some by researchers in other countries, and some by practitioners—especially the case-study work that Paine conducted with Britton, Pimm, and Raizen (2003)[2] and the collaborative work of Schwille, Dembele, and Schubert (2007). Also included in our review are papers and publications from 1980 to the present through our search in the Education Resources Information Center (ERIC) database for the keywords *international induction*.

To synthesize this diverse literature is challenging. In many settings questions of induction are not framed in the research literature but in policy briefings, program recommendations, and the like. Because of that we also draw on the consultation of colleagues who have shared with us their experiences and knowledge of induction. Here we do not pretend to be exhaustive, but instead we focus on broad patterns, contrasts, and selected examples.

While agreeing with Feiman-Nemser's conceptualization of induction as a phase, as policies, and as programs (2001), in our review we focus on induction in the form of a program instead of seeing it as simply a stage of a teacher's career or a process of socialization that inevitably occurs. In this way induction can be analyzed in terms of goals, a curriculum or sequence of opportunities to support those goals, and a range of pedagogical activities to enact what is intended. It can then be discussed in light of its costs and sustainability.

WHY INDUCTION, AND WHAT IS TO BE GAINED?

Teacher induction in the United States presumably serves a range of purposes, such as: reducing attrition, supporting novice teachers' well-being, responding to mandates and practical needs of educational systems, and more (Huling-Austin, 1990). However, reducing teacher attrition is often one of the major goals for teacher induction (Feiman-Nemser et al., 1999). Teacher shortages, attrition, and turnover were also policy concerns that argued for induction in many other countries (OECD, 2005). However, in still other settings the motivation for induction had little or nothing to do with teacher hiring or retention (Britton et al., 2003). Rather, it was valued as essential to the learning of new teachers.

Observing four international cases of comprehensive teacher induction, Paine et al. (2003) confirmed that induction was not primarily about fixing a problem like attrition. It was about building "something desirable: effective teachers, a strong teaching force, a vital profession, and optimum learning for students in schools" (80). Thus, the prominent concern of teacher induction should be with the learning needs of the beginning teacher (Janssens and Kelchtermans, 1997; Jesus and Paixao, 1996). Based on data from five national sites, Britton et al. (2003) found that there was unusual, broad, cross-national agreement about what teachers need to learn in their first several years of teaching and the help that they need to do so. Even in settings like Switzerland, where preservice preparation was extensive in both subject specialization and pedagogy, it was assumed that a beginning teacher, even one with substantial preservice training, had much to learn.

Earlier U.S. literature often characterized mentoring and induction as matters of emotional support and helping each teacher find his or her own style of or approach to teaching (Feiman-Nemser et al., 1999; Janssens and Kelchtermans, 1997).[3] While induction from New Zealand to Switzerland and England to Singapore took as a starting point that beginning teaching was stressful and needed emotional and social support, the purpose of induction in these countries was more than offering emotional and psychological support to these newcomers. Instead, they emphasized the professional knowledge and skill that beginning teachers needed to develop in order to become more competent and treated beginning teachers as adult learners (Paine et al., 2003a,b). In China there is evidence that mentors of novice teachers were much more likely to take on the role of master teacher and coach and provide more direct, explicit guidance on what it takes to teach well according to the professional goals instead of honoring beginning teachers' personal preferences (Wang, 2001; Wang, Strong, and Odell, 2004).

In the United States, literature on teacher induction paid relatively rare attention to the specific subject matter of teaching. In contrast, beginning mathematics teachers in France, who already had a university degree in mathematics and were among the elite group to pass an extremely advanced and competitive test of mathematics (the CAPES), spent a day per week at the university institute, or IUFM, learning pedagogical content knowledge of mathematics. Furthermore, at the end of their initial induction year, these teachers must defend before a jury a yearlong action research project that focuses on the specifics of teaching mathematics, known as a professional memoir.

Induction internationally is also about learning to work with others in school and community and to develop personal traits and strengths of importance to teachers. Norway, for example, organized beginning teacher gatherings with teachers from many local area schools to discuss challenging issues, including relations with colleagues (OECD, 2005). In Alberta, Canada, district-led induction sessions focused on parent issues in preparation for parent-teacher conferences (Teacher Induction Programs in Alberta, 2008). The Swiss induction programs asked its beginning teachers to write a *Standortbestimmungen* to reflect not only on their teaching but also on their development as a person.

Finally, teacher induction occupies a special place, uniquely influenced by looking backward to preservice teacher preparation and forward to the career of teaching (Feiman-Nemser, 2001). A key characteristic of induction in the international context that emerges from our review is the close relationship among preservice, induction, and professional development.

An Educational Testing Service review of teacher induction in eight countries (Wang et al., 2003) reported that some preservice programs, such as those in Switzerland, provided extensive and repeated field experiences in elementary or secondary schools as well as instruction in pedagogy or didactics. Others, such as Korea and France, provided extremely little time in the field and concentrated on the learning of subject matter rather than on how it is taught. The role of induction in these countries was, therefore, to complement what comes before, to build on the practicum and professional training that novice teachers had, and to provide more for those novices who did not have this experience.

When Japanese educators began developing special induction programs in the 1960s, beginning teachers were considered well prepared in content knowledge but not in dealing with their students or with demands on the school from parents or society at large. Consequently, induction in Japan was practically oriented. The Monbusho guidelines, for example, specified six broad categories of content in the induction program, all closely related to working with pupils, managing classrooms, working with parents, and participating in the school community (Monbusho, 1991; Padilla and Riley, 2003).

The Swiss case (Raizen, Huntley, Britton, 2003) illustrated two organizational links between preservice and induction. In the canton of Zurich, at the primary school level, the same institutions (the *seminars*) were set up to be responsible for both preservice and induction. In Lucerne, at the secondary level (*gymnasium*), the mentors for preservice teachers were also mentors for them at induction level. Concern about institutional connections was also visible in more recent induction policy in Taiwan in which preservice institutions and faculty continued to work with graduates in their induction period.

In the Shanghai region of China, even though preservice teacher education allowed for very little field experience, certain activities, tasks, and texts created a continuity between preservice and induction in the sense that preservice students concentrated more on studying the school curriculum they would teach than was the case in various other countries. These students also developed an analytical lens to this curriculum that they would continue to study and use as practicing teachers. "Central to their work as future teachers is their developing understanding of what are called the 'important' points (*zhongdian*), 'difficult' points (*nandian*) and 'hinges' or 'hinge' points (*guanjian*) of teaching particular content" (Paine, Fang, and Wilson, 2003, 35).

These international cases together encourage U.S. research, policy, and practice to consider a more ambitious set of goals than we often do. They suggest that personal support of the new teacher need not be at the expense of encouraging their learning subject-specific content and pedagogy as well as more general pedagogical knowledge. They remind us to consider induction in the context of the broader trajectory of teacher learning and expand our sense of possible support for new-teacher learning that can be connected to preservice and ongoing professional development.

WHERE ARE INDUCTION PROGRAMS TO BE FOUND, AND HOW LONG ARE THEY?

Induction is not always an organized practice across countries, nor is there substantial literature about induction in those countries that lack formal programs. For example, of the twenty-five countries reviewed for the OECD

Teachers Matter (OECD, 2005), only ten had mandatory induction programs (Australia—certain states, England and Wales, France, Greece, Israel,
Italy, Japan, Korea, Switzerland, and Northern Ireland).[4] In six countries
schools could elect to offer induction programs. Interestingly, in Scotland
individual teachers made this choice. Finally, in eight of the countries there
were no formal induction programs at all.

A similar variation is found in terms of where within a country's education system induction is housed. Induction programs were most commonly
offered by schools among the countries in the OECD report (2005). However, in Israel, Japan, Switzerland, and Northern Ireland, teacher education
institutions and schools provided induction programs jointly. A smaller
comparative study of induction in five countries (Britton et al., 2003)
found similar variations across France; New Zealand; Japan; Shanghai,
China; and three cantons in Switzerland. Induction was carried out in very
diverse institutions—school-based, university-based, induction-specific
centers, district-based settings, and in several cases in more than one of
these institutions.

Likewise, there has been no consensus on the duration of induction—formal or informal. In the OECD study (2005), the length of the
programs varied from seven months in Korea to two years in Quebec and
Switzerland. In fact, educational systems were not even consistent in what
they consider a beginning teacher to be—much less on how long this stage
should be considered to last.

HOW IS IT ARRANGED?

There is no single approach to organizing the learning opportunities for
induction at the international level. Different patterns emerge across settings that include variation in activities within a program, intensive learning opportunities organized within or around classrooms, opportunities
for reflection and personal development, and activities with a longer-term,
broader view of education.

Variations to Provide a Balanced Menu for Learning

The complex learning goals of induction help explain the great variety of
activities in certain induction programs. In Shanghai, for example, induction included both school-based and district-based activities (Paine, Fang,
and Wilson, 2003). First, at the school level, formal contractlike agreements set goals and laid out work for all novice-mentor combinations.
These agreements included: school-based mentoring (with one mentor) in
subject-matter teaching; school-based mentoring (with a different mentor)

in working with students; visiting students' homes in the company of experienced teachers; and a summer orientation for teachers who might come from one school or many schools in the same vicinity.

Second, district-based activities in the Shanghai region required a minimum of one hundred hours from each novice. They consisted of workshops and courses for new teachers, district-provided mentoring, and teaching competitions for new teachers. In one district a hotline was established for subject-matter specialists who answered phoned-in questions from new teachers.

Third, there were activities offered by both school and district, often in a coordinated fashion. These activities included: peer observation by the mentor and novice of other teachers in the same school and other schools; public lessons observed and discussed by the novice or a group of novices as well as others; "talk" lessons in which novice and experienced teachers talked through a lesson without actually teaching it and then provided justification for what was presented; action research projects by new teachers with support from others at school or district level; and the use of a handbook developed by the school or district for new teachers and their mentors.

In such comprehensive and robust systems of induction, participating in multiple activities within the same program is the norm and is seen as critical. "Beginning teachers, these programs believe, need a range of different approaches—different formats and different teachers—to support the broad range of learning and development required of novices" (Britton et al., 2003, 319).

Intensive Opportunities in and through the Classroom

Induction programs create opportunities to learn from classrooms that novice teachers would not otherwise have at the international level. In the programs reviewed, new teachers observed and were observed, mentors and others discussed individual lessons with new teachers, and novice teachers were encouraged to talk about particular pupils learning particular content. Three arrangements were especially common: mentoring, peer group activities, and work that promoted reflection.

Working with a Mentor

Induction programs typically enable the beginning teacher to work one-on-one with an experienced teacher. The OECD review (2005) found that of fifteen countries with induction programs, thirteen had mentors as either the key person with whom the novice worked or as one of the primary people responsible for supporting them. The analysis of mentoring is increasingly common in the literature (Harrison, Dymoke, and Pell, 2006; Lee and Feng, 2007; Lindgren, 2005; Rippon and Martin, 2006; Schwille, 2008; Tang and Choi, 2005; Vonk, 1995). Not surprisingly, the terms used to describe the mentor varied by site. Different connotations are associated with each term.

The words used in Shanghai—"guiding teacher," "old teacher," or "master"—are associated with traditional culture and show that in some sense the new teacher is a "disciple" of the master. In France, mentors are called "pedagogic advisors," a title that communicates the focus of their work, while in New Zealand, they are "advice and guidance advisors," department heads, or "buddy" teachers, which suggest mentoring roles of a different sort.

Working with Peers

Another common activity that emerged from the literature was that novices discussed, planned, and explored with other beginners. Peer observation, shared reflection, and joint inquiry projects, such as the memoir in France, reinforced the idea that novices can learn from each other. In Singapore, in addition to school-based mentoring and "practice-oriented courses," novices with an 80 percent teaching load participated in the Singapore-wide Teacher Network, a center housing all professional development, including induction (Gopinathan et al., 2008). The Teacher Network established an online "café" created by novice teachers to help provide the learning, support, and dialogue for more recently hired teachers.

In Alberta, Canada, many districts organized their beginning teachers into cohorts for networking with peers (Teacher Induction Programs in Alberta, 2008). In Israel, the mandatory induction program included peer group workshops as one of its main components (Lazovsky and Reichenberg, 2006). In Switzerland, "practice groups" allowed first- and second-year teachers from different schools to voluntarily join a face-to-face group to discuss problems of practice three to four hours each time and eight times a year. The novices set the direction of the discussion, identified the problems they wanted to engage, and facilitated the group discussions about classroom teaching based on observation.

Reflecting on Practice

In many countries beginning teachers were encouraged to reflect and inquire about their teaching and to develop a reflective stance personally and professionally. In Switzerland, the options for novice teachers included practice groups, individual counseling, observation of other teachers, seminars, and courses, and a reflective activity called *Standort-bestimmungen,* a process of "self-evaluation of self-competence, social competence, and competence in one's area of teaching. It is intended to lead to a determination of next steps in self- and professional development, with a number of choices possible (including leaving teaching)" (Raizen et al., 2003, 118).

The French professional memoir embodies an expectation for novice teachers to develop analytical and reflective skills that they could bring to bear on aspects of their own emerging practice, including—in the case of mathematics—the design and the use of curriculum materials and pedagogic resources (Pimm, Chazan, and Paine, 2003).

Management of Different Kinds of Tensions

Learning in and from one's own classroom is a vital part of induction. For many countries induction learning also takes place outside one's own teaching context. For example, beginning teachers regularly visited another teacher's classroom through the "accompanied practice" in France, the occasional seminar in New Zealand, or the practice group in Switzerland. Even more far-ranging, each year in Japan a cruise ship takes about 20 percent of the nation's new teachers for a summer cruise that emphasizes cultural activities. These induction activities rest on the belief that beginners need some distance from the immediacy of the classroom to be able to see their teaching in new ways.

Induction internationally also takes on the long-standing theory versus practice issue. Although in the U.S. literature there is a tendency to regard preservice programs as a period of theoretical learning and induction as a phase of practical learning, in reality mentors often have to manage a continuing tension between giving the novice the assistance needed to resolve immediate problems of teaching while helping the novice to take a longer and deeper view of teaching (Schwille, 2008; Wang, Odell, and Schwille, 2008).

Using data from international contexts as a base, Britton and colleagues (2003) argued that induction "must be grounded in practice, yet it requires . . . the perspective of research away from immediate practice, which allows formulation and discussion of general principles, theories and abstractions. . . . These activities involve not only experienced teachers in schools, but also those in universities, colleges, district offices, special institutions, and elsewhere who can offer a different perspective. They are in a position to share knowledge and facilitate conversation and insights that might not otherwise occur, given the press of teaching, the 'clamor of immediacy,' especially in the beginning years" (326).

HOW MUCH TIME, AND AT WHAT COST?

There are considerable differences among countries in terms of the time allocated to formal induction. In England and Singapore, reduction in teaching loads is limited to no more than 90 and 80 percent, respectively, while the time required in China for off-job training is a minimum of 150 class periods of about fifty minutes each in addition to time spent in school-based mentoring (Gang and Meilu, 2007). In Japan, the out-of-school induction component alone involves ninety days, which is equal to three out of every eight days considering a school year of 240 days. French first-year mathematics teachers, one could argue, have their entire week devoted to formal induction—with a day and a half at the IUFM, solo teaching of a single class in one school throughout the entire year, developing and presenting a professional memoir, and supporting and observing weekly at another school for twelve weeks.

These cases indicate that one of the critical policy issues for induction is how much to deduct from the teaching loads of beginning teachers. Such deductions will increase the cost of induction dramatically since the salaries of teachers—even parts of these salaries—can easily outweigh the cost of other support for induction.

In Germany, for participating in the second institution, novice teachers got half the salary of a regular teacher for teaching a certain number of classes. This cost could be compared with the cost of assigning regular teachers to teach these same classes. In France, a regular teacher had a full load of eighteen weekly contact hours, but a beginning teacher had only one-third of this teaching load (six contact hours) while using the remaining two-thirds for their study, research, and observation. Likewise, beginning teachers in Japan and Shanghai spent a half day a week on coursework for their own learning while their counterparts in New Zealand spent a fifth of their time for the year in school-based professional development programs. All of these teachers also received full pay.

The OECD report (2005) showed that six of the national sites in their study used reduced loads for beginning teachers as an approach to supporting their induction while eight countries did not, including Japan and Switzerland. Thus, reduced teaching loads were not the norm even among relatively affluent countries, and even where there was a reduction, it might be minimal.

Cost is an elephant in the room of teacher induction. In the economics of education, there is a literature on the costs of on-the-job training, of which induction is an example (Villar and Strong, 2007). According to this literature, both the trainees and their employing institutions are willing to invest in on-the-job training if they can anticipate future returns to this investment that are comparable to what they earn on other investments of the same resources. Although this conceptual apparatus can be problematical when applied to the monopolistic hiring practices of most public educational institutions, it still contains ideas that should be taken seriously.

Simply stated, it would seem as if there is no on-the-job training without cost. If an institution employs a novice, it will presumably get less in the way of results than if it employs a fully qualified person. However, if novices accept lower salaries in order to learn what they can from their initial job experience, the institution would realize a better return because novices would become more fully qualified at initially lower salaries (Villar and Strong, 2007).

However, in public education, the training of novices is not always funded based on considerations of cost return. Indeed, we find little scholarship that addresses fiscal issues in relation to teacher induction. In some settings, protected time allocations for induction—as in New Zealand—have a long history and seem impervious to economic and political changes. In other settings there is no load time allocated for induction and no discussion about whether this could or should be justified.

When we turn from beginning teacher salary costs to other salary costs, notably the costs of a formally assigned mentor's time, many additional questions appear. How is this cost accounted for? How much time do mentors actually devote to induction? How much does this reduce their productivity in other respects? If mentors work longer than nonmentors, are they compensated for this additional time or not?

Good analyses of these costs in various countries by knowledgeable economists of education would quickly show, we believe, that formal induction programs and reduced teaching loads are an advantage that can be enjoyed only by affluent nations. Low-income countries, which have great difficulty finding enough resources to build, equip, and staff all the schools, would not be able to create and sustain such programs. Yet, the need for helping novices learn how to improve their practice is obviously important for all countries, not just affluent ones. It would be helpful to examine examples of induction in low-income regions, such as some rural regions of China, to determine whether less expensive forms of induction programs can be devised and tested to meet the needs of low-income countries. Such work might yield implications for how to reduce the cost of teacher induction in the United States as well.

WHERE DOES THIS LEAD?

Induction programs are not universally present in all countries. Yet the presence of induction programs in many countries reminds us of induction's potential to support teacher learning. Reviewing the implementation of induction across many countries expands our sense of the possible and perhaps encourages imaginative solutions to constraints and pressures that we feel at home.

Although there is no single "silver bullet" in terms of approach, philosophical orientation, or actors in induction, this review suggests that robust induction requires variation, coordination, sustained effort, and much attention on the part of policy makers and providers. In addition to the anecdotal reports that are increasingly available, there needs to be much more systematic research on induction in different contexts with better conceptualization and more rigorous data collection and assessment.

REFERENCES

Breaux, A. L., and H. K. Wong. 2003. *New teacher induction: How to train, support, and retain new teachers.* Mountain View, CA: Harry K. Wong Publications.

Britton, E., L. Paine, D. Pimm, and S. Raizen. 2003. *Comprehensive teacher induction: Systems for early career learning.* Dordrecht, The Netherlands: Kluwer Academic Publishing.

Feiman-Nemser, S. 2001. From preparation to practice: Designing a continuum to strengthen and sustain teaching. *Teachers College Record* 103(6):1013–55.

Feiman-Nemser, S., C. Carver, S. Schwille, and B. Yusko. 1999. *Beyond support: Taking new teachers seriously as learners.* Alexandria, VA: Association for Supervision and Curriculum Development.

Fideler, E., and D. Haselkorn. 1999. *Learning the ropes: Urban teacher induction programs and practices in the United States.* Belmont, MA: Recruiting New Teachers, Inc.

Gang, D., and S. Meilu. 2007. The qualifications of the teaching force in China. In *A comparative study of teacher preparation and qualifications in six nations,* eds. R. Ingersoll, S. Boonyananta, H. Fujita, D. Gang, E. G. Kim, K. C. Lai, R. Maynard, P. Siribanpitak, S. Tan, and A. F. L. Wong, 19–27. Philadelphia: Consortium for Policy Research in Education.

Gold, Y. 1996. Beginning teacher support: Attrition, mentoring and induction. In *Handbook of research on teacher education,* eds. J. Sikula, T. J. Buttery, and E. Guyton. New York: Macmillan.

Gopinathan, S., S. Tan, F. Yanping, L. Devi, C. Ramos, and E. Chao. 2008. In *Transforming teacher education: Redefined professionals for 21st century schools.* Singapore: National Institute of Education, Nanyang Technical University.

Harrison, J., S. Dymoke, and T. Pell. 2006. Mentoring beginning teachers in secondary schools: An analysis of practice. *Teaching and Teacher Education* 22(8):1055–67.

Huling-Austin, L. 1990. Teacher induction programs and internships. In *Handbook of research on teacher education,* ed. R. W. Houston, 535–48. New York: Macmillan.

Janssens, S., and G. Kelchtermans. 1997, April. *Subjective theories and professional self of beginning teachers.* Paper presented at the annual meeting of the American Educational Research Association, Chicago, IL.

Jesus, S. N., and M. P. Paixao. 1996. *The "reality schock" of the beginning teachers*. Paper presented at the International Conference of FEDORA, Coimbra, Portugal.

Lazovsky, R., and R. Reichenberg. 2006. The new mandatory induction programme for all beginning teachers in Israel: Perceptions of inductees in five study tracks. *Journal of Education for Teaching* 32(1):53–70.

Lee, J. C. K., and S. Feng. 2007. Mentoring support and the professional development of beginning teachers: A Chinese perspective. *Mentoring & Tutoring: Partnership in Learning* 15(3):243–62.

Lindgren, U. 2005. Experiences of beginning teachers in a school-based mentoring program in Sweden. *Educational Studies* 31(3):251–63.

Monbusho. 1991. *Basic outline for the beginning teacher training implementation*. Tokyo: Ministry of Education, Science, Sports, and Culture.

OECD. (Orgaisation for Economic Co-operation and Development). 2005. *Teachers matter: Attracting, developing, and retaining effective teachers*. Paris: OECD.

Padilla, M., and J. Riley. 2003. Guiding the new teacher: Induction of first-year teachers in Japan. In *Comprehensive teacher induction: Systems for early career learning*, eds. E. Britton, L. Paine, D. Pimm, and S. Raizen, 261–96. Dordrecht, the Netherlands: Kluwer Academic Publishing.

Paine, L., Y. Fang, and S. Wilson. 2003a. Entering a culture of teaching: Teacher induction in Shanghai. In *Comprehensive teacher induction: Systems for early career learning*, eds. E. Britton, L. Paine, D. Pimm, and S. Raizen, 20–82. Dordrecht, Netherlands: Kluwer Academic Publishing.

Paine, L., D. Pimm, E. Britton, S. Raizen, and S. Wilson. 2003b. Rethinking induction: Examples from around the world. In *Keeping good teachers*, ed. M. Scherer, 67–80. Alexandria, VA: Association for Supervision and Curriculum Development.

Pimm, D., D. Chazan, and L. Paine. 2003. Being and becoming a mathematics teacher: Ambiguities in teacher *formation* in France. In *Comprehensive teacher induction: Systems for early career learning*, eds. E. Britton, L. Paine, D. Pimm, and S. Raizen, 194–260. Dordrecht, the Netherlands: Kluwer Academic Publishing.

Raizen, S., M. A. Huntley, and E. Britton. 2003. Co-operation, counseling and reflective practice: Swiss induction programs. In *Comprehensive teacher induction: Systems for early career learning*, eds. E. Britton, L. Paine, D. Pimm, and S. Raizen, 83–140. Dordrecht, the Netherlands: Kluwer Academic Publishing.

Rippon, J. H., and M. Martin. 2006. What makes a good induction supporter? *Teaching and Teacher Education* 22(1):84–99.

Schwille, S. 2008. The professional practice of mentoring. *American Journal of Education* 115(1):139–67.

Schwille, J., M. Dembele, and J. Schubert. 2007. *Global perspectives on teacher learning: Improving policy and practice*. Paris: UNESCO, IIEP.

Smith, T. M., and R. M. Ingersoll. 2004. What are the effects of induction and mentoring on beginning teacher turnover? *American Educational Research Journal* 41(3):681–714.

Tang, S. Y. F., and P. L. Choi. 2005. Connecting theory and practice in mentor preparation: Mentoring for the improvement of teaching and learning. *Mentoring and Tutoring* 13(3):383–401.

Teacher Induction Programs in Alberta. 2008. Unpublished report.

Villani, S. 2002. *Mentoring programs for new teachers: Models of induction and support.* Thousand Oaks, CA: Corwin.

Villar, A., and M. Strong. 2007. Is mentoring worth the money? A benefit-cost analysis and five-year rate of return of a comprehensive mentoring program for beginning teachers. *ERS Spectrum* 25(3):1–17.

Vonk, J. H. C. 1995, April. *Conceptualizing novice teachers' professional development: A base for supervisory interventions.* Paper presented at the annual meeting of the American Educational Research Association, San Francisco, CA.

Wang, J. 2001. Contexts of mentoring and opportunities for learning to teach: A comparative study of mentoring practices. *Teaching and Teacher Education* 17(1):51–73.

Wang, A. H., A. B. Coleman, R. J. Coley, and R. P. Phelps. 2003. *Preparing teachers around the world.* Princeton, NJ: Educational Testing Service.

Wang, J., S. J. Odell, and S. A. Schwille. 2008. Effects of teacher induction on beginning teachers' teaching. *Journal of Teacher Education* 59(2):132–52.

Wang, J., M. Strong, and S. J. Odell. 2004. Mentor-novice conversations about teaching: A comparison of two U.S. and two Chinese cases. *Teachers College Record* 106(4):775–813.

NOTES

1. The authors thank Sigrid Blömeke, Ted Britton, Brian DeLany, Martial Dembélé, Yanping Fang, David Pimm, and Sharon Schwille for their considerable help in the development of this piece. We also clearly owe gratitude to Dan Chazan, Senta Raizen, and Suzanne Wilson for their significant contribution to the Middle Grades Mathematics and Science Induction study, which helped launch some of the thinking discussed here. The U.S. National Science Foundation (NSF Award #9814083) provided financial support for that MGM project, for which we are grateful. While appreciative of the assistance of many, we take all responsibilities for any errors in this text.

2. The Britton et al. (2003) study involved case studies of induction policies, programs, and practices in five national settings: China (Shanghai), France, Japan, New Zealand, and Switzerland. This involved extensive interviewing, observation, and document analysis of induction programs and activities.

3. Given the diversity across induction programs in this country we cannot say that all programs take this emphasis as their main one. More recent efforts at induction actively challenge this. But we do suggest that historically a U.S. emphasis on emotional and social support has had important implications for the design and orientation of induction.

4. This finding has a parallel in the work of the Middle Grades Mathematics and Science study led by Raizen, Britton, and Paine. Preliminary literature review and interview work with colleagues in eleven countries suggested that in many countries there was either no formal nationwide program of induction or no long-standing induction schemes.

3

School Cultures and Organizations and Teacher Induction

Maria Assunção Flores, University of Minho, Braga, Portugal

Workplace conditions play a key role in influencing teacher learning and development in schools, which in turn shape the quality of education provided to students (Day, 1999; Cole, 1991). High-quality teachers and high-quality teaching and learning in schools are dependent upon the ways in which teachers are trained (Calderhead and Shorrock, 1997; Flores, 2000), the ways in which teacher professionalism is defined and framed (Hargreaves, 2000), and the opportunities for teacher learning and development in and out of school (Day, 1999; Lieberman, 1996).

Workplace conditions, school culture, and leadership also impact teachers' learning and professional development (Cole, 1991; Flores, 2004; Williams, Prestage, and Bedward, 2001) and teacher commitment, morale, and retention (Weiss, 1999). The early years of teaching are crucial in (re)shaping teachers' understanding and practice of teaching (Vonk, 1993, 1995). The intense learning impacts upon the ways in which professional identity is (re)constructed as teachers' personal beliefs, values, and perspectives are revisited and challenged against the powerful influences of the workplace. As Day (1999) argued:

> These first few years of teaching have been described as a two-way struggle in which teachers try to create their own social reality by attempting to make their work match their personal vision of how it should be, whilst at the same time being subjected to the powerful socializing forces of the school culture (59).

THEORETICAL FRAMEWORK

Teacher socialization theory highlights the complexity of the process by which new teachers become members of a teaching community in their schools. The interplay among the characteristics of the teaching profession itself, new teachers' personal characteristics, and the institutional and contextual factors (Flores, 2001; Jordell, 1987; Lacey, 1977, 1995) has been conceptualized from different theoretical stances, which draw upon different methodological orientations and methods (Vonk and Schras, 1987; Zeichner and Gore, 1990). Functionalist and normative approaches assign a central role to the existing structures and cultures by which novices adapt. Interpretative and interactive approaches view adaptation as a mutual interaction between the person and the workplace, which change both individual professional behavior and the work context.

Different, and sometimes contradictory, perspectives fill the literature on teacher socialization regarding the impact of different contexts and factors. The classic work by Lortie (1975) highlighted the powerful influence of the *apprenticeship of observation* that occurs when teachers are elementary and high school students. Learning about how to teach prior to teacher education is then activated during preservice teacher education and persists during early field experiences and student teaching. Related to this theory is the argument that formal teacher education has a weak impact on new teachers' preexisting personal beliefs and images of teaching. In other words, student teaching reinforces rather than challenges prior beliefs (Kagan, 1992).

Others point to the more direct influences of the workplace on teacher socialization (Feiman-Nemser, 1983; Feiman-Nemser and Remillard, 1996; Jordell, 1987; Rust, 1994). Looking at learning to teach as a socialization process, Feiman-Nemser and her colleagues (1999) argued that research should focus "attention on the occupational setting and professional community, within which new teachers are entering, the messages they receive about what it means to be a teacher, and how these messages influence their emerging identity and practice" (4). According to this perspective, teacher socialization is directly influenced by the characteristics of the school as a workplace, their colleagues, evaluators, and administrators.

Different factors in the workplace may have different kinds or levels of influences. The influence of colleagues can be rather limited in isolated and individualist cultures where new teachers receive little assistance (Huberman, 1991; Vonk and Schras, 1987). Achinstein, Ogawa, and Speiglman (2004) concluded that state policy impacts on new teachers' socialization and that "local schools and district contexts exert a profound influence on teacher socialization both directly and by mediating the impact of state instructional and accountability policies" (589). Jordell (1987) stressed that a strong impact of structures in teachers' work can be detrimental to personal factors in beginning teachers' socialization.

Much recent research adopts an interactionist view of socialization, emphasizing the ways in which new teachers both shape and are shaped by their work context (Flores and Day, 2006; Kuzmic, 1994; Kelchtermans and Ballet, 2002; Rust, 1994). In other words, teacher socialization is seen "not simply as passively sliding into an existing context, but rather as an interpretative and interactive process between the new teacher and the context" (Kelchtermans and Ballet, 2002, 106). Both formal structures and workplace cultures have an impact upon new teachers' socialization, learning, and development. This chapter explores the ways in which different kinds of school cultures and organizations influence novice teachers' induction experiences.

METHOD FOR REVIEW AND FINDINGS

The methodology for this review included both manual searches through journals and electronic searches of databases such as Educational Resources Information Center (ERIC). The main descriptors were school culture and organizations, induction, teacher socialization, and new teachers. Only the studies that addressed directly the issues of the influence of school cultures and organizations on new teachers' learning to teach and induction were selected for inclusion in this review. These studies address two questions. What are the connections between different school cultures, organizations, and mentoring relationships in induction? What are the influences of these relationships on new teachers' learning to teach and retention?

SCHOOL CULTURES AND ORGANIZATIONS AND MENTORING RELATIONSHIPS IN INDUCTION

In a longitudinal study carried out in Portugal with new teachers over a two-year period, Flores (2006a, 2006b, 2006c) concluded that most of them received no information or support from school leaders and colleagues. Even when some support did exist at their schools (e.g., welcome meetings), the target audience was not newcomers in many cases. Seeking advice from more experienced colleagues was not easy for novices due to the recurring dilemma of being aware of their lack of knowledge about the tasks they had to perform while, at the same time, needing to be perceived as professionals who were aware of and knowledgeable about their duties as teachers.

New teachers were often treated as a separate category from their more experienced colleagues, pointing to hierarchical, formal relations (De Lima, 2003). Such a distinction was illustrated by a novice teacher who reported on the lack of interaction between the dinosaurs at her school and the newcomers (Flores, 2004). These studies mirrored the general literature on teacher professional cultures, which points to the lack of support, guidance, and collaboration for the new teachers and the isolated and impersonal ways they were socialized, which led to feelings of being lost (Flores, 2004).

Other research noted that many novice teachers, whether or not they were participating in formal induction and mentoring programs, often identified peers as most supportive during their first year. These peers might have been mentors, relatives, or former teachers (Marable and Raimondi, 2007). In some cases and among other factors, beginning teachers did not perceive support from their induction tutors or mentors as being adequate (Jones, 2003) due to lack of time (Rhodes, Nevill, and Allan, 2005).

In a study of mentoring in primary schools in England, Moyles, Suschitsky, and Chapman (1999) examined the perceptions of mentors, new entrants, and principals concerning formal and informal support structures for mentoring that existed at their schools. The authors found that mentoring was judged to be most successful when the ethos of the school was characterized by genuine support systems for all staff. Novice teachers received more informal mentoring, and more staff members were involved in informal mentoring processes when collaboration was a strong element in the school ethos. Similarly, in research conducted in China, Lee and Feng (2007) identified that collegial cultures, teaching workload, and style of mentor-protégé interactions were among the factors that affected the nature of mentoring support for new teachers in secondary schools.

In England, Williams, Prestage, and Bedward (2001) studied formal induction arrangements for newly qualified teachers (NQTs), particularly the significance of teacher culture to first-year teachers' experiences. The authors found that the schools with individualistic cultures were problematic for novice teachers, while the schools with spontaneously collaborative cultures provided novice teachers with supportive and development-oriented atmospheres, regardless of any mandatory induction requirements. They concluded that induction arrangements for NQTs made the greatest impact when schools enabled "collaborative activity that arises from organization procedures" (264).

Conversely, De Lima (2003) studied student teachers' views and collaborative practices within two different departmental cultures during their practicum. Despite formal arrangements and existing discourse on the virtues of collaboration, the student teachers were socialized into isolationist professional cultures. His findings point to the importance of the department in student teachers' socialization, and he argued that, even in highly structured programs intended to foster collaboration, traditional norms and practices instead of joint work tended to be reinforced.

Drawing upon research in England, Jones (2005) argued that not only do new teachers have to become expert technically but also they need to develop the professional capability to establish positive relationships with their colleagues and reconcile their idealistic expectations with school reality. Cole (1991), in research conducted with thirteen new teachers on relationships in the workplace, found that beginning teachers' socialization was facilitated by a sense of belonging, security, support, and learning from colleagues.

In a recent review of mentoring beginning teachers, Hobson, Ashby, Malderez, and Tomlinson (2009) concluded that the success of mentoring programs and mentoring relationships is dependent upon the existence of collegial and learning cultures in schools. Similarly, in a recent review of the effects of induction on beginning teachers' conceptions and practice of teaching on their students' learning, Wang, Odell, and Schwille (2008) concluded that the different components of teacher induction did not independently influence novices' teaching and learning, but they were mediated by social, cultural, and organizational contexts of the schools in which they operate.

The studies described above suggested that the nature of school culture and the characteristics of school organization are key mediating factors in shaping the socializing influence of colleagues and the quality of the mentoring relationship in new teacher induction. They supported three conclusions. First, there is a paradox of teacher socialization and continuing education in which the importance of formal and informal collaborative school structures and cultures mismatches with the isolation and lack of support that characterizes many settings in which teachers begin teaching. Even within contexts where induction and mentoring arrangements are mandatory, the absence of a collaborative culture can undermine the mandates. Second, the interplay between the formal and the informal dimensions of mentoring seem to be more evident in supportive and collaborative school cultures. And third, mentoring relationships are framed within existing organizational structures (such as departments) and cultures wherein the value of induction may or may not be valued as part of teachers' professional cultures.

SCHOOL CULTURES AND ORGANIZATIONS AND NOVICE TEACHERS' LEARNING TO TEACH AND RETENTION

In a longitudinal study of fourteen beginning teachers in Portugal, Flores (2005) found that ten participants lost their idealism and increased their

compliance under the poor working conditions and the lack of clear expectations in the school environments. They struggled with problems in
classroom management and student control and with external and internal
pressures to conform to school practices. These struggles led them to an
outcome-led orientation to teaching and to compliance with practices they
did not support. Four of the teachers, however, were still motivated and
committed to teaching and learning in their second year of teaching because
of the supportive atmosphere and informative and collaborative school cultures and leadership in their workplaces. Other researchers have also noted
beginning teachers' challenges to maintain their initial beliefs and images
as they became socialized into the ethos of the school (Burk and Fry, 1997;
Choi and Tang, 2005; Powell, 1997; Puk and Haines, 1999).

Kardos, Johnson, Peske, Kauffman, and Liu (2001) identified three
patterns of school culture, each of which had different influences on the
new teachers. In the veteran-oriented school culture, experienced faculty
members enforced the prevailing norms of privacy and autonomy. In the
novice-oriented culture, the views and values of new teachers, which were
marked by idealism and energy, predominated the professional culture.
The integrated school culture encouraged ongoing and two-way interaction
among novices and experienced teachers. Novice teachers were more likely
to remain in teaching when they worked in the integrated professional culture. In this culture special status was given to novice teachers and support
for their needs in learning to teach was a shared responsibility among the
teachers with different levels of experiences.

Studies from across nations suggested that the mismatch between beginning teachers' original expectations and the reality they faced as they
began teaching in their own classrooms forced a struggle between finding
a balance between their images of the teaching profession and the reality
of schools (Avalos and Aylwin, 2007; Findlay, 2006; Flores and Ferreira,
2009; De Lima, 2003). In a study carried out in Canada, Goddard and
Foster (2001) found that novices often felt overwhelmed by the "realities
of schools" and their jobs as teachers, and they often struggled with disil-
lusionment and blamed the students for their struggles. In Portugal, Flores
and Day (2006) found that school administrators often assumed that new
teachers already had the basic skills and knowledge to handle all the duties required of them. This had a negative influence on novices' first year
of teaching, with implications for their further learning to teach and their
commitment to the teaching profession (Flores and Day, 2006).

In the United States, Kardos and Johnson (2007) found that novices were
often "solo practitioners" in their schools, especially in the veteran-oriented
school cultures. This was also found among new teachers in the Chilean
schools (Avalos and Aylwin, 2007). Drawing on the narrative-biographies
of new teachers, Findlay (2006) investigated new teachers' experience in
England, finding that in spite of formal induction offered to them, they

often felt alienated and isolated in the school context. Kelchtermans and Ballet (2002) analyzed the ways in which Belgian beginning teachers confronted the micropolitical reality of their job situations and experienced struggle and conflict in collaboration and coalition building. They argued that "the challenges of the induction period are to an important degree determined by the organizational contexts and the working conditions in which beginning teachers find themselves" (160).

In summary, there are tensions and conflicts and contradictory messages to new teachers that are directly influenced by school cultures and organizations. This is especially problematic in the places where isolation and lack of collaboration characterize school or department norms. New teachers' images of what it means to be a teacher and their values of teaching as a profession can be revisited, reinforced, challenged, or reshaped through their interaction with their workplaces, and this has implications for teacher learning and retention.

CONCLUSION AND IMPLICATIONS

This chapter examined some of the ways in which school cultures and organizations influenced new teacher induction. Many new teachers struggled with difficulties during their early years in the profession and failed to receive adequate support from colleagues, school leaders, and mentors in their schools, whether or not a formal induction system was in place. Some novices found supportive cultures and benefitted from induction arrangements and supportive mentoring relationships; other new teachers were isolated and had to find their own ways of coping with the complexities of teaching and the realities of schools. This relates directly to issues of professional culture, which is influenced by both formal and informal structures for all teachers (Kardos and Johnson, 2007).

The studies in this review highlight the importance of the ways in which mentoring relationships are framed within existing organizational structures and cultures and the extent to which induction is recognized as a valued part of the school's professional culture. The existence of a supportive and collaborative workplace makes a difference both formally and informally and, unfortunately, isolation and lack of support still characterize many beginning teachers' induction into teaching. New teachers' initial views of what it meant to be a teacher and their values regarding teaching as a profession were often challenged by school settings that were not supportive, which had implications for their further learning to teach and retention as they interacted with their school cultures and organizations.

While some school leaders recognized new teachers' learning and information needs and supported their socialization process and development, others played a minor role in new teacher induction and mentoring. Without any guidance and support from leaders and colleagues in the schools, new teachers were pushed toward more traditional and conservative beliefs and teaching practices (Flores and Day, 2006). When they did find supportive and collaborative leaders and colleagues in the school environment, they more often became self-confident and committed to their work (Flores and Ferreira, 2009). Organizational cultures were found to be one of the most influential factors on the nature and kinds of induction and mentoring (Curry et al., 2008; Johnson and Birkeland, 1993; Schempp, Sparkes, and Templin, 1993). If collaboration does exist in school cultures, it benefits and enhances support structures.

Although induction and mentoring have been identified as valuable experiences for new teachers in many studies (Feiman-Nemser, 2001; Kelly, 2004; Lazovsky and Reichenberg, 2006; Lofstrom and Eisenschmidt, in press; Robinson, 1998), this review supports the notion of linking formal induction to the larger context of policies that promote ongoing professional development for all teachers that are embedded within supportive school cultures and organizations. This is valid for countries, states, or districts in which there are formal induction requirements, such as those in England, Scotland, USA, Israel, New Zealand, and Australia, as well as in countries in which they do not exist at the present time, such as Portugal and Chile. In other words, support programs for new teachers need to be embedded and nurtured within contexts comprising supportive, collaborative, and learning-oriented school cultures.

More studies are needed in order to find out the impact of and interaction among formal and informal mentoring processes and their effect upon new teachers' learning, commitment, and retention. It is also important to examine the influence of the micropolitical realities of schools and departments on new teachers' learning to teach and mentoring. The interactions between mentors and mentees and among new teachers and other staff members should be examined in terms of improved teaching practices and teacher retention. Finally there should be more in-depth studies on the kinds of support that mentors get at school and how the mentoring processes affect and are affected by school cultures and organizations.

Policy makers need to give more attention to induction by recognizing the unique nature of beginning teaching and by adopting consistent and global policies linked to teacher education as a lifelong enterprise. It is important to move beyond the rhetoric of recognizing the institutional and political interest in investing in the induction of new teachers by providing them with effective opportunities for learning and professional growth, especially in countries in which induction is still nonexistent.

Quality induction needs to be framed within the context of a whole-school policy that acknowledges the particular situation of new teachers but that also locates induction within a wider framework for teacher and school development. There is a need to provide education for school leaders and experienced teachers, especially mentors that will enable them to provide new teachers with guidance and support, both formally and informally. Finally, the ways in which novices are welcomed, supported, and helped to develop and the ways school cultures are open to their contributions may foster cultures in which collaborative work and learning become a reciprocal process. As Tickle (2001) noted, "If new teachers are to play a creative and active role in shaping educational quality, the nature of their participation in their own work and their (self-) development will need to be re-imagined and revised" (52). Overlooking induction will have costs and implications for teacher commitment and retention, and, ultimately, for the quality of education provided to children and young people in schools.

REFERENCES

Achinstein, B., R. T. Ogawa, and A. Speiglman. 2004. Are we creating separate and unequal tracks for teachers? The effects of state policy, local conditions, and teacher characteristics on new teacher socialization. *American Educational Research Journal* 41(3):557–603.

Avalos, B., and P. Aylwin. 2007. How young teachers experience their professional work in Chile. *Teaching and Teacher Education* 23(4):515–28.

Burk, D. I., and P. G. Fry. 1997. Autonomy for democracy in a primary classroom: A first year teacher's struggle. *Teaching and Teacher Education* 13(6):645–58.

Calderhead, J., and S. Shorrock. 1997. *Understanding teacher education case studies in the professional development of beginning teachers.* London: Falmer Press.

Choi, P. L., and S. Y. F. Tang. 2005. Role management strategies of beginning teachers in Hong Kong. *Teacher Development* 9(3):369–87.

Cole, A. L. 1991. Relationships in the workplace: Doing what comes naturally? *Teaching and Teacher Education* 7(5/6):415–26.

Curry, M., K. Jaxon, J. L. Russell, M. A. Callahan, and J. Bicais. 2008. Examining the practice of beginning teachers' micropolitical literacy within professional inquiry communities. *Teaching and Teacher Education* 24(3):660–73.

Day, C. 1999. *Developing teachers: The challenges of lifelong learning.* London: Falmer Press.

De Lima, J. A. 2003. Trained for isolation: The impact of departmental cultures on student teachers' views and practices of collaboration. *Journal of Education for Teaching* 29(3):197–218.

Eldar, E., N. Nabel, C. Schechter, R. Talmor, and K. Mazin. 2003. Anatomy of success and failure: The story of three novice teachers. *Educational Research* 45(1):29–48.

Feiman-Nemser, S. 2001. Helping novices learn to teach: Lessons from an exemplary support teacher. *Journal of Teacher Education* 52(1):17–30.

———. 1983. Learning to teach. In *Handbook of teaching and policy*, eds. L. Shulman and G. Sykes. New York: Longman.

Feiman-Nemser, S., and J. Remillard. 1996. Perspectives on Learning to Teach. In *The teacher educator's handbook. Building a knowledge base for the preparation of teachers*, ed. F. B. Murray, 63–91. San Francisco, CA: Jossey-Bass Publishers.

Feiman-Nemser, S., S. Schwille, C. Carver, and B. Yusko. 1999. *A conceptual review of literature on new teacher induction.* College Park, MD: National Partnership for Excellence and Accountability in Schooling.

Findlay, K. 2006. Context and learning factors in the development of teacher identity: A case study of newly qualified teachers during their induction year. *Journal of In-Service Education* 32(4):511–32.

Flores, M. A. 2006a. *Teacher change: A student perspective.* Paper presented at the annual meeting of the American Educational Research Association, San Francisco, CA.

———. 2006b. Being a novice teacher in two different settings: Struggles, continuities, and discontinuities. *Teachers College Record* 108(10):2021–52.

———. 2006c. Induction and mentoring: Policy and practice. In *Research on Teacher Induction*, ed. J. R. Dangel, 37–66. Lanham, MD: Rowman & Littlefield Education.

———. 2005. Mapping new teacher change: Findings from a two-year study. *Teacher Development* 9(3):389–412.

———. 2004. The impact of school culture and leadership on new teachers' learning in the workplace. *International Journal of Leadership in Education* 7(4):1–22.

———. 2001. Person and context in becoming a new teacher. *Journal of Education for Teaching* 27(2):135–48.

Flores, M. A. 2000. *A indução no ensino: Desafios e constrangimentos.* Lisboa: Instituto de Inovação Educacional.

Flores, M. A., and C. Day. 2006. Contexts which shape and reshape new teachers' identities: A multi-perspective study. *Teaching and Teacher Education* 22(2):219–32.

Flores, M. A., and F. I. Ferreira. 2009. The induction and mentoring of new teachers in Portugal: Contradictions, needs, and opportunities. *Research in Comparative and International Education* 4(1):63–73.

Fresko, B., and F. N. Alhija. 2009. When intentions and reality clash: Inherent implementation difficulties of an induction program for new teachers. *Teaching and Teacher Education* 25(2):278–84.

Goddard, J. T., and R. Y. Foster. 2001. The experiences of neophyte teachers: A critical constructivist assessment. *Teaching and Teacher Education* 17(3):349–65.

Hargreaves, A. 2000. Four ages of professionalism and processional learning. *Teachers and Teaching: Theory and Practice* 6(2):151–82.

Hebert, E., and T. Worthy. 2001. Does the first year of teaching have to be a bad one? A case study of success. *Teaching and Teacher Education* 17(8):897–911.

Hobson, A. J., P. Ashby, A. Malderez, and P. D. Tomlinson. 2009. Mentoring beginning teachers: What we know and what we don't. *Teaching and Teacher Education* 25(1):207–16.

Huberman, M. 1991. Survivre à la première phase de la carrière. *Cahiers Pédagogiques* 290:15–17.

Johnson, S. M., and S. E. Birkeland. 1993. Pursuing a "sense of success": New teachers explain their career decisions. *American Educational Research Journal* 40(3):581–617.

Jones, M. 2005. Fitting in, feeling excluded or opting out? An investigation into the socialization process of newcomers to the teaching profession in secondary schools in England. *Journal of In-service Education* 31(3):509–25.

———. 2003. Reconciling personal and professional values and beliefs with the reality of teaching: Findings from an evaluative case study of 10 newly qualified teachers during their year of induction. *Teacher Development* 7(3):385–401.

Jordell, K. O. 1987. Structural and personal influences in the socialization of beginning teachers. *Teaching and Teacher Education* 3(3):165–77.

Kagan, D. M. 1992. Professional growth among preservice and beginning teachers. *Review of Educational Research* 62(2):129–69.

Kardos, S. M., and S. M. Johnson. 2007. On their own and presumed expert: New teachers' experiences with their colleagues. *Teachers College Record* 109(9):2083–106.

Kardos, S. M., S. M. Johnson, H. G. Peske, D. Kauffman, and E. Liu. 2001. Counting on colleagues: New teachers encounter the professional cultures of their schools. *Educational Administration Quarterly* 37(2):250–90.

Kelchtermans, G., and K. Ballet. 2002. The micropolitics of teacher induction: A narrative-biographical study on teacher socialization. *Teaching and Teacher Education* 18(1):105–20.

Kelly, L. M. 2004. Why induction matters. *Journal of Teacher Education* 55(5):438–48.

Kuzmic, J. 1994. A beginning teacher's search for meaning: Teacher socialization, organizational literacy, and empowerment. *Teaching and Teacher Education* 10(1):15–27.

Kyriacou, C., and A. O'Connor. 2003. Primary newly qualified teachers' experience of the induction year in its first year of implementation in England. *Journal of In-Service Education* 29(2):185–200.

Lacey, C. 1995. Professional socialization of teachers. In *International encyclopedia of teaching and teacher education*, ed. L. W. Anderson, 616–20. Oxford: Pergamon.

———. 1977. *The socialization of teachers*. London: Methuen and Co.

Lazovsky, R., and R. Reichenberg. 2006. The new mandatory induction programme for all beginning teachers in Israel: Perceptions of inductees in five study tracks. *Journal of Education for Teaching* 32(1):53–70.

Lee, J. C., and S. Feng. 2007. Mentoring support and the professional development of beginning teachers: A Chinese perspective. *Mentoring and Tutoring: Partnership in Learning* 15(3):243–62.

Lieberman, A. 1996. Practices that support teacher development. Transforming conceptions of professional learning. Pp. 185–201 in *Teacher learning: New policies, new practices*, eds., M. W. McLaughlin and I. Oberman. New York: Teachers College Press.

Lofstrom, E., and E. Eisenschmidt. In press. Novice teachers' perspectives on mentoring: The case of the Estonian induction year. *Teaching and Teacher Education* 25(5):681–89.

Lortie, D. 1975. *Schoolteacher: A sociological study*. Chicago: University of Chicago Press.

Marable, M. A., and S. L. Raimondi. 2007. Teachers' perceptions of what was most (and least) supportive during their first years of teaching. *Mentoring and Tutoring: Partnership in Learning* 15(1):25–37.

Moir, E., and J. Gless. 2001. Quality induction: An investment in teachers. *Teacher Education Quarterly* 28(1):109–14.

Moyles, J., W. Suschitsky, and L. Chapman. 1999. Mentoring in primary schools: Ethos, structures and workloads. *Journal of In-Service Education* 25(1):161–72.

Patterson, N. C., and J. A. Luft. 2002. Informing expectations for induction: Explorations of attrition among supported beginning secondary science teachers in the United States. *Teacher Development* 6(2):205–24.

Powell, R. R. 1997. Teaching alike: A cross-case analysis of first-career and second-career beginning teachers' instructional convergence. *Teaching and Teacher Education* 13(3):341–56.

Puk, T. G., and J. M. Haines. 1999. Are schools prepared to allow beginning teachers to reconceptualize instruction? *Teaching and Teacher Education* 15(5):541–53.

Rhodes, C., A. Nevill, and J. Allan. 2005. How will this help me? Evaluating an accredited programme to enhance the early professional development of newly qualified teachers. *Journal of In-Service Education* 31(2):337–52.

Rippon, J., and M. Martin. 2003. Supporting induction: Relationships count. *Mentoring and Tutoring: Partnership in Learning* 11(2):211–26.

Robinson, G. W. 1998. *New teacher induction: A study of selected new teacher induction models and common practices.* Paper presented at the annual meeting of the Midwestern Educational Research Association, Chicago, IL.

Rust, F. O. 1994. The first year of teaching: It's not what they expected. *Teaching and Teacher Education* 10(2):205–17.

Schempp, P. G., A. C. Sparkes, and T. J. Templin. 1993. The micropolitics of teacher induction. *American Educational Research Journal* 30(3):447–72.

Smith, T. M., and R. M. Ingersoll. 2004. What are the effects of induction and mentoring on beginning teacher turnover? *American Educational Research Journal* 41(3):681–714.

Tickle, L. 2001. Professional qualities and teacher induction. *Journal of In-Service Education* 27(1):51–64.

Vonk, J. H. C. 1995. *Conceptualizing novice teachers' professional development: A base for supervisory interventions.* Paper presented at the annual meeting of the American Educational Research Association, San Francisco, CA.

———. 1993. *Mentoring beginning teachers: Development of a knowledge base for mentors.* Paper presented at the annual meeting of the American Educational Research Association, Atlanta, GA.

Vonk, J. H. C., and G. A. Schras. 1987. From beginning to experienced teacher: A study of the professional development of teachers during their first four years of service. *European Journal of Teacher Education* 10(1):95–110.

Wang, J., S. J. Odell, and S. A. Schwille. 2008. Effects of teacher induction on beginning teachers' teaching: A critical review of the literature. *Journal of Teacher Education* 59(2):132–52.

Weiss, E. M. 1999. Perceived workplace conditions and first-year teachers' morale, career choice commitment, and planned retention: A secondary analysis. *Teaching and Teacher Education* 15(8):861–79.

Williams, A., S. Prestage, and J. Bedward. 2001. Individualism to collaboration: The significance of teacher culture to the induction of newly qualified teachers. *Journal of Education for Teaching* 27(3):253–67.

Yusko, B., and S. Feiman-Nemser. 2008. Embracing contraries: Combining assistance and assessment in new teacher induction. *Teachers College Record* 110(5):923–53.

Zeichner, K. M., and J. M. Gore. 1990. Teacher socialization. In *Handbook of research on teacher education*, ed. R. Houston, 329–48. New York: Macmillan.

4

Teacher Induction for Diverse, Urban Contexts

Peter Youngs, Hong Qian, and Richard Holdgreve-Resendez,
Michigan State University

Student populations in many urban school districts in the United States are characterized by high levels of diversity with regard to race/ethnicity, family income, family composition, language, religion, and other factors (Steinberg and Kincheloe, 2004). In such settings, beginning teachers must address students' individual and cultural differences, establish productive learning environments, plan instruction, translate subject matter knowledge into appropriate curriculum, and assess student learning (Wideen, Mayer-Smith, and Moon, 1998). These challenges are often compounded in urban districts by the range of student needs, learning styles, and behaviors and factors such as poverty, unemployment, and residential mobility (Fideler and Haselkorn, 1999).

The working conditions in urban settings lead many beginning teachers to develop coping strategies that can negatively impact their instruction, their commitment to teaching in urban contexts, and student learning. In addition, these conditions can lead to high rates of turnover. Data from the Schools and Staffing Survey (SASS), a nationally representative survey of U.S. teachers, indicated that 16 percent of first-year teachers in high-poverty schools in 1999–2000 left teaching at the end of the year while 13 percent migrated to other schools or districts (Smith and Ingersoll, 2004). Further, research has found that urban districts often have lesser-qualified teachers than other districts (Lankford, Loeb, and Wyckoff, 2002).

The past two decades have witnessed several responses to the challenges facing beginning teachers in urban settings as well as the inequitable distribution of qualified teachers across districts. Many urban districts have established programs to recruit teaching candidates from among paraprofessionals, community college students, and others with similar racial/ethnic or linguistic backgrounds as urban students. Teach for America is a national program that places graduates from selective universities in high-poverty schools in urban areas. And many urban districts actively recruit midcareer professionals into teaching.

Along with efforts to recruit teachers to urban settings, many districts and states have focused on mentoring and induction to increase teacher effectiveness and retention, especially in urban districts. Many novice teachers are formally assigned to trained mentors, have access to school-based colleagues, and participate in orientations, workshops, and seminars (*Education Week*, 2009; Smith and Ingersoll, 2004). The assumption is that proper support will increase the likelihood that beginning teachers will learn to teach effectively, promote student achievement, and remain in their districts of origin. But recent research by Glazerman and colleagues (2008) has raised questions about the effects of mentoring and induction programs on teacher instruction, retention, and effectiveness, particularly for new teachers in urban settings.

The purpose of this review chapter is to explicate the roles of mentors, colleagues, and administrators in new teachers' experiences in urban settings. We first present the theoretical framework that we employed in the review. The framework suggests that in research on induction in urban settings, scholars need to attend to the characteristics and roles of mentors, colleagues, and administrators; school organizational conditions; and the degree of alignment or fit between novices and others in their schools. Next, we draw on the framework to review several research studies on mentoring and induction in diverse, urban contexts. Finally, we conclude by explicating the implications of this review for practitioners, policy makers, and researchers.

THEORETICAL FRAMEWORK

The theoretical framework employed in this review emphasizes the need for induction research in urban contexts to address the characteristics and roles of mentors, colleagues, and administrators, as well as school organizational conditions. Further, the framework also stresses the importance of considering the degree of alignment or fit between new teachers and those who make up the social system of their schools.

The characteristics of teachers who serve as formally assigned mentors can influence the nature of their interactions with their mentees (i.e., the beginning teachers with whom the mentors are formally matched) as well as the effectiveness of their assistance. Relevant characteristics include years of teaching experience; content areas or grade levels taught; areas of certification; knowledge of curriculum, pedagogy, and assessment; and expertise, including successful teaching experience in diverse, urban contexts (Achinstein and Barrett, 2004; Ladson-Billings, 2001). In addition, scholars have argued that effective urban teachers are able to deal effectively with disruptive student behavior, limited resources, and challenging bureaucratic environments (Haberman, 1994; Zeichner, 1993). Further, such teachers tend to be focused on student learning, have a strong sense of identity, include diverse cultural perspectives in their curriculum, and have strong interpersonal skills (Guyton and Hidalgo, 1995).

Similarly, for colleagues who work with beginning teachers, important traits include years of teaching experience; content areas or grade levels taught; areas of certification; knowledge of pedagogy and assessment; expertise in urban settings; and whether they have taught the same content area or grade level as their mentee. Finally, studies of principals' characteristics have focused on school leaders' knowledge of content, pedagogy, and assessment; professional training; and prior experience (Youngs, 2007b).

Research on mentors' roles in urban settings indicates the importance of assistance with teaching and assessment strategies, classroom management, district policies and procedures, and communication with parents (Athanases and Achinstein, 2003, 2004; Feiman-Nemser, 2001). Studies also find value in opportunities to collaborate with colleagues on pedagogical issues (Kapadia, Coca, and Easton, 2007; Smith and Ingersoll, 2004) and instructional support from principals (Desimone and Smith, 2008; Youngs, 2007b).

New teacher outcomes can also be shaped by the organizational conditions in their schools, including school culture and relational trust. Research by Johnson and colleagues (2004) identified three types of professional school cultures: veteran-oriented, novice-oriented, and integrated. In contrast to schools with veteran- or novice-oriented cultures, schools with integrated professional cultures are marked by frequent opportunities for new teachers to talk with experienced colleagues about curriculum, instruction, and assessment (Kardos et al., 2001).

Relational trust operates at multiple levels within schools. At the intrapersonal level, it is based in a complex cognitive activity in which actors discern others' intentions. These discernments occur within a set of role relations that are influenced by the institutional structure of schooling and by the characteristics of an individual school community. These role relations include teacher-principal relations and teacher-teacher relations; and they can have important consequences at the organizational (i.e., school) level.

Bryk and Schneider (2002) provided evidence that high levels of teacher-teacher and teacher-principal trust were related to higher levels of student achievement and improvements in student performance over time. In urban schools with high levels of relational trust, the framework posits that beginning teachers will be more likely than novices in other schools to discuss instruction with colleagues and to maintain high levels of commitment and efficacy.

In sum, the framework suggests that research on induction should address the characteristics and roles of mentors, colleagues, and administrators, as well as the organizational conditions in new teachers' schools. At the same time, the framework contends that researchers also need to collect data on beginning teachers' characteristics and the extent to which their beliefs about effective urban teaching are aligned or fit with the expectations of their mentors, colleagues, and administrators (Kristof, 1996; Roehrig and Luft, 2006; Wang and Odell, 2007). The first of these aspirations is associated with psychic rewards related to teaching (Bandura, 1977; Hargreaves, 1993; Lortie, 1975) while the latter two involve the degree of social fit between oneself and one's colleagues (Bidwell, 2000; Zhao and Frank, 2003; McLaughlin and Talbert, 2001). The ways in which beginning teachers in urban settings address differences between their beliefs and the expectations placed on them can affect key outcomes, including their instruction, commitment, and retention, and student learning.

In this review, we draw on the framework presented here to explicate what is known about the characteristics and roles of mentors, colleagues, and administrators in effective urban induction programs. In particular, we focus in the next three sections on research published in peer-reviewed journals that met the following criteria:

1. Research included measures of beginning teachers and mentors(-ing), colleagues, and/or principals
2. Research conducted in the United States
3. Research published between 2000 and 2009

Later in the chapter, we draw on theoretical and empirical work between 2000 and 2009 to consider how school organizational conditions and alignment or fit potentially affect key outcomes for beginning teachers in diverse, urban contexts and their students.

CHARACTERISTICS AND ROLES OF MENTORS IN DIVERSE, URBAN SETTINGS

This section examines the types of assistance with instruction, assessment, and student learning that are consequential for beginning teachers in urban settings. In particular, we review several studies that have considered in detail novices' induction experiences in diverse, urban contexts and the characteristics of effective mentors in such contexts and the activities in which they engage. With regard to the latter, we focus on mentoring practices that addressed or promoted the following among novice teachers: reflective, student-centered instruction, subject matter knowledge, the use of formative assessment, analyses of student learning, and/or culturally relevant teaching.

In one study, Luft and Roehrig (2005) explored the beliefs, instructional practices, and experiences of three white, first-year secondary science teachers who worked primarily with urban and rural Hispanic students. The researchers concluded that the beginning teachers' intentions did not always translate into reality and that they used familiar, less effective practices to make their environments less uncertain.

Further, the novices' enthusiasm for working in diverse communities did not result in the enactment of reform-based practices. In general, the new teachers did not have a cultural point of reference with regard to their students; instead, they often moved through their science units with little attention to the cultural relevance of the curriculum or their instruction. The study suggested that novices working in communities different than their own backgrounds require strong preservice and induction programs that promote beliefs and effective practices for working with diverse students (Luft and Roehrig, 2005).

In another study, Achinstein and Barrett, (2004) investigated the patterns of and differences in frames (managerial, human resource, and political) used by mentors and novices to view linguistically and culturally diverse elementary students and challenges of practice. The study featured three case study vignettes that clearly highlighted the distinct frames and reframing exhibited across elementary teacher-mentor pairs in diverse California districts.

Achinstein and Barrett, (2004) concluded that mentors introduced novices to new ways of seeing challenges of practice and students through the use of multiple frames. In particular, the mentors promoted reframing as a way to interpret experiences, address problems, and to expose the underlying values held by teachers. The researchers also found that the mentors helped new teachers understand that reframing their problems, by considering relationships with students and the school political context, could help them adjust their approaches. Along those lines, they used student observations, student work analyses, and teacher-student transcripts to help new teachers focus on the needs of culturally diverse students. By reframing novices' views, mentors were able to help make hidden or ignored dynamics affecting student learning more apparent (Achinstein and Barrett, 2004).

In a third study, Athanases and Achinstein (2003) examined two beginning elementary teacher-mentor pairs from a two-year study of twenty such pairs in diverse California districts. The investigation of these two pairs illuminated the complex challenges that mentors face in focusing new teachers on student learning, including low-performing students.

The researchers concluded that the mentors in the study used two main strategies to focus beginning teachers on the learning of individual and underperforming students. First, the mentors activated knowledge of student and teacher learning and numerous domains of assessment, including knowledge of student assessment, content standards, curricular alignment, and formative assessment of new teachers. Second, the mentors helped beginning teachers enact and refine pedagogical strategies based on their accumulated knowledge of students' learning styles and needs (Athanases and Achinstein, 2003). When mentors addressed such knowledge and strategies in their interactions with novices, the novices, in turn, were more able to use scaffolding and grouping strategies to meet their students' learning needs (Athanases and Achinstein, 2003).

The studies by Achinstein and colleagues provide some insight into effective mentoring practices in diverse, urban contexts. In particular, they suggest mentors can promote student-centered instruction and attention to the needs of diverse learners by probing novices' thinking, focusing on students, reframing new teachers' views, drawing on knowledge of assessment, and analyzing student learning. At the same time, it is less clear from these studies how particular mentoring practices may be associated with district policies or broader cultural practices. Next, we discuss studies that considered associations between mentoring and such factors.

In one study, Youngs (2007a) addressed this question by examining mentoring for first- and second-year teachers in two urban, high-poverty school districts in Connecticut. For this study, the researchers interviewed beginning teachers and mentors throughout the 2000–2001 school year. In one of the districts, three of the four novices in the study had frequent opportunities to address instructional issues with their mentors. Mentoring assistance included helping novices understand the purposes of teaching reading, writing, and math at different grade levels; focusing on students' knowledge and abilities in planning instruction and analyzing student work in these content areas; and helping novices examine the relationship between their lesson plans and instructional decisions during class and student engagement and behavior. In the other district, beginning teachers had much fewer opportunities to address instructional issues with their mentors. Differences in the novices' experiences in these two districts seemed related to variations between the districts in a) the degree to which they focused on teaching expertise in selecting mentors, b) the degree to which they assigned each new teacher to a mentor who taught in the same grade level and/or content area, and c) the understandings of induction held by mentors (Youngs, 2007a).

In a study that did not focus on mentoring in urban school contexts, Strong and Baron (2004) analyzed the pedagogical suggestions made by sixteen mentors in conversations with their mentees and how the beginning teachers responded. Each of the pairs typically participated in a conversation before and after a lesson that the mentor observed.

The researchers reported that mentors avoided giving direct advice. Instead, they provided indirect suggestions, including ones that elaborated responses from the new teachers, thereby resembling an open-ended interview. These indirect suggestions included expressions of possibility, including such words as "perhaps," "could," "might," or "maybe" (Strong and Baron, 2004). The researchers found that the mentees accepted their mentor's suggestions 80 percent of the time. The most frequent suggestion topics related to teaching (70 percent of the time) and students (18 percent of the time). Strong and Baron (2004) suggest that the conversational patterns might be explained by the induction program (in which all sixteen mentor-mentees participated), which was based on a cognitive coaching model.

Other research has considered how U.S. mentoring practices may differ from practices in other countries. In one study that did not focus on mentoring in urban contexts, Wang, Strong, and Odell (2004) examined the content and forms of mentor-novice conversations among two U.S. and two Chinese elementary mentor-novice pairs. Compared to the Chinese pairs, the conversations among the U.S. mentor-novice pairs focused less on subject-matter content and more on individual students. In terms of conversation forms, the U.S. mentors tended to ask questions about what happened and to describe what they saw in novices' lessons while the Chinese mentors tended to provide new teachers with specific critiques and suggestions regarding their lessons.

Wang and his colleagues (2004) argued that these differences were likely related to the structure of curriculum and the organization of teaching and mentoring in each country. In the U.S. mentor-novice pairs in this study, inconsistent curricular materials and guidance and individualized teaching may have made it difficult for the mentors to focus on subject matter and provide concrete feedback.

This not only contrasts with the Chinese mentor-novice pairs in the Wang, Strong, and Odell (2004) study, it also differs from mentors in structured U.S. induction programs who generally focus in their work with novices on curriculum, formative assessment, and student learning. Examples of structured induction programs in the United States include the Pathwise/Danielson Framework for Teaching; the New Teacher Center's Formative Assessment System; peer assistance and review programs; and Connecticut's BEST (Beginning Educator Support and Training) program.

For an overview of structured induction programs in the United States, see Youngs, Pogodzinski, and Low (in press).

In sum, recent qualitative studies of mentoring in diverse, urban contexts indicate that mentors can promote several important outcomes among beginning teachers. More specifically, mentors can help novices reframe the challenges they face, modify their instructional and assessment practices, and analyze and promote student learning. In addition, some large-scale survey research suggests that mentoring can increase teacher commitment and retention (Kapadia, Coca, and Easton, 2007; Smith and Ingersoll, 2004). In the next section, we consider the results from these studies.

RECENT LARGE-SCALE RESEARCH ON MENTORING

This section describes recent large-scale studies that investigated the effects of mentoring and other induction activities on several outcomes for beginning teachers. In a study using the 1999–2000 SASS, Smith and Ingersoll (2004) found that having a mentor in one's field reduced the likelihood of leaving teaching at the end of the first year by 30 percent. The authors also reported that turnover among teachers did not vary by school location; i.e., whether the teacher's school of origin was urban, suburban, or rural (Smith and Ingersoll, 2004).

Recent work by Kapadia, Coca, and Easton (2007) and Glazerman and colleagues (2008) has built on Smith and Ingersoll's study by analyzing the induction experiences of new teachers in diverse, urban contexts. Kapadia and her colleagues (2007) collected survey data in 2004–2005 from novice (i.e., first- and second-year) teachers in the Chicago Public Schools (CPS). The researchers found that novice elementary teachers (i.e., in grades K–8) receiving "strong" mentoring "were much more likely (than other novices) to report a good experience, intend to continue teaching, and plan to remain in the same school" (Kapadia, Coca, and Easton, 2007, 28).

Strong mentoring included help with teaching and assessment strategies, classroom management, CPS policies and procedures, observation and discussion of teaching, and communication with parents. Teachers receiving *average* levels of mentoring experienced most types of assistance and found them somewhat or very helpful, and teachers receiving *weak* mentoring either received no mentoring assistance or they received some mentoring activities, but found them at best somewhat helpful.

In some ways, a recent study by Glazerman and colleagues (2008) challenged findings of other research on mentoring and induction. In their study, the researchers employed random assignment to compare a group of beginning elementary school teachers who experienced "comprehensive" induction with an equivalent group exposed to their districts' conventional induction activities.

The teachers in the treatment group participated in comprehensive induction programs from either the Educational Testing Service (ETS) or the New Teacher Center (NTC) at the University of California-Santa Cruz. These programs featured full-time, trained mentors, weekly meetings with mentors, professional development opportunities, and formative assessments that featured observations and constructive feedback (Glazerman et al., 2008). Seventeen districts in thirteen states participated in the study, each of which had more than 50 percent of its students eligible for free or reduced-price lunch. In each district, elementary schools were assigned to either the control group or one of two treatments (selected by the district). In their analyses, Glazerman and colleagues (2008) considered the teachers who received comprehensive induction through the ETS and NTC programs to be part of one treatment group.

Based on the first year of data collection (2005–2006) and analysis, Glazerman and colleagues (2008) reported "no statistically significant differences between treatment and control group teachers' performance on any of the three domains of classroom practices" on which they focused: lesson implementation, lesson content, and classroom culture" (2008, xv). With regard to the effects of comprehensive induction on teacher effectiveness, "the average impacts across all grades were not significantly different from zero for math or reading" (Glazerman et al., 2008, xvi). Finally, they reported, "comprehensive teacher induction had no statistically significant impact on teacher retention" (Glazerman et al., 2008, xvi). The researchers do note, though, that analyses based on the second year of their data collection (when complete) may indicate some statistically significant long-term effects of comprehensive induction programs.

In sum, recent large-scale survey research on induction provides some insights into the impact of mentoring on beginning teachers in diverse, urban contexts. Smith and Ingersoll (2004) reported an effect of within-field mentoring on teacher retention while Kapadia, Coca, and Easton (2007) found that strong mentoring was related to important outcomes for novice elementary teachers in Chicago. At the same time, analyses by Glazerman and colleagues (2008) raised questions about the impact of comprehensive induction programs on first-year teachers in urban, high-poverty districts. While findings from the latter study may seem dismaying to advocates of high-quality induction, they also indicate a need for induction scholars to expand the foci of their research designs to include measures of colleagues, principals, and school organizational conditions.

HOW COLLEAGUES, ADMINISTRATORS, AND SCHOOL ORGANIZATIONAL CONDITIONS SHAPE INDUCTION IN DIVERSE, URBAN SETTINGS

In urban contexts, along with formally assigned mentors, beginning teachers' colleagues and administrators can play an important role in their induction experiences. In addition, school organizational conditions, including school culture and relational trust, can also impact novices in diverse settings. This section explicates the results from several studies that have considered how colleagues, principals, and school conditions can affect outcomes for novices.

In one study, Kardos and colleagues (2001) identified three types of professional cultures within schools: veteran-oriented, novice-oriented, and integrated professional cultures. This study was based on interview data gathered from fifty beginning teachers in a wide range of Massachusetts public school settings, 60 percent of which were urban schools. In different types of professional cultures, novices experienced varying levels of support. In schools with veteran-oriented cultures, new teachers were given no special status, which seemed to result in little orientation, induction, or support. In schools labeled as having novice-oriented cultures, the majority of the teachers were new to the profession, but few formal induction supports were offered and there was a general lack of expertise (Kardos et al., 2001).

Unlike novices in schools with veteran- or novice-oriented cultures, Kardos and colleagues found that beginning teachers in integrated professional cultures received sustained support and had frequent exchanges with colleagues across experience levels. This study also illustrated the important role that principals can play in developing integrated professional cultures where the particular needs of novice teachers are addressed. As described by new teachers, the principals in schools with integrated professional cultures were actively involved, focused on improving teaching and learning, and promoted collaboration and teamwork (Kardos et al., 2001).

In related research, Johnson and colleagues focused in-depth on a teacher who was teaching in a small, urban secondary school. His school served primarily low-income students and was characterized by an integrated professional culture. From the novice's perspective, the school emphasized high expectations for students, teacher collaboration, and continuing professional development, all geared toward promoting high student performance. At this school, novices received ongoing assistance as they learned to teach, and teachers across experience levels frequently discussed teaching (Johnson and PNGT, 2004).

In their study using the 1999–2000 SASS, Smith and Ingersoll (2004) found that for first-year teachers, collaborating with colleagues on instruction reduced the risk that they would leave teaching at the end of the year by 43 percent. In addition, the authors reported that collaborating with colleagues lowered the risk of migration to other schools by 25 percent (Smith and Ingersoll, 2004).

Other research is addressing the role of principals and school conditions in the induction of particular groups of beginning teachers. In the study by Kapadia, Coca, and Easton (2007), the authors found that "(e)ncouragement and assistance from the principal, regularly scheduled opportunities to collaborate with peers in the same field, and participation in a network of new teachers" made elementary novices more likely to have a good teaching experience and to plan to remain in the same school (Kapadia, Coca, and Easton, 2007, p. 30).

Other research by Youngs (2007b) considered elementary principals' approaches to supporting beginning teachers in diverse, urban contexts. The study featured interviews with and observations of six elementary principals from three Connecticut districts and novice teachers, mentors, and other teachers from the principals' schools. The study found that three of the principals strongly promoted new teachers' instructional growth in their direct interactions with them and by facilitating their work with mentors and grade-team members; in contrast, the other three school leaders had much less of a positive impact on new teachers.

These differences in beginning teachers' experiences seemed related to variations in the principals' professional backgrounds and their beliefs and actions regarding leadership, induction, and teacher evaluation. In particular, principals with strong backgrounds in context knowledge, teacher assessment, and professional development were more likely to promote new teacher learning in urban contexts than other school leaders (Youngs, 2007b).

Another key aspect of the social context for beginning teachers in diverse, urban schools is the degree of relational trust among teachers at their schools and between teachers and their administrators (Bryk and Schneider, 2002). As noted, relational trust can be conceptualized as an emergent property of the everyday interactions between and among adults in the school setting. When relational trust is high among teachers and between teachers and administrators, a given school is likely to support the practices and growth of new teachers and to reduce their sense of vulnerability, which can have a significant effect on their self-efficacy and commitment. Further, new teachers' efforts to put their own beliefs about instruction into practice can be strengthened and reinforced when they discern high levels of integrity and competence among their mentors, colleagues, and principals.

In sum, recent research suggests the need for induction researchers to include measures of the beliefs, practices, and support provided by new teachers' colleagues and principals and the relations among them. Further, advances in scholarship indicate the need for future induction studies that take account of the school cultures and professional communities in which novices work. But this recent work neglects to consider the extent to which beginning teachers are aligned or fit in with their colleagues, principals, and/or broader school and district contexts. In the next section, we discuss recent research on induction that addresses these questions.

DEGREE OF FIT BETWEEN NEW TEACHERS IN DIVERSE, URBAN CONTEXTS AND THEIR MENTORS, COLLEAGUES, AND ADMINISTRATORS

The theoretical framework employed in this review posits that induction researchers should not only investigate mentors, colleagues, principals, and school organizational conditions; in order to understand how these factors affect outcomes for beginning teachers in diverse, urban contexts, it is also important to examine the degree of fit or alignment between novices and the individuals who make up the social system of their schools. In this section, we review three empirical studies that considered the extent to which new teachers are aligned or fit in with key members of their social contexts.

In one study, Achinstein, Ogawa, and Speiglman (2004) showed how differences in two new teachers' characteristics, their alignment with mentors and colleagues, and their opportunities for collaboration seemed to influence their initial labor market decisions as well as the teaching skills they acquired. One novice, Liz, grew up in the urban district where she taught, attended a nearby large public university, and began teaching while she completed her certification.

District A, in which Liz worked, recruited teachers from the local community to reflect the population of the students, even though they may have initially lacked full teaching credentials. In contrast, the other novice, Sam, was from an affluent community and received a teaching certificate from a research university. District B, in which Sam worked, recruited teachers from such universities who shared a teaching philosophy consistent with that of the district. Achinstein, Ogawa, and Speiglman reported that "(t)he types of teachers employed by the two districts were the result of an interaction between the new teachers' backgrounds, which affected their educational and employment choices, and the districts' hiring practices" (2004, 576).

Liz and Sam were each assigned a mentor during their first two years of teaching. Liz focused more with her mentor on issues related to classroom management and parents than on instruction. While Liz's beliefs about teaching were aligned with those of her mentor, her mentor did not help her improve her teaching. The expectations placed on Liz by her colleagues and district policy were to follow routines, curricula, and assessments designed by the state and district. According to Achinstein, Ogawa, and Speiglman, "(t)he literacy coordinator agreed that novices could simply enact the curriculum without having to understand it" (2004, 578). Further, the induction program in Liz's district focused on implementing the literacy curriculum.

In contrast, Sam met weekly with his mentor to coplan instruction, and he benefited from grade-team collaboration, working with a district instructional coach and participating in an action research group. In addition, he enjoyed numerous professional development activities that emphasized inquiry (Achinstein, Ogawa, and Speiglman, 2004). In sum, in the cases of both Liz and Sam, there was a strong degree of fit between novices and their school and district contexts, but the consequences of having high levels of fit differed considerably for these two novices.

In a second study, Roehrig and Luft (2006) investigated the effects of a science-focused induction program on beginning secondary science teachers who had completed different teacher education programs. The sixteen study participants were all first-year secondary science teachers who had graduated the previous year from one of four different preparation programs. The researchers collected data on all of the participants during their first year of teaching as they participated in the induction program in order to examine their teaching beliefs, instructional practices, and experiences in the classroom.

Roehrig and Luft (2006) found that the novice science teachers' preservice training influenced the types of assistance they sought and took away from the induction program. In addition, during the year of data collection, those participants who had graduated from a preparation program with two science methods courses and an extended student teaching experience expressed beliefs in the efficacy of student-centered instruction and enacted more reform-based practices than the other teachers (Roehrig and Luft, 2006).

In a third study, Youngs, Frank, and Pogodzinski (2009) used survey data to examine how early career teachers' perceptions of fit between themselves and their schools were associated with their commitment. The sample included eleven urban school districts in Michigan and Indiana and 184 teachers in grades 1–8 who were in their first three years of teaching. The authors found that stronger person-organization fit was associated with commitment to one's grade level, commitment to one's school, and one's overall commitment to teaching (Youngs, Frank, and Pogodzinski, 2009).

In sum, these studies suggest that based on their professional training and their beliefs and practices, beginning teachers will fit in with their school and district contexts to varying degrees and that the degree of fit they experience can have important consequences for their instruction and commitment.

CONCLUSION AND IMPLICATIONS

In conclusion, the findings from this review suggest a number of implications for practitioners, policy makers, and researchers. With regard to practitioners, the studies reviewed in the second section of this chapter demonstrate several ways that mentors can promote new teacher development in diverse, urban settings. In particular, mentors can foster growth among novices by probing their thinking, helping them to focus on students, using knowledge of assessment, reframing novices' perspectives, and analyzing student work (Achinstein and Barrett, 2004; Athanases and Achinstein, 2003).

Such mentoring practices can help novices to engage in student-centered, culturally relevant teaching; strengthen their knowledge of subject matter; employ formative assessment; and use student performance data to modify their instruction. Further, effective mentoring practices seem to be possibly related to mentors' background knowledge, district selection and assignment policies, and the use of cognitive coaching models in induction (Strong and Baron, 2004; Youngs, 2007a).

But research from urban school districts reviewed in the third and fourth sections indicated some limitations of the influence of mentors on beginning teachers, even in comprehensive induction programs. In particular, recent research by Glazerman et al. (2008); Johnson and colleagues (2004); and Kapadia, Coca, and Easton (2007) suggested a need for policy makers and researchers to conceptualize induction in broader ways than mentoring.

As noted, in a large-scale, experimentally designed study, Glazerman and colleagues (2008) found little impact in urban districts on first-year teacher instruction, retention, or effectiveness of induction that featured intensive, structured support from mentors; formative teacher assessment; and frequent professional development. At the same time, research by Johnson and colleagues (Johnson and PNGT, 2004; Kardos et al., 2001) and Kapadia, Coca, and Easton (2007) found that regular opportunities to collaborate with colleagues and assistance from principals were associated with more positive teaching experiences and higher commitment levels for first- and second-year teachers at both the elementary and secondary school levels.

The fifth section of the chapter featured three studies that suggested a need for policy makers, district and school administrators, and researchers to attend to the degree of alignment or fit between new teachers and the social contexts in which they work. As noted, degree of fit refers to the extent to which a beginning teacher's beliefs about effective teaching and instructional practices are aligned with those of their mentor, colleagues, and administrators.

Two of the studies reviewed here found that the degree of fit experienced by novices affected their instructional practices (Achinstein, Ogawa, and Speiglman, 2004; Roehrig and Luft, 2006) while the third reported that degree of fit was associated with commitment (Youngs, Frank, and Pogodzinski, 2009). In our view, unless administrators and policy makers focus more directly on the issue of fit between beginning teachers and the social contexts of their schools, efforts to provide structured, formal support through mentoring and other forms of assistance are unlikely to have consistent, significant effects on novices, as evidenced by the results from Glazerman et al. (2008).

REFERENCES

Achinstein, B., and A. Barrett. 2004. How new teachers and mentors view diverse learners and challenges of practice. *Teacher College Record* 106(4):716–46.

Achinstein, B., R. T. Ogawa, and A. Speiglman. 2004. Are we creating separate and unequal tracks of teachers? The impact of state policy, local conditions, and teacher characteristics on new teacher socialization. *American Educational Research Journal* 41(3):557–603.

Athanases, S. Z., and B. Achinstein. 2003. Focusing new teachers on individual and low performing students: The centrality of formative assessment in the mentor's repertoire of practice. *Teacher College Record* 105(8):1486–1520.

Bandura, A. 1977. Self-efficacy: Toward a unifying theory of behavioral change. *Psychological Review* 84:191–215.

Bidwell, C. E. 2000. School as context and construction: A social psychological approach to the study of schooling. In *Handbook of the sociology in education*, ed. M. T. Hallinan, 15–36. New York: Kluwer Academic.

Bryk, A., and B. Schneider. 2002. *Trust in schools: A core resource for improvement.* New York: Russell Sage Foundation.

Desimone, L. M., and T. M. Smith. 2008. *Improving middle-school math instruction and student achievement.* Paper presented at the annual meeting of the American Educational Research Association, New York.

Education Week. 2009. *Portraits of a population: How English-language learners are putting schools to the test. Quality Counts 2009.* Washington, DC: Editorial Projects in Education.

Feiman-Nemser, S. 2001. From preparation to practice: Designing a continuum to strengthen and sustain teaching. *Teachers College Record* 103(6):1013–55.

Fideler, E. F., and D. Haselkorn. 1999. *Learning the ropes: Urban teacher induction programs and practices in the United States.* Belmont, MA: Recruiting New Teachers, Inc.

Glazerman, S., S. Dolfin, M. Bleeker, A. Johnson, E. Isenberg, J. Lugo-Gil, M. Grider, E. Britton, and M. Ali. 2008. *Impacts of comprehensive teacher induction: Results from the first year of a randomized controlled study.* Washington, DC: U.S. Department of Education, Institute of Education Sciences.

Guyton, E., and F. Hidalgo. 1995. Characteristics, responsibilities, and qualities of urban school mentors. *Education and Urban Society* 28(1):40–47.

Haberman, M. 1994. Gentle teaching in a violent society. *Educational Horizons* 72(3):1–13.

Hargreaves, A. 1993. Individualism and individuality: Reinterpreting the teacher culture. In *Teachers' work: Individuals, colleagues, and contexts,* eds. J. Little and M. McLaughlin, 51–76. New York: Teachers College Press.

Johnson, S. M., and The Project on the Next Generation of Teachers (PNGT). 2004. *Finders and keepers: Helping new teachers survive and thrive in our schools.* San Francisco: Jossey-Bass.

Kapadia, K., V. Coca, and J. Q. Easton. 2007. *Keeping new teachers: A first look at the influences of induction in the Chicago Public Schools.* Chicago: Consortium on Chicago School Research, University of Chicago.

Kardos, S. M., S. M. Johnson, H. G. Peske, D. Kauffman, and E. Liu. 2001. Counting on colleagues: New teachers encounter the professional cultures of their schools. *Educational Administration Quarterly* 37(2):250–90.

Kristof, A. 1996. Person-organization fit: An integrative review of its conceptualizations, measurement, and implications. *Personnel Psychology* 49:1–49.

Ladson-Billings, G. 2001. *Crossing over to Canaan: The journey of new teachers in diverse classrooms.* San Francisco: Jossey-Bass.

Lankford, H., S. Loeb, and J. Wyckoff. 2002. Teacher sorting and the plight of urban schools: A descriptive analysis. *Educational Evaluation and Policy Analysis* 24(1):37–62.

Lortie, D. C. 1975. *Schoolteacher: A sociological study.* Chicago: University of Chicago Press.

Luft, J. A., and G. Roehrig. 2005. Enthusiasm is not enough: Beginning secondary science teachers in primarily Hispanic settings. *School Science and Mathematics* 105(3):116–26.

McLaughlin, M. W., and J. E. Talbert. 2001. *Professional communities and the work of high school teaching.* Chicago: University of Chicago Press.

Roehrig, G. H., and J. A. Luft. 2006. Does one size fit all? The induction experience of beginning science teachers from different teacher preparation programs. *Journal of Research in Science Teaching* 43(9):963–85.

Smith, T. M., and R. M. Ingersoll. 2004. Reducing teacher turnover: What are the components of effective induction? *American Educational Research Journal* 41(3):681–714.

Steinberg, S. R., and J. L. Kincheloe, eds. 2004. *19 urban questions: Teaching in the city.* New York: P. Lang.

Strong, M., and W. Baron. 2004. An analysis of mentoring conversations with beginning teachers: Suggestions and responses. *Teaching and Teacher Education* 20:47–57.

Wang, J., and S. J. Odell. 2007. An alternative conception of mentor-novice relationships: Learning to teach in reform-minded ways as a context. *Teaching and Teacher Education* 23:473–89.

Wang, J., M. Strong, and S. J. Odell. 2004. Mentor-novice conversations about teaching: A comparison of two U.S. and two Chinese cases. *Teacher College Record* 106(4):775–813.

Wideen, M., J. Mayer-Smith, and B. Moon. 1998. A critical analysis of the research on learning to teach: Making the case for an ecological perspective on inquiry. *Review of Educational Research* 68(2):130–78.

Youngs, P. 2007a. District induction policy and new teachers' experiences: An examination of local policy implementation in Connecticut. *Teachers College Record* 109(3):797–837.

———. 2007b. How elementary principals' beliefs and actions influence new teachers' induction experiences. *Educational Administration Quarterly* 44(2):101–37.

Youngs, P., K. A. Frank, and B. Pogodzinski. 2009. *The role of person-organization fit in beginning teacher commitment.* Paper presented at the annual meeting of the American Educational Research Association, San Diego.

Youngs, P., B. Pogodzinski, and M. Low. In press. The role of formative assessments in new teacher induction. In *Teacher assessment and the quest for teacher quality: A handbook,* ed. M. Kennedy. San Francisco: Jossey-Bass.

Zeichner, K. M. 1993. *Educating teachers for cultural diversity.* East Lansing, MI: National Center for Research on Teacher Learning, Michigan State University.

Zhao, Y., and K. A. Frank. 2003. An ecological analysis of factors affecting technology use in schools. *American Educational Research Journal* 40(4):807–40.

5

Teacher Induction Policies at National and State Levels

Edward G. Pultorak, Southern Illinois University
Richard E. Lange, National-Louis University

Pam Brown, superintendent of a medium-sized rural school district, looked across her desk at Sally Kenshaw, one of the district's new teachers. Sally just completed what Pam thought was her first successful year of teaching. The three formal evaluations from the principal were very positive, parents and colleagues were extremely pleased with her involvement in extracurricular activities, and the student body seemed to look forward to her classes. Sally, however, had submitted her letter of resignation.

"What would provoke such a letter?" thought the superintendent. Brown turned toward the young teacher, who began to express her deep sadness for this decision—a decision that was also confusing for her to express. Although she enjoyed her job as teacher, she began to explain that the stress and expectations were more than she had anticipated. The superintendent began to remember that as a "highly recommended" individual for this position, she thought it would be acceptable to provide Ms. Kenshaw with a larger class even though the class consisted of several challenging students. Further, because of the nature of her assignment, she was not likely to have many opportunities to interact with other teachers. With regret, the superintendent accepted her letter and wished her well.

Sally was left with several options. She could quit the teaching profession, but Sally's love for teaching and working with students had deepened during her first year, and she wished to pursue this career. She had considered applying for a similar position in a different district. However, the innumerable thoughts of the anxiety and pressure experienced during her first teaching position led to further confusion. And so, Sally selected her final option. She had heard from former classmates that a neighboring state provided support programs for beginning teachers that included a mentor and class-size reduction.

After a few interviews in different states, Sally was successful and gained employment as a teacher in a school very similar to her first teaching assignment except that it provided an induction program for novice teachers. The pattern of Sally's teaching success continued. In fact, her new superintendent rated her as one of the top teachers in the school district. This time Sally was also content with her employment choice, not feeling as overwhelmed by her teaching responsibilities as a result of having reduced class size and a mentor to guide her through more challenging situations.

Though fictitious, the above scenario is based on a similar situation that did occur. Unfortunately, first-year teachers are frequently left in a "sink or swim" position with little support from colleagues and few opportunities for professional development (Darling-Hammond, 2006). The purpose of this chapter is to provide a better understanding of the trends of teacher induction policy at the national and state levels. To meet this purpose, we define *policy*, provide information as it relates to induction program policy at the national level, identify states requiring support programs for beginning teachers, and discuss induction program policies in four states that serve as a cross section of policies across the United States.

INTRODUCTION

Some of the most successful educational reforms of the early 1980s were new teacher mentoring and induction programs. Furtwengler (1995) explains, "Key goals of these programs were to retain new teachers in the profession and help those teachers advance through Berliner's identified stages of competent, proficient, or expert" (1). As the eighties progressed, "beginning teacher programs took on various ownerships at the local and state level . . . but the major policy initiative for their emergence occurred at the state level" (Furtwengler, 1995, 1). It became increasingly evident by the late 1980s that induction and mentoring programs were necessary to retain teachers. The trend continued into the nineties as professional development was paired with new teacher programs to ensure that teachers were not only retained but also developed mastery of teaching skills (Furtwengler, 1995).

The magnitude of these reforms can be seen in the number of states that have developed programs since 1984. "At that time, eight states reported the operation of [new teacher] programs. By 1991, 31 states reported that they had launched beginning teacher programs" of some sort (Furtwengler, 1995, 2). In the early 1990s, pilot programs were in place and many states conducted their own research regarding effective programs. This created much experimentation into the most effective ways to promote teacher induction and mentoring programs; some states added funding and/or mandates while others dropped them. To illustrate the unpredictability of these trends, since 2006, five states have stopped mandating new teacher programs but nine states have begun to contribute funding (Editorial Projects in Education Research Center, 2008; Klemick, 2008; Russell, 2006).

Presently, Klemick (2008) reports that "25 states require and finance mentoring for all beginning teachers and 20 of those states have some form of mentoring program standards for selecting, training, and/or matching mentors to novice teachers" (61). Still, there are great disparities among the states regarding the type of programs available and the amount of funding (Russell, 2006). While these numbers indicate that fewer states are currently mandating new teacher programs than in the past, particularly during the explosion of new programs in the early nineties, in fact, more teachers are involved in them overall. Russell (2006) gives credence to this trend in reporting that "more than 80 percent of new teachers participate in some kind of program, up from 40 percent in 1990–91" (1). Further, two states, South Carolina and North Carolina, also have a reduced-workload policy for first-year teachers (Editorial Projects in Education Research Center, 2008).

The following is a list of states that have a requirement for all new teachers to participate in a state-funded induction program: Alabama, Arkansas, California, Connecticut, Delaware, Indiana, Iowa, Kentucky, Louisiana, Maine, Massachusetts, Michigan, New Jersey, New Mexico, North Carolina, Ohio, Oklahoma, Pennsylvania, South Carolina, Utah, West Virginia, and Wisconsin. Virginia, New York, and Missouri require a state-funded mentoring program but not an induction program. Further, all the states listed above, with the exception of Michigan, Missouri, New Mexico, New York, and Pennsylvania, have state standards for selecting, training, and/or matching mentors (Editorial Projects in Education Research Center, 2008).

However, the effectiveness of new teacher induction programs is debatable. Because of the diversity in programs among states, research regarding their effectiveness is just beginning to appear. Regardless, initial data suggest that effective teacher mentoring and induction programs are cost-effective and increase teacher retention (Russell, 2006; Villar and Strong, 2007). Further research must be conducted to ascertain if induction programs affect other areas such as quality of teaching and, in turn, quality of student learning (Russell, 2006).

This chapter does not provide analyses of emerging data; rather, the purpose is to paint a picture of the diversity of support programs by providing a cross section of four states for examination. These states were selected inasmuch as they illustrate the variety of state policies in place to support beginning teachers across the United States at the time of this writing. Further, for clarification, as we discuss teacher induction policies at national and state levels in this chapter, policy is defined as "a program of action adopted by an individual, group, or government, or the set of principles on which they are based" (Soukhanov, 2001).

INVOLVEMENT AT THE NATIONAL LEVEL

Currently, individual states set policies that determine what, if any, type of new teacher support programs are available in their states. The national government is interested in these programs, although it neither mandates nor funds programs of its own. Russell (2006) reports that "the U.S. Department of Education's Institute of Education Services began a five-year evaluation study examining the effects" of new teacher programs on schools, particularly the learning of students and the quality of instruction (3). This study should provide much-needed research-based evidence for the effectiveness of the nation's new teacher induction programs. From this, one hopes that each state's data will be represented and effective methods will be shared among states. In this way, the U.S. Department of Education can take a passive, yet important, role in policy making at the state level.

In addition to important research studies, the United States Department of Education webpage (www.ed.gov) provides literature to help new teachers in their first years. Although the government does not fund specific programs, it has used qualitative data to help new teachers. For instance, Sallie Mae First Class Teacher award winners (outstanding new teachers from each U.S. state and territory) have been interviewed and their advice published in the "Survival Guide for New Teachers" (DePaul, 2000).

The impetus for this type of support, as DePaul (2000) explains, arises because the U.S. Department of Education has "a keen interest in the issues of teacher induction, quality, and retention and is taking steps to improve the American teaching force: supporting legislation to improve teacher education; connecting with teachers through a National Teacher Forum and listserv; and working with college presidents to call attention to teacher education" (7). Obviously, the U.S. government plays a part in new teacher mentoring and induction, though currently it has a more passive role than state governments that play the largest, most active roles in these programs.

CALIFORNIA

The largest state in the country by population, California is one of the leaders in promotion and legislation of new teacher programs. Beginning in 1983 with the Hughes-Hart Educational Reform Act, California sought to expand rewards and opportunities in teaching, attract and retain capable teachers, and expand resources supporting staff development and school improvement in the state (Sweeny, 1998). At the time, California had a large number of teachers who began their career through alternative certification, particularly in its urban districts. This created a need for a more structured mentoring and induction program as many new teachers were entering the profession without backgrounds in educational studies.

By 1986, California had functioning new teacher programs that could be critically examined. Although thousands of teachers volunteered to be mentors, the programs were not working to their best potential. Mentors were still not providing the services that the state had hoped for when passing the Hughes-Hart Act. Sweeny (1998) explains that the "problems found were lack of clarity in leadership and helping roles between mentors and principals, concerns about excessive time away from students, use of implementation funds for many things with only an indirect effect on instruction, and that the egalitarian nature of schools created a dilemma for mentors. That dilemma is that to be an effective mentor required a counter-culture assertion that a mentor can only make a difference by assuming a very different role from the mentor's own peers" (7). The root of the problem was that while programs were clearly in place, specific procedures and sufficient funding were missing.

The solutions to these problems were threefold. First, the state provided more funding. In 1992, California's legislature created the Beginning Teacher Support and Assessment (BTSA) program that provided enough finances to support approximately 7 percent of California's beginning teachers (Villar and Strong, 2007). Although only a small percentage of the state's beginning teachers, those supported rose by several thousand from a few years previously.

The number of new teachers and mentors was steadily on the rise. Second, the state recognized that finding mentors was only part of the process. The need to prepare teachers to become effective mentors became apparent. This took California to a whole new level as far as new teacher programs and professional development were concerned. Education for experienced teachers became just as important as that for new teachers.

The third step in California's problem solving was to involve educational institutions and agencies that were specifically dedicated to new teacher support programs. In 1988, the California New Teacher Project (NTP) was implemented with the goal of testing different induction, mentoring, and assessment program models that targeted support for beginning teachers and helped define the benefits and results attained. California school districts were experiencing difficulty in attracting and retaining qualified teachers.

The California Department of Education and the California Commission on Teacher Credentialing launched a four-year pilot program to address these concerns and point the way for new policy directions in new teacher development (The New Teacher Center, 2005a). This group was continuously able to collect data, experiment with practice, and guide new teacher program policy across the state. By 1991 these findings led directly to the piloting of thirty-seven programs for new teachers and opportunities for local districts to apply for competitive grants (Furtwengler, 1995).

The information gleaned from these pilot programs was subsequently infused into BTSA. BTSA now provides formative assessment, individualized support, and advanced content for newly credentialed, beginning teachers, and it is the preferred pathway to a California Professional (Clear) Teaching Credential. The BTSA induction program is coadministered by the California Department of Education and the California Commission on Teacher Credentialing.

Since 2004, all beginning certified teachers are eligible to receive support from the BTSA program (Villar and Strong, 2007). Perhaps much of the success of this program is because it encourages collaboration among local school districts, county offices of education, colleges, and universities to organize and deliver professional development for beginning teachers. BTSA induction programs provide much of the framework for California's new teachers. The BTSA objectives, listed below, are precise and based on the State of California's Standards for Quality and Effectiveness for Professional Teacher Induction Programs.

- Provide an effective transition into the teaching career for first- and second-year teachers in California.
- Improve the educational performance of students through improved training, information, and assistance for participating teachers.
- Enable beginning teachers to be effective in teaching students who are culturally, linguistically, and academically diverse.
- Ensure the professional success and retention of new teachers.
- Ensure that a support provider offers intensive individualized support and assistance to each participating beginning teacher.
- Ensure that an individual induction plan is in place for each participating beginning teacher and is based on an ongoing assessment of the development of the beginning teacher.
- Ensure continuous program improvement through ongoing research, development, and evaluation (California BTSA, 2008).

The New Teacher Center (2005a) states that "California requires that BTSA Induction Programs ensure all new teachers are mentored for two years and receive additional professional development. The mentors employ a formative assessment system that must meet Standard 13 of the Standards of Quality and Effectiveness for Teacher Induction Programs" (1). Although a costly venture, California sees the investment as profitable. In fact, when BTSA was first state funded, it received $4 million for mentoring support; by 1999 that amount had grown to $85 million, and the state currently funds over $4,000 per new teacher (Moir, 2008; Villar and Strong, 2007).

The state of California determined through cost analysis that this approach is financially effective as it reduces the teacher attrition rate and saves money on recruitment, rehiring, and retraining (Villar and Strong, 2007). Perhaps there are other significant benefits for new and mentor teachers, as well as their students, that exceed the financial benefits described here. Hanson and Moir (2008) suggest that the mentors benefit from induction programs as they receive new knowledge, skills, and values that can positively influence students, other teachers, school organizations, and the teaching profession. The New Teacher Center (2005a) believed that California was fortunate as there was an ongoing legislative mandate with funding for new teacher induction that did not appear to be in jeopardy at that time.

Sweeny (1998) described California's new teacher program as "a comprehensive vision of a well-supported professional growth effort that is focused on the pursuit of quality teaching. What is most heartening is the parallel effort to provide the support necessary for beginning teachers to succeed in this complex work" (8). Written in the late 1990s, these words seemed still relevant a decade later.

KENTUCKY

Kentucky created its first new teacher induction program in 1984. The program was then mandated and funded in 1985 as the Kentucky Beginning Teacher Internship Program (KBTIP). New teachers and out-of-state teachers who had less than two years of experience were required to enter into a one-year internship program (Sweeny, 1998). Currently, KBTIP is described as an internship program designed to provide assistance to new teachers (Education Professional Standards Board, 2006). The main goal of this support program is to help new teachers experience a successful first year in the classroom.

The internship period for new teachers is a rigorous process aimed at developing and assessing educator skills. Furtwengler (1995) describes the process:

> Beginning teachers are issued a provisional certificate for their internship year. The teacher internship committee consists of three members: the principal, resource teacher, and a teacher educator. All members are trained to use a separate supervision and assessment process for the beginning teacher. The Classroom Observation Instrument was developed by the state. The team observes the beginning teacher at least three times for one hour or one class period and meets a minimum of four times. The resource teacher, who serves as a mentor, is appointed by the Department of Education and spends a minimum of 70 hours working with the intern, that consists of 20 hours inside the classroom and 50 hours outside the classroom. The teacher educator is appointed by a regional university (14).

All members of the internship committee are compensated by the state, and any funds required for substitute teachers to accommodate the process are also funded by the state (Furtwengler, 1995). A final decision regarding successful completion of the internship is made after a third round of observations. The completed report is sent to the State Internship Office and then is forwarded to the Division of Certification that grants a four-year extension of the initial limited certificate.

The rigor and intensity of the program has come under scrutiny, as the people charged with assisting and developing new teachers are the same people that evaluate the interns. As Sweeny (1998) points out, "Such a high-stakes evaluative role for the committee has often been shown to compromise the safety a new teacher needs to feel to take the risks of seeking help, discussing their problems, and becoming vulnerable in order to learn to teach" (18). A very high percentage of interns pass this process during the first attempt.

The State Department reports that only 1.5 percent of the interns fail, and they are provided a second opportunity to pass if they are employed a second year. If they do not pass the second year, their only option to receive certification in Kentucky is to teach two years in another state, receive that state's certification, and then return to Kentucky. A similar induction program is in place for new administrators.

The quality of Kentucky's induction programs can be inferred from its standards for new teachers. A list of these standards, revised in February 2008, follows.

Standard 1: The teacher demonstrates applied content knowledge.
Standard 2: The teacher designs and plans instruction.
Standard 3: The teacher creates and maintains learning climate.
Standard 4: The teacher implements and manages instruction.

Standard 5: The teacher assesses and communicates learning results.
Standard 6: The teacher demonstrates the implementation of technology.
Standard 7: The teacher reflects on and evaluates teaching and learning.
Standard 8: The teacher collaborates with colleagues/parents/others.
Standard 9: The teacher evaluates teaching and implements professional development.
Standard 10: The teacher provides leadership within school/community/profession (Education Professional Standards Board, 2008).

Kentucky evaluates new teachers based on an initial level of performance and experienced teachers based on an advanced level of performance in each of these areas. For example, standard 1.1 states that an effective teacher communicates concepts, processes, and knowledge. A new teacher accurately and effectively communicates concepts, processes, and/or knowledge and uses vocabulary that is clear, correct, and appropriate for students. An experienced teacher accurately and effectively communicates an in-depth understanding of concepts, processes, and/or knowledge in ways that contribute to the learning of all students (Education Professional Standards Board, 2008).

Further, Kentucky currently uses technology to enhance and make more convenient the internship process:

> The Intern Management System (IMS) is an electronic system used to collect data on the progress and final result of each teacher in the Kentucky Teacher Internship Program (KTIP). Each KTIP District Coordinator is provided a copy of the Intern Management System (IMS) User Manual and trained on how to operate within IMS. Each KTIP Committee member must have a user name and password to access IMS and has specific responsibilities for inputting data and providing electronic signatures [that] provide legally binding electronic signatures (Education Professional Standards Board, 2006, 2).

Kentucky was at the forefront of teacher induction programs in the early 1980s and remains there with its in-depth, ever-evolving internship process.

IOWA

According to the Iowa Department of Education (2008a), The Iowa Mentoring and Induction Program began as part of the Iowa Teacher Quality legislation enacted in 2001. Every new teacher in the first or second year of the profession was to enter into a two-year induction program that addressed the teacher's personal and professional needs and trained her or him on Iowa's eight teaching standards.

Although Iowa was not at the forefront of developing new teacher programs, it definitely has instituted an in-depth policy, as described below.

A mentor is assigned to each teacher—not to evaluate for employment purposes, but to observe, critique, and provide support and advice on effective teaching practices. In 2006, guidance counselors, teacher librarians, and interns (hired under alternative licensure) were approved to participate in the mentoring and induction program in addition to classroom teachers. Iowa pays $1,300 for each first or second year teacher—$1,000 of those funds are paid to the mentor and the remaining dollars can be used by the district or AEA (Area Education Agencies) to pay for related program costs, including FICA or IPERS (Iowa Department of Education, 2008a, 2).

After the two-year induction program, the new teacher receives a standard license in most cases. The state fully funds induction for the required two years. If a teacher does not meet the requirements after two years, a third year in the induction program can be granted by the district, but it must be funded by the district. If a teacher does not successfully complete the program after the third year, that teacher cannot receive a license and cannot continue to teach in the state.

During the 2005–2006 school year, approximately 3,360 new teachers participated in the state-funded Iowa Mentoring and Induction Program. This total is comprised of both first- and second-year teachers in Local Education Agencies (LEAs) and AEAs statewide (Iowa Department of Education, 2008a). Iowa has the same type of program in place for its administrators, funded at $1,500 per new administrator. As the Iowa Department of Education (2008b) explains:

> The legislation for the Beginning Administrator Mentoring and Induction Program was created to promote excellence in school leadership, improve classroom instruction, enhance student achievement, build a supportive environment within school districts, increase the retention of promising school leaders, and promote the personal and professional well-being of administrators. The program is intended to provide qualified mentors and support for beginning (first-time) administrators (2).

Iowa has a policy that requires all educators in new positions to go through induction programs; however, the state does not specify a particular program that new teachers must go through. Instead, local districts are responsible for tailoring their own programs around state criteria. The approval process is based on how well programs meet and plan to measure state-developed requirements. State funds given to districts are contingent on the approval of induction programs. The Iowa Department of Education (2008c) gives guidelines for these plans:

> The goals must be aligned with state legislative goals for beginning educator mentoring and induction programs and support the Iowa Teaching Standards. Program goals should be realistic and measurable. Please remember that pro-

gram goals should align with Program Evaluation in Section G of the application. Carefully consider the number of goals for your program, as the district will need to assess and evaluate the degree to which program goals are met (goals section, paragraph 2).

Below is the list of goals for the Beginning Educator Mentoring and Induction Program followed by the Iowa Teaching Standards. The goals are to: promote excellence in teaching; enhance student achievement; build a supportive environment within school districts; increase the retention of promising beginning educators; promote the personal and professional well-being of classroom educators; and support continuous improvement.

The eight Iowa Teaching Standards include: demonstrates ability to enhance academic performance and support for implementation of the school district's student achievement goals; demonstrates competence in content knowledge appropriate to the teaching position; demonstrates competence in planning and preparing for instruction; uses strategies to deliver instruction that meet the multiple learning needs of students; uses a variety of methods to monitor student learning; demonstrates competence in classroom management; engages in professional growth; and fulfills professional responsibilities established by the school district (Iowa Department of Education, 2008c).

TEXAS

Texas started piloting new teacher induction programs between 1988 and 1990. One pilot program, developed by the Texas Commissioner's Advisory Committee on Teacher Induction (TCACTI), included a one-year-long program consisting of cooperative supervision of new teachers by mentors (with no previous experience required), administrators, and university faculty members, and included an advanced orientation session and specialized professional development opportunities for novice teachers.

Later, TCACTI published a mentoring program framework titled, "Beginning Teacher Induction Plan for Texas Schools." This publication resulted from pilot programs and included guidelines that encouraged mentors and novice teachers to observe each other, districts to provide release time for such activities, and districts to provide ongoing support seminars and sharing sessions as well as other collaborations.

In 1991, the Texas Induction Year Program for Beginning Teachers (TIYPBT) was mandated. Sweeny (1998) provides an overview of the program:

The TIYPBT consisted of 7 goals including retention, socialization, improved instruction, and K–16 collaboration. State guidelines suggest collaborative governance of the local programs and support focused on the needs of new teachers, mentors and mentor training, and program evaluations. A part of that collaboration was the state's interest in involving teacher education institutions in mentoring programs (12).

Similar to other mandated programs in the early 1990s, sufficient funding to support more than the pilot programs was not available, which effectively eliminated the mandate. The state, however, was able to develop a statewide network of Centers for Professional Development and Technology. By 1997, several centers were fully functional and included 43 universities, 15 service centers, and 113 school districts (Sweeny, 1998).

Financially, the state continues to struggle with how best to provide aid for now optional induction programs. In 2007, the state provided $13 million to support such programs through grants (Texas Education Agency, 2007). All school districts are eligible to apply for funds, but not all districts receive funding (Glynn, Dumas, and Zavala, 2007).

The grant money is conditional and based upon how well the district addresses accountability measures, such as the program's external evaluation process, and how well it documents the success in improving new teacher quality. Schools may use their grant funds for mentor teacher stipends, scheduled time for mentoring, and/or mentor support provided by approved mentor training providers. Further, districts have the option of subcontracting with commissioner-approved providers who offer training for mentor teachers.

IMPLICATIONS AND SUMMARY

The mentoring of new teachers and the diverse new teacher induction programs, as described for the states mentioned in this chapter, have a wide range of implications for the practitioner, researcher, and policy maker. With few guidelines provided at the national level, the quality and quantity of administrative support provided for new teachers varies considerably among states. Further, it is important to note that state policies are often in flux. That is, they change frequently and sometimes without warning. Considering the mobility of our society, and with new teachers transferring from one school system to another becoming more common, the variances or lack of any kind of mentoring standard from state to state, let alone from district to district, could negatively impact the quality and attrition of new teachers (Smith and Ingersoll, 2004).

Because of the diversity among state programs, it is difficult to generalize research about the effectiveness of new teacher induction programs. Obviously, there is a need for large-scale quality research investigations, similar to those completed in 2007 by Villar and Strong, regarding the impact of support programs for beginning teachers on student learning, teacher performance and attrition, and the cost-effectiveness of such programs (Fletcher, Strong, and Villar, 2008).

One desideratum is to advocate for greater cooperation among states that have policies regarding support programs for new teachers and to encourage nonmandating states to begin to explore what standards, goals, and model programs they need to establish to ensure that new teachers are highly qualified to work with our nation's children. Such institutions as the New Teacher Center in Santa Cruz, California, have already had a major impact not only in the United States but also in other countries as they set the tone and standard for quality support programs for novice teachers.

Prospective new teachers who are searching for their first teaching positions need to consider seriously the type of induction program available to them. Candidates must be aware that their beginning years are most important to their continuing success as educators. Therefore, new teachers should prudently consider which states are better for seeking employment based on the quality of support available. As this occurs, nonmandating states are likely to begin to look at policy as it relates to support programs and perhaps revise their current position. More importantly, states are more likely to retain high-quality beginning teachers, like Sally Kenshaw, and provide better-prepared teachers for the complexities involved in educating all children.

REFERENCES

California Beginning Teacher Support and Assessment. 2008, January 29. *BTSA basics*. Retrieved January 29, 2008, from http://www.btsa.ca.gov/BTSA_basics.html.

Darling-Hammond, L. 2006. *Powerful teacher education*. San Francisco: Jossey-Bass.

DePaul, A. 2000. *Survival guide for new teachers: How new teachers can work effectively with veteran teachers, parents, principals, and teacher educators*. Washington, DC: U.S. Department of Education Office of Educational Research and Improvement.

Duff, V. 2004. *Side by side: A mentoring newsletter*. Retrieved from www.state.nj.us/njded/profdev/mentor/newsletter/mentoring1.pdf.

Editorial Projects in Education Research Center. 2008. The teaching profession: Building and supporting capacity. Special issue: Quality counts 2008. *Education Week* 2718:54–56.

Education Professional Standards Board. 2008. *Kentucky teacher standards: Approved 2–2008*. Retrieved from http://www.kyepsb.net/documents/EduPrep/Kentuckyteacherstandards.doc.

———. 2006. *Kentucky teacher internship programs*. Retrieved February 15, 2008, from http://www.kyepsb.net/internships/index.asp.

Fletcher, S. H., M. Strong, and A. Villar. 2008. An investigation of the effects of variations in mentor-based induction on the performance of students in California. *Teachers College Record* 110(10): 227–89.

Furtwengler, C. B. 1995. Beginning teachers programs: Analysis of state actions during the reform era. *Education Policy Analysis Archives* 3(3):1–20.

Glynn, R., L. A. Dumas, and G. Zavala. 2007, May 17. *Commissioner's rules*. Retrieved January 21, 2008, from http://www.tea.state.tx.us/rules/commissioner/adopted/0507/153-1011-ltradopt.html.

Hanson, S., and E. Moir. 2008. Beyond mentoring: Influencing the professional practice and careers of experienced teachers. *Phi Delta Kappan* 89(6):453–58.

Iowa Department of Education. 2008a, January 7. *Mentoring and induction*. Retrieved February 4, 2008, from http://www.iowa.gov/educate/index.php?option=com_content&task=view&id=1674&Itemid=2479.

———. 2008b, January 7. *Administrator mentoring and induction*. Retrieved February 15, 2008, from http://www.iowa.gov/educate/index.php?option=com_content&task=view&id=1448&Itemid=2447.

———. 2008c, January 7. *Technical assistance for Iowa teacher mentoring and induction program*. Retrieved February 15, 2008, from http://www.iowa.gov/educate/index.php?option=com_content&task=view&id=1674&Itemid=2479#Technical Assistance.

Klemick, E. 2008. Mentoring support for new teachers. Special issue: Quality counts 2008. *Education Week* 27(18):60–62.

Moir, E. 2008, January 12. *Dear Ellen: Induction policy drives program quality*. Retrieved January 21, 2008, from http://www.edutopia.org/node/ 5140/print.

The New Teacher Center. 2005a. *California: Induction policy survey*. Retrieved January 21, 2008, from http://newteachercenter.org.

———. 2005b. New Jersey: Induction policy survey. Retrieved January 21, 2008, from http://newteachercenter.org/policy_induction_newjersey.php.

Russell, A. 2006, October. *Policy matters: Teacher induction programs, trends and opportunities*. Retrieved on January 28, 2008, from http://www.aascu.org/policy_matters/pdf/v3n10.pdf.

Smith, T. M., and R. M. Ingersoll. 2004. What are the effects of induction and mentoring on beginning teacher turnover? *American Educational Research Journal* 41(3):681–714.

Soukhanov, A. H., ed. 2001. *Microsoft Encarta college dictionary*. New York: St. Martin's Press.

Sweeny, B. 1998, March. *What's happening in mentoring and induction in each of the United States?* Retrieved January 21, 2008, from http://teachermentors.com/RsrchStateList.php.

Texas Education Agency. 2007. *$13 million granted to districts for beginning teacher induction and mentoring programs*. Retrieved February 16, 2008, from http://www.tea.state.tx.us/press/07btimfinal.pdf.

Villar, A., and M. Strong. 2007. Is mentoring worth the money? A benefit-cost analysis and five-year rate of return of a comprehensive mentoring program for beginning teachers. *ERS Spectrum* 25(3):1–17.

II

COMPONENTS AND IMPACTS
OF TEACHER INDUCTION

6

Characteristics of Beginning Teacher Role Quality

Connections to Satisfaction and Commitment

Alan J. Reiman, Kristen A. Corbell, Erin T. Horne, and Dina Walker-DeVose, North Carolina State University

This chapter complements Smith and Finch (this volume) and extends their discussion by examining sources of teacher satisfaction and commitment to teaching. This review focuses on recent empirical literature on the characteristics of beginning teacher role quality with connections to perceptions of success, satisfaction, and commitment to teaching. Two questions guided the review:

1. What are the domains of beginning teachers' perceptions of success?
2. How does beginning teacher satisfaction and professional commitment influence retention decisions?

During the last two decades, substantial research focused on the characteristics of beginning and experienced teachers for insights in determining which kinds of teachers were more inclined to remain in the classroom. For example, males were less likely to leave teaching than females (Ingersoll, 2001). Minority teachers were less likely to quit than majority teachers (Guarino, Santibanez, and Daley, 2006; Kirby, Berends, and Naftel, 1999). Single teachers were more likely to remain in teaching, particularly when compared with newly married beginning teachers with a young child (Borman and Dowling, 2008).

College graduates with college entrance examinations in the bottom three quartiles who became teachers were more likely to remain in teaching than college graduates with college entrance examinations in the top quartile who became teachers (Henke, Chen, Geis, and Knepper, 2000; Lankford,

Loeb, and Wyckoff, 2002; Podgursky, Monroe, and Watson, 2004). Kirby et al. (1999) found that teachers with a bachelor's degree were more likely to remain in the classroom than beginning teachers with advanced degrees.

Research that investigated the characteristics of teachers' roles with attention to role quality and role change suggested that adults assumed multiple roles (parent, partner, caregiver, employee), and these multiple roles could have beneficial effects depending on *role quality* (Barnett and Baruch, 1985; Barnett and Hyde, 2001; Crosby and Jaskar, 1993). However, there were upper limits to the benefits of multiple roles, and role quality was more important than number of roles (Perry-Jenkins, Repetti, and Crouter, 2000).

Much of the current research on teacher role change was triggered by the high-stakes accountability climate for teachers. Scholars noted intensified teacher expectations, and these observations led to subsequent research (Finnigan and Gross, 2007; Kelley, Heneman, and Milanowski, 2002; Leithwood, Steinbach, and Jantzi, 2002; Ofoegbu, 2004; Valli and Buese, 2007). The literature also noted increased societal expectations for which teachers assumed responsibility; for example, the prosocial and character development of students (Goodman and Lesnick, 2001; Lapsley and Power, 2005; Solomon, Battistich, and Watson, 2001). Other studies suggested that psychological factors influenced teacher decision making and decisions to remain in the classroom (Johnson and Birkeland, 2003; Johnson and Reiman, 2007; Marso and Pigge, 1997).

Largely drawing on the social-cognitive work of Bandura (1977, 1993), research on teachers' decisions examined protective factors and support systems that contributed to an individual's self-complexity and self-efficacy. Self-efficacy included personal goals and increased feelings of control over one's actions. Scholars argued that such self-complexity and self-efficacy built a success orientation. Bandura (1993) noted, however, ". . . people who perform poorly may do so because they lack the skills or they have the skills but they lack the sense of efficacy to use them well" (119). New teacher studies found that persistence and efficacy affected beginning teachers' decisions to remain in the classroom (Marso and Pigge, 1997; Tschannen-Moran and Hoy, 2007).

Ingersoll (2001) analyzed the 1990–1991 National Center for Educational Statistics (NCES) Schools and Staffing Survey (SASS), as well as the 1991–1992 Teacher Follow-up Study (TFS) data. He found that 42 percent of all departures reported job dissatisfaction (i.e., inadequate administrative support, poor salary, student discipline problems, lack of faculty influence, lack of student motivation, unrealistic assignments, lack of community support, lack of professional competence of colleagues, and intrusions on teaching time) as their reason for leaving. This research was influential due to national sampling and sample size.

Subsequent research with a nationally representative sample (Smith and Ingersoll, 2004) confirmed trends in the 2001 findings and concluded that teacher dissatisfaction and the role it played in the workplace warranted further study. Although the research acknowledged the relationship among teacher characteristics such as specialty field, age, and turnover, these characteristics were immutable. They recognized, implicitly, that a characteristic such as teacher role quality was modifiable and depended on associations between the teacher and the school organization.

The review begins with the conceptual framework around which our comments are organized and, based on this framework, the methods for selecting and evaluating research for this review. We then review the literature we selected and that pertain to teachers' perceptions of success and the relationship between their perceptions and their professional commitment and their retention decisions. We conclude with suggestions for further research.

CONCEPTUAL FRAMEWORK

Beginning teacher satisfaction and commitment are two central aspects of work roles. From the standpoint of districts and schools that hire teachers, beginning teacher satisfaction and commitment have a direct impact on whether these teachers remain in teaching. The framework for this review is derived from social role theory (Barnett and Hyde, 2001) and conceptions of teacher work role change (Valli and Buese, 2007). As such, we integrated two important lines of theory and research in social psychology and teacher work roles.

We defined *multiple roles* as the variety of adult roles educators can assume, including that of teacher, parent, spouse/partner, caregiver, or public service. Within these roles and as jobs or working conditions change, work roles may also change. Such work role changes may include *role increase*—more tasks; *role intensification*—heightened responsibility for teaching and learning driven by policy directed at the classroom; and *role expansion*—greater scope of responsibilities outside of the classroom.

Beginning teachers' *perceptions of success* are their perceptions of personal and professional well-being. Factors within their perceptions include those personal, professional, and organizational factors that contribute to perceptions of success. *Satisfaction* is related to beginning teachers' perceptions of their workplace conditions. Job satisfaction is associated with individuals' persistence in a job as well as their willingness to work effectively within an organization (Ostroff, 1992). It represents one dimension of commitment (Johnson and Birkeland, 2003; Reyes and Shin, 1995).

We drew on the work of Firestone and Pennell (1993) and Reyes (1989) for our definition of teacher commitment. *Commitment* represents the strength of a beginning teacher's identification with and involvement in the school. It has three major qualities: (a) a strong belief in and acceptance of the school's goals and values, (b) a willingness to exert significant effort on behalf of the school, and (c) a strong intent to remain in the school or in education. Some recent work makes the distinction between a teacher's commitment to school, labeled as organizational commitment, and commitment to teaching, labeled as professional commitment (Ebmeier, 2003; Somech and Bogler, 2002). Finally, beginning teachers' *retention intentions* are a measure of beginning teachers' self-identified intentions to remain in the teaching profession. In contrast, *retention* represents a beginner teacher's actual decision to remain in the classroom for another year.

A basic assumption guiding our concepts and definitions is the following: beginning teachers will remain in the classroom if they experience relatively moderate-to-high perceptions of success. Perceptions of success are macrocharacteristics, are mutable, promulgate satisfaction and commitment, and drive retention decisions.

METHOD

Our literature review included all studies from 1998 to 2008 that met three criteria: (a) relevance, (b) empirical in nature, and (c) quality. To assess the relevance of the study, we first determined whether the reported studies provided insight into the research questions for our review. We limited studies to those performed in the United States and those that were empirical in nature. We excluded theoretical or opinion works. Thus, articles that outlined a new teacher support program but were not analytical or evaluative were excluded from this review.

To determine quality, we applied the following questions: (a) Are the research questions or hypotheses clearly identified? (b) Is the sample appropriate to the subsequent analyses performed? (c) Is the method aligned with the research questions or hypotheses? (d) Are findings sufficient to support conclusions? (e) Is subsequent interpretation warranted by the findings? If answers to these questions were positive, we included the study in our review.

We began with a thorough review of multiple databases, including Academic Search Premier, PsycINFO, JSTOR, and Social Sciences Citation Index. The search terms included *beginning teacher satisfaction, new teacher satisfaction, beginning teacher commitment, new teacher commitment, beginning teacher retention,* and *new teacher retention.* The initial search yielded 381 publications. After initial review, we reduced the potential set to 104 publications, after removing duplicate publications and those studies not assisting with our research questions. We also reviewed additional works known through our previous research on beginning teachers and role quality. We only focused on studies of beginning teachers and the work role quality, satisfaction, commitment, and retention that pertained to in-service teachers, but not preservice or student teachers. This reduced the total to thirty-five publications.

Our method for analyzing and grouping studies into representative themes was guided by both theory and cross-study synthesis. As noted earlier, social role theory (Barnett and Hyde, 2001) and teacher work role change (Valli and Buese, 2007) were foundational to our thinking. Additionally, we employed cross-study synthesis to generate a final set of studies related to beginning teacher role quality, satisfaction, commitment, and retention. The synthesis incorporated research trends from across the studies. Overall groupings and generalizations then were assigned.

SUMMARY OF FINDINGS

The research revealed fairly consistent evidence that beginning teachers' changing roles, perceptions of success, and satisfaction with teaching were associated with professional autonomy and administrative support. Beginning teachers tended to have higher levels of satisfaction and perceptions of success when such support and autonomy were present. Findings also suggested that participation in student teaching and more intensive specialized undergraduate teacher education programs led to beginning teachers' perceptions of success, particularly with regard to instructional planning and formative assessment of learners.

Multiple Roles and Role Quality

One of the most dramatic changes of the late twentieth and early twenty-first century has been the transformation in work and family roles in the United States. Women now expect to spend at least thirty years in the paid labor force, and the modal American family is the dual-earner family (White and Rogers, 2000). Expansionist theorists in social psychology have found a number of beneficial effects of multiple roles, including buffering, added income, social support, expanded frame of reference, and increased self-complexity (Barnett and Hyde, 2001).

These beneficial effects are reflected in mental health (Barnett, Marshall, and Pleck, 1992), physical health (Waldron and Jacobs, 1989), and relationship health (Oppenheimer, 1997). Multiple roles increase opportunities for social support, which increase well-being. For example, Polasky and Holahan (1998) found that social support at work was negatively correlated with anxiety and depression. Social support can also act as a buffer when there are expanded responsibilities in the role (Cohen and Wills, 1985). With respect to beginning teachers, numerous studies have found that support groups can ameliorate the work-related stress of beginning teachers (Babinski and Rogers, 1998; Gold, 1998; Thies-Sprinthall and Gerler, 1990).

Although there are certain conditions under which multiple roles are beneficial, beyond certain upper limits, however, overload and distress may occur (Voydanoff and Donnelly, 1999). Role quality is more important than number of roles or expanded responsibilities in roles (Perry-Jenkins et al., 2000). When persons commit long hours to the workplace, psychological benefits only accrue if there are moderate-to-high perceptions of success. In fact, low perceptions of workplace success and the perception of limited opportunity were the strongest predictors of job turnover for both men and women (Barnett and Brennan, 1995; Stroh, Brett, and Reilly, 1992). Alternatively, challenge, variety in tasks and supports, autonomy, and salary were predictors of higher perceptions of success in the American workforce (Loscocco, 1990).

An important assumption of research on multiple roles is that changes in one role interact with other roles. These interactions can be beneficial. Reiman, Sprinthall, and Thies-Sprinthall (1999) noted the importance of support, challenge, and guided or scaffolded reflection as the person engaged in a new role. Rosenblatt (2001) investigated the mediating effect of two hundred seventh through twelfth grade teachers' skill flexibility on multiple roles (extracurricular school roles) and work attitudes (burnout, intent to leave, and organizational commitment). A path analysis revealed that skill flexibility mediated the effect of holding multiple roles on burnout, and it mediated the effects of demographic variables (age, education, nationality, and school size) on work attitudes. Skill flexibility refers to "the mastery of various skills, and the ability to switch easily from one job to another while engaging different skills as required" (Atkinson, 1984, 28).

Perceptions of Success

In a study of beginning teachers in their first three years of experience in New Jersey schools, Manning (2004) found that beginning teacher autonomy and feelings of influence corresponded with self-reported perceptions of success. Success was characterized as certainty, school enthusiasm, and enthusiasm about work. Alternatively, Manning found factors such as principal leadership, adequate resources, and collegiality corresponded only with job satisfaction. In addition, workplace conditions were positively associated with a beginning teacher's perception of success as well as satisfaction and teacher retention (Corbell, 2008; Ingersoll, 2001; Johnson and Birkeland, 2003; Murnane, Singer, Willett, Kemple, and Olsen 1991).

Corbell, Reiman, and Nietfeld (2008) developed a survey called the Perceptions of Success Inventory for Beginning Teachers and conducted an exploratory factor analysis of the survey. Their analysis identified the following factors: mentor support, colleague and instructional resource support, administrative support, classroom management, student success, assignment and workload, parental contacts, and commitment. They also found high levels of convergent validity with the Teacher's Sense of Efficacy Scale (Tschannen-Moran and Hoy, 2001). In a second study Corbell (2008) revised the Perceptions of Success Inventory for Beginning Teachers using a confirmatory factor analysis.

The following distinct workplace factors were associated with beginning teachers' perceptions of success, and these factors were supported by additional research:

- mentor support (Bauer and LeBlanc, 2002; Johnson and Birkeland, 2003);
- colleague support (Johnson and Birkeland, 2003; Kardos, Johnson, Peske, Kauffman, and Liu, 2001; Louis and Marks, 1998; O'Brien and Christie, 2005; Smith and Ingersoll, 2004);
- administrative support (Johnson and Birkeland, 2003; Kardos et al., 2001; Stockard and Lehman, 2004; Youngs, 2007);
- classroom management (Hertzog, 2000; Johnson and Birkeland, 2003; Liu and Meyer, 2005; Weiss, 1999);
- reduced assignment and workload (Ingersoll and Smith, 2004; Johnson and Birkeland, 2003; Stockard and Lehman, 2004);
- instructional resources (Hertzog, 2000; Johnson and Birkeland, 2003; Kauffman, 2005; Kauffman, Johnson, Kardos, Liu, and Peske, 2002);
- encouraging student success (Johnson and Birkeland, 2003); and
- parental support (Greenwood and Hickman, 1991; Martin, 2003).

How Does Satisfaction and Commitment Influence Retention Decisions?

Commitment to one's work has many positive outcomes, including higher job satisfaction (Freund, 2005) and lower turnover rates (Blau and Lunz, 1998). Firestone and Pennell (1993) conducted a comprehensive review of teacher commitment and satisfaction. The literature provided fairly consistent evidence regarding this relationship.

Commitment

A recent study by Chan, Lau, Nie, Lim, and Hogan (2008) used multigroup, structural equation modeling to test and validate the mediation model across two samples of teachers. Teacher efficacy and identification with school mediated the relationship among teaching experience, perceived organizational politics, and reflective dialogue to commitment. They also found a positive relationship between teaching experience and teacher commitment, with increased experience associated with stronger commitment. Teacher perceptions of professional community and reflective dialogue (e.g., learning-centered discourse with colleagues) had significant positive path coefficients with secondary teachers' commitment.

Corbell (2008) found beginning teachers' perceptions of success to be predictive of satisfaction ($F_{(8,433)}$ = 46.17, p < 0.001, R^2 = .50) and commitment ($F_{(9,433)}$ = 24.23, p < 0.01, R^2 = .34), as measured by the factors of the Perceptions of Success Inventory for Beginning Teachers. This study found administration support, classroom management, assignment and workload, instructional resources, and parental contacts factors to predict commitment, satisfaction, and retention intentions. Beginning teachers with higher perceptions of success experienced greater satisfaction and commitment, and satisfaction and commitment predicted intent to remain in teaching.

Ingersoll and Alsalam (1997), in their multilevel analysis of more than 53,000 teachers in more than 11,000 schools in the 1990–1991 Schools and Staffing Survey, found that self-reported commitment to the teaching profession was positively associated with school-level measures of teacher autonomy and faculty influence. Thus, teacher satisfaction as measured by autonomy and faculty influence appeared to be associated with teacher commitment. They also found that self-reported commitment to the teaching profession among working teachers was positively associated with the maximum possible salary level in the school.

Satisfaction

Weiss (1999), using data on first-year teachers from the SASS in 1987–1988 and 1990–1991, found that new teachers' perceptions of professional autonomy were connected to school leadership and school culture. Sense of autonomy and the perception of administrative support were the main factors predicting high teacher satisfaction. These first-year teachers also acknowledged that high satisfaction fostered a sense that it was worthwhile to give teaching their best effort. These first-year teachers' perceptions of satisfaction were predictors of teachers' intent to remain in the classroom.

Similarly, Stockard and Lehman (2004), in their study of beginning teachers from the SASS in 1990–1991, the 1991–1992 Teacher Follow-up

Study, and their survey of beginning teachers in one western state, found that new teachers who reported less autonomy and limited administrative support had less satisfaction with teaching. Beginning teacher reports of high rates of classroom behavioral problems were associated with decreased perceptions of satisfaction.

Oh, Ankers, Llamas, and Tomjoy (2005), using survey data from 204 K–12 beginning teachers, found new teachers who had traditional student teaching experiences were more likely to have a higher level of job satisfaction than those who did not have student teaching experience. Beginning teachers who completed student teaching reported higher levels of confidence in their ability to foster student learning in a variety of positive ways than beginning teachers who did not have a student teaching experience. Freeman, Brookhart, and Loadman (1999), using a two-group comparison design with 1,700 beginning teachers and 10 teacher preparation institutions, compared the perceptions of beginning teachers in racially/ethnically diverse schools and those who taught in schools with low levels of racial/ethnic diversity. Beginning teachers in high diversity schools reported lower levels of satisfaction than teachers in low diversity schools.

Maloch et al. (2003) found that graduates of specialized undergraduate teacher education programs with a major or minor in reading, as compared with graduates of undergraduate general education programs, were more focused on learner needs, instructional activities, and formative assessment processes. The findings were consistent for all three teacher education programs. Beginning teachers from the specialized undergraduate teacher education programs self-reported higher levels of confidence and satisfaction with teaching.

Role Intensification, Satisfaction, and Commitment

In a two-year, qualitative study of eighteen new language arts teachers, Smethem (2007) found that the intensification of beginning teachers' work roles reduced job satisfaction and consequent commitment to teaching. Beginning teachers consistently reported that work intensification was adversely affecting their intent to remain in the classroom.

Valli and Buese (2007) found that beginning and experienced teachers perceived expanded roles due to high-stakes testing. In their three-year qualitative study, the magnitude of change and the nature of changed roles were greater than predicted. Ironically, teachers' institutional roles expanded further than their instructional roles. They described teachers' roles as dynamic, expanding in intellectual and social complexity, yet limited in workplace autonomy and adequate support. They recommended that as policy makers created new policies, developed new curricula, and initiated new plans for increasing student achievement, they needed to carefully consider the impact of such policies on both teachers' roles and subsequent unintended changes. Role increases, role expansion, and role intensification encouraged even experienced teachers to question whether they were good teachers.

Peske, Liu, Johnson, Kauffman, and Kardos's (2001) analysis of interviews with first- and second-year teachers suggested that new teachers tended to approach the profession of teaching tentatively or conditionally. A majority of the beginning teachers did not consider teaching to be a lifelong commitment. Additionally, Kauffman et al. (2002) reported that the standards and accountability movement created role intensification for beginning teachers that was not balanced by extra levels of support for teachers.

Weiss (1999), in a large-scale study of relationships between work intensification and beginning teacher satisfaction and commitment, found that a collaborative culture and teacher participation in decision making were most strongly associated with job satisfaction and professional commitment. The study also found that beginning teachers with strong job satisfaction and professional commitment demonstrated higher intent to remain in the classroom than beginning teachers with lower job satisfaction and commitment. This study, like many others, highlighted the importance of supportive workplace conditions during the initial year of teaching.

Satisfaction, Commitment, and Retention Intentions

Johnson and Birkeland (2003) found that teachers' decisions to stay in a school or in the profession were greatly dependent upon their satisfaction as well as the level of colleague and administrative support, availability of instructional resources, support with classroom management, student learning, and being provided a reduced assignment and workload compared to experienced teachers. Corbell (2008) found similar results in a study of 439 beginning teachers. Beginning teacher satisfaction, commitment, and intent to remain in teaching were significantly and positively associated with a number of school factors, including mentor support, colleague support, administrative support, classroom management, student success, instructional resources, assignment and workload, and parental contacts.

DISCUSSION AND CONCLUSION

Our review focused on beginning teacher characteristics that were mutable. Figure 6.1 portrays beginning teacher multiple roles, beginning teacher role changes, the influence of multiple roles and work role changes on beginning teacher perceptions of success, and the consequent pathways to two outcome variables (beginning teacher satisfaction, beginning teacher commitment) and retention intentions.

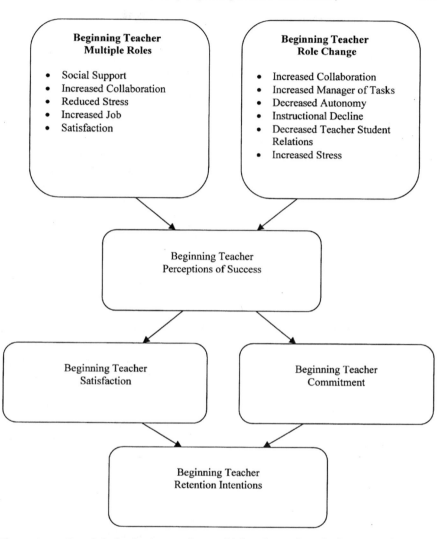

Figure 6.1.   Trends in beginning teacher multiple roles and work change: pathways to satisfaction, commitment, and retention.

Changing work roles for all teachers represent an emerging and important trajectory of further research by scholars and are portrayed at the top right of figure 6.1. This section of the figure summarizes the studied effects of teacher work role changes (e.g., increased collaboration, increased management of tasks, decreased autonomy, increased stress). We propose that teacher work role changes mediate beginning teachers' perceptions of success. Work role increases, intensification, and expansion due to high-stakes accountability movements (for example) are contributing to decreased beginning teacher satisfaction and commitment to the profession. Although such work role changes contribute to increased collaboration, they also increase managerial tasks associated with high-stakes accountability efforts, decrease autonomy, decrease instructional repertoire, increase stress, and may negatively impact teacher-student relations (Valli and Buese, 2007).

These results are corroborated in recent reviews of mentoring support and beginning teacher satisfaction and commitment (Wang and Odell, 2002), meta-analytic reviews of characteristics of beginning teachers as predictors of turnover (Borman and Dowling, 2008), and narrative reviews of teacher recruitment and retention studies (Guarino et al., 2006).

On the other end of the continuum, we introduced literature in the social psychology arena, which found that multiple roles could ameliorate work role stress. Beginning teachers' multiple roles are portrayed in the top-left frame of figure 6.1, suggesting that beginning teacher participation in multiple roles can contribute to increased social support, reduced stress, and increased job satisfaction. Multiple roles may also mediate beginning teachers' perceptions of success.

Several studies reviewed above suggested that when adults assume multiple roles (parent, partner, caregiver, and employee), these multiple roles can have beneficial effects depending on *role quality* (Barnett and Baruch, 1985; Barnett and Hyde, 2001; Crosby and Jaskar, 1993). In effect, multiple roles may buffer persons from the stresses that may be endemic to a particular role, such as beginning a career as a teacher. However, these studies also found that there were upper limits to the benefits of multiple roles, and role quality was more important than number of roles (Perry-Jenkins et al., 2000). Skill flexibility mediated the effect of holding multiple roles and role intensification (Rosenblatt, 2001).

Role quality for beginning teachers represents a needed and promising new trajectory of research, and beginning teachers' perceptions of success may characterize such role quality. Ingersoll's research (2001, 2003) indicated that beginning teacher satisfaction was positively associated with commitment to the organization and to the profession of teaching. Higher levels of satisfaction were associated with higher levels of commitment. More recent studies found that beginning teachers' perceptions of success contributed to satisfaction, commitment, retention intentions, and actual retention (Corbell, 2008; Johnson and Birkeland, 2003).

Similar to other studies and research reviews, our review found beginning teachers' perceptions of success to be associated with organizational conditions. Workplace supports (such as mentoring, mentors in one's content area, face-to-face time with administrators, collaboration time, beginning teacher seminars, reduced preparations and networking, and a teacher aide) may buffer beginning teachers from the work role intensification that is underway in America's schools. However, comprehensive support programs are rarely available to beginning teachers (Ingersoll, Smith, and Dunn, 2007).

As a result of our review, we are struck by an apparent dialectic. On the one hand, states and school systems are recognizing the need for more support for beginning teachers. Such support fosters a sense of professional autonomy and perceptions of success and satisfaction, which are associated with professional commitment and retention. Yet accountability initiatives and related new curriculum initiatives are prompting beginning teachers to feel less confident, less autonomous, more managerial, and more stressed, perhaps leading to premature attrition.

In the real world of schools, few trends emerge without ambiguity and potential unintended consequences. Public education represents a complex system, and it should not be surprising that work intensification interacts with the characteristics of beginning teachers in ways that defy easy explanation. The real question for future research is not whether change and work intensification will continue or accelerate. It will, but we need to gain understanding of these dynamics. Our success in supporting beginning teachers is, in part, a long-term commitment to applied research. Such research means in the end that we will move ahead while looking back at prior research trends.

We need to know more about how new curricular innovations affect beginning teachers' roles and perceptions of success and how intensive induction programs that attend to all of the perceptions of success factors might ameliorate the demands and stresses of the first three years of teaching. We need to be able to answer questions about what other kinds of support are needed as beginning teachers are expected to respond to increased professional demands associated with the accountability movement. We need to understand better the ways multiple roles do and do not buffer beginning teachers. Longitudinal research is needed to better understand the trends of beginning teachers' perceptions of success across the initial three years of induction and the influence of multiple roles.

It is not clear from the literature how these seemingly opposed dynamics of beginning teacher characteristics, multiple roles, and work intensification will ultimately play out in our nation's schools. It seems unlikely that accountability programs will change dramatically. It also is unclear whether states and school systems are prepared to increase funding for more comprehensive support programs without more evidence of the efficacy of such programs to ameliorate a number of the stresses associated with starting a career as a teacher. Certainly, the current economic downturn would suggest that resources at all levels of public education will be stretched very tight for the foreseeable future.

Our research review supports the notion that individual schools and districts can affect retention by increasing the perceptions of success of their beginning teachers through more comprehensive support programs. Still needed, however, are rigorous longitudinal and experimental studies of programs and/or policies evaluating which combination of supports will have the largest impact in a time of resource scarcity.

REFERENCES

Atkinson, J. 1984. Manpower strategies for flexible organizations. *Personnel Management* 16(8):28–31.

Babinski, L. M., and D. L. Rogers. 1998. Supporting new teachers through consultee-centered group consultation. *Journal of Educational and Psychological Consultation* 9:285–308.

Bandura, A. 1993. Perceived self-efficacy in cognitive development and functioning. *Educational Psychologist* 28(2):117–48.

———. 1977. Self-efficacy: Toward a unifying theory of behavioral change. *Psychological Review* 84(2):191–215.

Barnett, R. C., and G. K. Baruch. 1985. Women's involvement in multiple roles and psychological distress. *Journal of Personality and Social Psychology* 49(1):135–45.

Barnett, R. C., and R. T. Brennan. 1995. The relationship between job experiences and psychological distress. *Journal of Personality and Social Psychology* 49(1):135–45.

Barnett, R. C., and J. S. Hyde. 2001. Women, men, work, and family. *American Psychologist* 56(10):781–96.

Barnett, R. C., N. L. Marshall, and J. H. Pleck. 1992. Men's multiple roles and their relationship to men's psychological distress. *Journal of Marriage and the Family* 54(2):358–67.

Bauer, S. C., and G. LeBlanc. 2002, November. *Teachers' perceptions of the mentoring component of the Louisiana teacher assistance and assessment program.* Paper presented at the annual meeting of the Mid-South Educational Research Association, Chattanooga, TN.

Blau, G., and M. Lunz. 1998. Testing the incremental effect of professional commitment on intent to leave one's profession beyond the effects of external, personal, and work-related variables. *Journal of Vocational Behavior* 52(2):260–69.

Borman, G. D., and N. M. Dowling. 2008. Teacher attrition and retention: A meta-analytic and narrative review of the research. *Review of Educational Research* 78(3):367–409.

Chan, W. Y., S. Lau, Y. Nie, S. Lim, and D. Hogan. 2008. Organizational and personal predictors of teacher commitment: The mediating role of teacher efficacy and identification with school. *American Educational Research Journal* 45(3):597–630.

Cohen, S., and T. A. Wills. 1985. Stress, social support, and the buffering hypothesis. *Psychological Bulletin* 98(2):310–57.

Corbell, K. A. 2008. *Evaluating the perceptions of success inventory for beginning teachers and its connection to teacher retention.* PhD diss., North Carolina State University. (Publication No. AAT 3306570). Retrieved July 8, 2008, from http://www.lib .ncsu.edu/theses/available/etd-02262008-102151/unrestricted/etd.pdf.

Corbell, K. A., A. J. Reiman, and J. L. Nietfeld. 2008. The perceptions of success inventory for beginning teachers: Measuring its psychometric properties. *Teaching and Teacher Education* 24(6):1551–63.

Crosby, F. J., and K. L. Jaskar. 1993. Women and men at home and at work: Realities and illusions. In *Gender issues in contemporary society,* eds. S. Oskamp and M. Costanzo, 143–71. Newbury Park, CA: Sage.

Ebmeier, H. 2003. How supervision influences teacher efficacy and commitment: An investigation of a path model. *Journal of Curriculum and Supervision* 18(2):110–14.

Finnigan, K. S., and B. Gross. 2007. Do accountability policy sanctions influence teacher motivation? Lessons from Chicago's low performing schools. *American Educational Research Journal* 44(3):594–629.

Firestone, W. A., and J. R. Pennell. 1993. Teacher commitment, working conditions, and differential incentive policies. *Review of Educational Research* 63(4):489–525.

Freeman, D. J., S. M. Brookhart, and W. E. Loadman. 1999. Realities of teaching in racially/ethnically diverse schools: Feedback from entry-level teachers. *Urban Education* 34(1):89–114.

Freund, A. 2005. Commitment and job satisfaction as predictors of turnover intentions among welfare workers. *Administration in Social Work* 29(2):5–21.

Gold, Y. 1998. Beginning teacher support: Attrition, mentoring, and induction. In *Second handbook of research on teacher education,* ed. J. Sikula, 548–94. New York: Macmillan.

Goodman, J. F., and H. Lesnick. 2001. *The moral stake in education: Contested premises and practices.* New York: Addison Wesley Longman.

Greenwood, G. E., and C. W. Hickman. 1991. Research and practice in parent involvement: Implications for teacher education. *Elementary School Journal* 91(3):279–88.

Guarino, C. M., L. Santibanez, and G. A. Daley. 2006. Teacher recruitment and retention: A review of the recent empirical literature. *Review of Educational Research* 76(2):173–208.

Henke, R. R., X. Chen, S. Geis, and P. Knepper. 2000. *Progress through the teacher pipeline: 1992–1993 college graduate and elementary/secondary teaching as of 1997* (NCES 2000-152). Washington, DC: National Center for Education Statistics.

Hertzog, H. S. 2000, April. *When, how, and who do I ask for help? Novices' perceptions of learning and assistance.* Paper presented at the annual meeting of the American Educational Research Association, New Orleans, LA.

Ingersoll, R. 2003. *Who controls teachers' work?* Cambridge, MA: Harvard University Press.

———. 2001. Teacher turnover and teacher shortages: An organizational analysis. *American Educational Research Journal* 38(3):499–534.

Ingersoll, R., and N. Alsalam. 1997. *Teacher professionalization and teacher commitment: A multilevel analysis* (NCES 97-069). Washington, DC: National Center for Education Statistics.

Ingersoll, R., and T. M. Smith. 2004. Do teaching induction and mentoring matter? *NASSP Bulletin* 88(638):28–40.

Ingersoll, R., T. M. Smith, and A. Dunn. 2007, April. *Who gets quality induction?* Paper presented at the annual meeting of the American Educational Research Association, Chicago, IL.

Johnson, L. E., and A. J. Reiman. 2007. Beginning teacher disposition: Examining the moral/ethical domain. *Teaching and Teacher Education* 23(5):676–87.

Johnson, S., and S. Birkeland. 2003. Pursuing a "sense of success": New teachers explain their career decisions. *American Educational Research Journal* 40(3):581–617.

Kardos, S. M., S. M. Johnson, H. G. Peske, D. Kauffman, and E. L. Liu. 2001. Counting on colleagues: New teachers encounter the professional cultures of their schools. *Educational Administration Quarterly* 37(2):250–90.

Kauffman, D. 2005. Curriculum support and curriculum neglect: Second-year teachers' experiences. *NGT working paper*. Cambridge, MA: Project on the Next Generation of Teachers. Retrieved March 4, 2007, from http://www.gse.harvard.edu/~ngt.

Kauffman, D., S. Johnson, S. Kardos, E. Liu, and H. Peske. 2002. "Lost at sea": New teachers' experiences with curriculum and assessment. *Teachers College Record* 104(2):273–300.

Kelley, C., H. Heneman, and A. Milanowski. 2002. Teacher motivation and school based performance awards. *Educational Administration Quarterly* 38(3):372–401.

Kirby, S., M. Berends, and S. Naftel. 1999. Supply and demand of minority teachers in Texas: Problems and prospects. *Educational Evaluation and Policy Analysis* 21(1):47–66.

Lankford, H., S. Loeb, and J. Wyckoff. 2002. Teacher sorting and the plight of urban schools: A descriptive analysis. *Educational Evaluation and Policy Analysis* 24(1):37–62.

Lapsley, D. K., and F. C. Power. 2005. *Character psychology and character education.* Notre Dame, IN: University of Notre Dame Press.

Leithwood, K., R. Steinbach, and D. Jantzi. 2002. School leadership and teachers' motivation to implement accountability policies. *Educational Administration Quarterly* 38(1):94–119.

Liu, X. S., and J. P. Meyer. 2005. Teachers' perceptions of their jobs: A multilevel analysis of their teacher follow-up survey for 1994–1995. *Teachers College Record* 107(5):985–1003.

Loscocco, K. A. 1990. Reactions to blue-collar work: A comparison of women and men. *Work and Occupations* 17(2):152–77.

Louis, K. S., and H. M. Marks. 1998. Does professional community affect the classroom? Teachers' work and student experiences in restructuring schools. *American Journal of Education* 106(4):532–75.

Maloch, B., A. Flint, D. Eldridge, J. Harmon, R. Loven, J. Fine et al. 2003. Understandings, beliefs, and reported decision-making of first-year teachers from different reading teacher preparation programs. *Elementary School Journal* 103(5):431–57.

Manning, K. M. 2004. Beginning teacher job satisfaction in high socioeconomic contexts. PhD diss., Teachers College, Columbia University. *Dissertation Abstracts International*, 65(6-A), 2040. Columbia, NY.

Marso, R., and F. Pigge. 1997. A longitudinal study of persisting and nonpersisting teachers' academic and personal characteristics. *Journal of Experimental Education* 65(3):243–54.

Martin, W. M. 2003. *Parent involvement and the beginning teacher: The story of three elementary educators.* Unpublished PhD diss., West Virginia University, Morgantown.

Murnane, R. J., J. D. Singer, J. B. Willett, J. J. Kemple, and R. J. Olsen. 1991. *Who will teach? Policies that matter.* Cambridge, MA: Harvard University Press.

O'Brien, J., and F. Christie. 2005. Characteristics of support for beginning teachers: Evidence from the new teacher induction scheme in Scotland. *Mentoring and Tutoring* 13(2):189–203.

Ofoegbu, F. I. 2004. Teacher motivation: A factor for classroom effectiveness and school improvement in Nigeria. *College Student Journal* 38(1):81–89.

Oh, D. M., A. M. Ankers, J. M. Llamas, and C. Tomyoy. 2005. Impact of pre-service student teaching experience on urban school teachers. *Journal of Instructional Psychology* 32(1):82–98.

Oppenheimer, V. K. 1997. Women's employment and the gain to marriage: The specialization and trading model. *Annual Review of Sociology* 23:431–53.

Ostroff, C. 1992. The relationship between satisfaction, attitudes, and performance: An organizational level analysis. *Journal of Applied Psychology* 77(6):963–74.

Perry-Jenkins, M., R. L. Repetti, and A. C. Crouter. 2000. Work and family in the 1990s. *Journal of Marriage and the Family* 62(4):981–98.

Peske, H. G., E. L. Lui, S. M. Johnson, D. Kauffman, and S. M. Kardos. 2001. The next generation of teachings: Changing conceptions of a career in teaching. *Phi Delta Kappan* 83(4):304–12.

Podgursky, M., R. Monroe, and D. Watson. 2004. The academic quality of public school teachers: An analysis of entry and exit behavior. *Economics of Education Review* 23(5):507–18.

Polasky, L. J., and C. K. Holahan. 1998. Maternal self-discrepancies, interrole conflict, and negative affect among married professional women with children. *Journal of Family Psychology* 12(3):388–401.

Reiman, A. J., N. A. Sprinthall, and L. Thies-Sprinthall. 1999. The conceptual and ethical development of teachers. In *Human development across the life span: Educational and psychological applications*, eds. R. Mosher, D. Youngman, and J. Day, 203–18. Westport, CT: Praeger.

Reyes, P. 1989. The relationship of autonomy in decision making to commitment to schools and job satisfaction: A comparison between public school teachers and mid-level administrators. *Journal of Research and Development in Education* 22(2):62–69.

Reyes P., and H. S. Shin. 1995. Teacher commitment and job satisfaction: A causal analysis. *Journal of School Leadership* 5(1):22–39.

Rosenblatt, Z. 2001. Teachers' multiple roles and skill flexibility: Effects on work attitudes. *Educational Administration Quarterly* 37(5):684–708.

Smethem, L. 2007. Retention and intention in teaching careers: Will the new generation stay? *Teachers and Teaching* 13(5):465–80.

Smith, T. M., and R. Ingersoll. 2004. Reducing teacher turnover: What are the components of effective induction? *American Educational Research Journal* 41(3):687–714.

Solomon, D., V. Battistich, and M. Watson. 2001. Teaching and schooling effects on moral/prosocial development. In *Handbook of research on teaching*, 4th ed., ed. V. Richardson. Washington, DC: American Educational Research Association.

Somech, A., and R. Bogler. 2002. Antecedents and consequences of teacher organizational and professional commitment. *Educational Administration Quarterly* 38(4):555–77.

Stockard, J., and M. Lehman. 2004. Influences on the satisfaction and retention of 1st-year teachers: The importance of effective school management. *Educational Administration Quarterly* 40(5):742–71.

Stroh, L. K., J. M. Brett, and A. H. Reilly. 1992. All the right stuff: A comparison of female and male managers' career progression. *Journal of Applied Psychology* 77(3):251–60.

Thies-Sprinthall, L., and E. Gerler. 1990. Support groups for novice teachers. *Journal of Staff Development* 11(4):18–23.

Tschannen-Moran, M., and A. W. Hoy. 2007. The differential antecedents of self-efficacy beliefs of novice and experienced teachers. *Teaching and Teacher Education* 23(6):944–56.

———. 2001. Teacher efficacy: Capturing an elusive construct. *Teaching and Teacher Education* 17(7):783–805.

Valli, L., and D. Buese. 2007. The changing roles of teachers in an era of high-stakes accountability. *American Educational Research Journal* 44(3):519–58.

Voydanoff, P., and B. W. Donnelly. 1999. Multiple roles and psychological distress: The intersection of the paid worker, spouse, and parent roles with the role of the adult child. *Journal of Marriage and the Family* 61(3):725–38.

Waldron, I., and J. A. Jacobs. 1989. Effects of labor force participation on women's health: New evidence from a longitudinal study. *Journal of Occupational Medicine* 30(12):977–83.

Wang, J., and S. Odell. 2002. Mentored learning to teach according to standards-based reform: A critical review. *Review of Educational Research* 72(3):481–546.

Weiss, E. M. 1999. Perceived workplace conditions and first-year teachers' morale, career choice commitment, and planned retention: A secondary analysis. *Teaching and Teacher Education* 15(8):861–79.

White, L., and S. J. Rogers. 2000. *Economic circumstances and family outcomes: A review of the 90s* (Working paper no. 00-03). University Park: Pennsylvania State University.

Youngs, P. 2007. How elementary principals' beliefs and actions influence new teachers' experiences. *Educational Administration Quarterly* 43(1):101–37.

7

Influence of Teacher Induction on Teacher Retention

Thomas M. Smith and Maida Finch, Vanderbilt University

The goal of this chapter is to review and assess the literature on the relationship between beginning teacher induction and retention. Although numerous studies have explored variability in program design, relatively few have been sufficiently rigorous in design and methodology to offer conclusive results about the impact of induction support on desired outcomes, particularly turnover or teaching effectiveness (Ingersoll and Kralik, 2004; Lopez et al., 2004).

We begin this chapter by reviewing the findings of Ingersoll and Kralik (2004) and Lopez et al. (2004), the most recent reviews of the impact of induction support on teacher retention and other outcomes. Importantly, though the studies reviewed by each of these reports overlap significantly, they draw different conclusions. Ingersoll and Kralik concluded that there was empirical support for the claim that mentoring programs had a positive impact on teacher retention; the SRI study (Lopez, Lash, Schaffner, Shields, and Wagner, 2004) concluded that weak outcome measures (e.g, teacher self-reports of their intent to stay in teaching) and poor study designs (e.g., no comparison group) made it difficult to draw any conclusions about the impact of induction programs in general or mentoring in particular on teacher retention.

After examining the results reported by Ingersoll and Kralik (2004) and SRI (Lopez et al., 2004), we focused on studies that were published in the five years following these reviews, asking the following questions: What is the evidence that specific components of induction programs, including mentoring, influence retention of beginning teachers? What are the methodological weaknesses in this literature, and how should (a) policy makers interpret the findings and (b) researchers shift their focus to address previously unanswered questions?

FOUNDATIONAL RESEARCH

Ingersoll and Kralik's (2004) report on the impact of induction programs on teacher retention restricted the inclusion of studies to those that met three criteria: (a) used quantitative data; (b) offered an assessment of the impact of induction programs using well-defined outcomes; and (c) included a comparison group of teachers who were not mentored (or at least did not receive formal mentoring through the programs that were evaluated). Only ten studies met the criteria. They identified limitations in methodology that occurred with regularity, including lack (or absence) of rigor in statistical analysis and no control for other factors that may have caused estimates of induction effects to be biased. None of the studies used random assignment to determine participation, implying that even in the strongest studies selection bias could not be entirely eliminated.

Ingersoll and Kralik (2004) concluded that within the context of these limitations sufficient evidence suggested that induction and mentoring had a positive impact on increasing teacher retention rates. Teachers who were mentored intended to remain in teaching at higher rates than comparison groups (Brown and Wambach, 1987; Fuller, 2003). Three studies that included a control group (Cheng and Brown, 1992; Eberhard, Reinhardt-Mondragon, and Stottlemyer, 2000; Gold, 1987) indicated that teachers who had mentors planned to stay in teaching at higher rates than those who did not, but the studies did not include tests of statistical significance.

Overall, weaknesses in the research included reliance on teacher self-reports of intentions to stay in teaching rather than assessing whether teachers returned to teach the following year. Also, statistical tests did not meet traditional criteria for rejecting the null hypothesis of no impact, or there were no reports of statistical tests at all. Finally, studies that focused only on teacher intent to stay in teaching at the end of their first year are not able to determine whether induction and mentoring programs had long-term effects on reducing attrition rates (Ingersoll and Smith, 2003).

Most of the studies that followed beginning teachers over several years focused on differences in the intent to stay in the profession between teachers who participated in a specific mentoring program and those who did not (Eberhard et al., 2000; Fuller, 2003; Odell and Ferraro, 1992). For example, the Texas study of new teacher retention showed 90 percent of teachers who had a mentor planned to stay in teaching after the first year versus 63 percent of those who were not mentored. After the second year, the percentage of mentored teachers with plans to remain in the classroom dropped to 78 percent; the percentage of nonmentored teachers remained constant (Eberhard et al., 2000).

Odell and Ferraro (1992) found a 4 percent turnover rate for teachers four years after participating in an induction and mentoring program. Using statewide data, they found a 9 percent attrition rate for all beginning teachers. Because this study compared teachers who participated in a program with statewide data, it is unknown whether different induction programs were offered to the teachers in the comparison group or whether the comparison districts initially had lower attrition rates than the statewide average, making it difficult to draw conclusions about the effectiveness of the mentoring program in reducing attrition (Ingersoll and Kralik, 2004).

An evaluation of the Montana Beginning Teacher Support Program (Spuhler and Zetler, 1993, 1994, 1995) compared retention of beginning teachers who participated in the mentoring program with those who did not. The study evaluated three cohorts, although the first cohort did not have a comparison (or control) group. In the second cohort of the program, 92 percent of teachers continued teaching the following year, as compared to 73 percent of teachers who were not mentored. In the third cohort, 100 percent of the teachers who participated in the program returned to teach for a second year, whereas only 70 percent of those in the comparison returned. The number of participants was small, between eleven and twelve each year, so the results are not generalizable. The inclusion of a control group whose members did not receive any mentoring, along with verifying teacher responses with district retention rates, strengthened the findings, however.

One of the most rigorous analyses in this review was based on the National Center for Education Statistics' (NCES) 1993 Baccalaureate and Beyond Longitudinal Survey. College graduates were surveyed one year after graduation in 1993 and again three years later. The follow-up survey documented that 15 percent of the teachers who had participated in an induction program had left teaching, as compared to 26 percent of teachers who had not participated in an induction program (Henke, Chen, and Geiss, 2000). Although the results are compelling, generalizability is limited to a cohort of recent college graduates entering teaching for the first time as opposed to the entire cohort of new entrants to teaching in the early 1990s.

Ingersoll and Kralik's (2004) review highlighted a number of common problems in this line of research, including the failure of most of the studies to control for teacher or school characteristics that could differ between teachers participating in mentoring programs and those who did not. The absence of differentiation may have led to biased estimates of program effects (Brown and Wambach, 1987; Eberhard et al., 2000; Odell and Ferraro, 1992). Variability in the mentoring programs both within and across studies was also problematic.

Turnover analyses based on the 1990–1991 Schools and Staffing Survey (SASS) controlled for a range of factors that might contribute to selection bias, although the survey on which the study was based did not distinguish different components included in teachers' induction programs (Ingersoll, 2000, 2001; Ingersoll and Alsalam, 1997), which was also a shortcoming in the Baccalaureate and Beyond Survey (Henke et al., 2000). Sampling methods and numbers of participants were not provided either in the review or in the original research (Brown and Wambach, 1987; Cheng and Brown, 1992; Eberhard, et al., 2000; Fuller, 2003; Spuhler and Zetler, 1993, 1994, 1995). Other sampling problems occurred when participation in a study was voluntary, e.g., Eberhard, et al. (2000), or when the district selected the participants (Fuller, 2003).

Ingersoll and Kralik's (2004) review provided a picture of the state of the most rigorous research available at the time. One of the areas for future research they recommended was to assess what components of induction and mentoring programs were most effective in meeting the needs of beginning teachers. Another area recommended for future research was to examine the impact of mentoring on retention rates beyond the first year of teaching, an expansion of the initial work done by Eberhard et al., 2000; Odell and Ferraro, 1992; and Fuller, 2003.

SRI INTERNATIONAL'S REVIEW OF RESEARCH

SRI International (Lopez et al., 2004) also conducted a review of mentorship and induction, focusing on studies published between 1985–1994, plus one from 2002. They reported on many of the same studies reviewed by Ingersoll and Kralik (2004; e.g., Brown and Wambach, 1987; Cheng and Brown, 1992; Gold, 1987). Despite examining a number of the same studies, however, the two reviews drew different conclusions. Ingersoll and Kralik (2004) concluded that the research, though lacking in rigor and scope, was consistent enough to indicate that induction programs had positive effects on reducing attrition rates among beginning teachers. Conversely, SRI concluded that although the evidence did not suggest that mentoring and induction programs were unsuccessful in reducing attrition rates among new teachers, the evidence was not strong enough to say they were increasing retention rates.

One explanation for these differences is that Ingersoll and Kralik's (2004) review included more recent studies, particularly those based on nationally representative samples (e.g., Henke et al., 2000; Ingersoll and Smith, 2003) and teachers relatively new to the profession (Ingersoll, 2000, 2001). Another explanation is that SRI (Lopez et al., 2004) set a higher bar for design and statistical rigor. While disagreeing about the evidence of impact induction programs on retention rates, both reviews called for additional research on the topic coupled with more rigorous methodology.

MORE RECENT RESEARCH

Induction program components can include, but are not limited to, mentoring by one or more experienced teacher(s); common planning time; professional development focused on curriculum, content, and effective classroom management; and classroom observations (e.g., Alliance for Excellent Education, 2004; Brown and Wambach, 1987; Smith and Ingersoll, 2004; Spuhler and Zetler, 1993, 1994, 1995). Importantly, these components appear in a myriad of combinations and there is seldom a clear distinction between components specific to the induction program and supports in schools for all teachers (Smith and Ingersoll, 2004; Serpell and Bozeman, 1999; Hahs-Vaughn and Scherff, 2008). Over the five years since the reviews in the previous section, a number of studies have described the components of the induction programs in greater detail.

For this review, we conducted an online search of research published after 2003 using combinations of the words *mentors, mentoring, new teachers, retention,* and *attrition.* We also used a database of literature we have compiled in conjunction with another project studying the effects of mentoring on beginning math teachers. In this section, we reviewed the stronger of these studies, broadly applying the criteria used by Ingersoll and Kralik (2004) as our basis for inclusion. We divided the studies into those based on nationally representative samples and those that evaluated specific programs or groups of programs.

Studies Based on Nationally Representative Samples

Smith and Ingersoll (2004) compared the relationship between components of induction and teacher turnover in their study of a nationally representative sample of first-year teachers who completed the SASS in 1999–2000 and the Teacher Follow-up Survey (TFS) in 2000–2001. They identified eight components of induction: mentoring; participation in a beginning teacher seminar or classes; collaboration or common planning time with other teachers; participation in an external teacher network; regular, supportive communication with the principal or other administrators; reduced teaching load; reduced number of preparations; and access to a teacher's aide.

The study examined the supports that new teachers in both public and private schools received and the relationship between those supports and turnover. Although Smith and Ingersoll (2004) referred to these supports as components of induction, they extended beyond what might be considered part of the formal induction program in a school. For example, collaborating with other teachers in the same grade or subject area might be considered an effective component for supporting new teachers, yet it might not be considered part of a school's or district's induction program.

Nearly two-thirds of the teachers in Smith and Ingersoll's (2004) study reported having a mentor. Seven out of ten had a mentor in their field, and nine out of ten found their mentors to be helpful. Having a mentor in the same field (subject matter and/or grade level assignment) reduced the odds of leaving by 30 percent (p <.1). Teachers whose mentor was not in their field were also less likely to leave; however, this result was not statistically significant. Common planning time with other teachers or other regularly occurring opportunities for collaboration, participation in an external teacher network, and regular and supportive communication with administrators also decreased the odds of a teacher leaving the profession, although not all of the components were statistically significant. Participation in beginning teacher seminars or classes had a small but insignificant effect (Smith and Ingersoll, 2004).

Smith and Ingersoll (2004) created models that incorporated varying levels of induction components, which they labeled *packages*. Results indicated that as the number of components offered in an induction program increased, predicted rates for both moving to another school and leaving the profession decreased, but so did the number of teachers receiving the packages.

Only 3 percent of teachers in the study reported receiving no induction supports, but their attrition rate (combining teachers moving to another school and those leaving the profession) was over 40 percent. At the same time, the attrition rate for teachers who received the basic *induction package* (56 percent), which included a mentor and supportive communication with their principal or other administrators, was 39 percent. This outcome suggests that having a mentor without any additional supports may not be enough to effectively retain beginning teachers. Just over one-quarter of the teachers received the upgraded induction package, which included the components in the basic model plus regular opportunities for planning and collaboration with colleagues in their subject area and participation in a seminar for beginning teachers. This model lowered the likelihood of leaving to 27 percent.

Although a representative sample and use of statistical controls improved the internal validity and generalizability of the results, as a study of natural variation, selection bias remains a potential problem (e.g., principals assigned more resources to teachers who they thought needed them). In addition, the SASS surveys did not gather information about the quality of induction components, only whether or not they were present. As Smith and Ingersoll (2004) noted in their article, future research should explore issues of duration and frequency of these components as well as their costs and structures. Also, the study did not address the long-term effects of different induction supports on reducing attrition.

Hahs-Vaughn and Scherff (2008) conducted a study with the same data, focusing on turnover of teachers with less than five years of experience and who indicated that their primary assignment was in English or language arts. They replicated the models and combinations of packages presented by Smith and Ingersoll (2004), examining the relationship between language arts teacher attrition and participation in different aspects of teacher induction programs (mentoring, seminars, common planning time, participation in a teacher network, and reduced preparation).

In all of the models, the researchers found that only gender and salary were statistically significant in reducing attrition among these teachers. Although none of the variables associated with induction and mentoring had any significant impact on decreasing attrition, the power to detect effects was lower than in the Smith and Ingersoll (2004) study because of the reduced sample size.

Studies of Specific Induction Programs

Kelley (2004) examined retention rates of ten cohorts of beginning teachers from the Partners in Education (PIE) program four years after they completed the first year of teaching. Across the 10 cohorts, there were 161 new teachers in total. Of the 144 new teachers who could be found at the end of 4 years, 94 percent were still teaching. There was no comparison group, and there was possible selection bias. All of the teachers enrolled in the program chose to participate. This form of nonrandom selection may indicate that these teachers were more committed to the profession than other new teachers and more likely to remain in teaching. Similar results in other studies, however, (e.g., Fuller, 2003; Odell and Ferraro, 1992) supported the plausibility that induction was at least partially responsible for the higher retention rates.

The PIE program consisted of three components: cohort group networking, ongoing inquiry, and intensive mentoring by teachers released from their classroom to spend at least half a day in each new teacher's classroom each week (Kelley, 2004). Teachers in each of the ten cohorts were required to attend two monthly seminars and had opportunities to share and plan lessons and problem solve real classroom challenges. The PIE program study did not include an analysis specifically exploring the link between collaborative activities and retention rates, yet the low attrition rates and the relationships between collaboration and reduced attrition in other studies suggested that this could be an important component.

In an evaluation of the New York City Department of Education's (NYC DOE) program for new teachers, Rockoff (2008) assessed the impact of induction (provided by the New Teacher Center [NTC]) on reducing turnover and increasing student achievement. Rockoff's analysis focused on the intensive mentoring component. The induction program applied to all new teachers, so it was not possible to establish randomized or matched comparison groups in the implementation year. Instead, Rockoff used a difference-in-differences strategy to compare the new teachers without prior experience with new teachers with experience who were hired at the same time (and, thus, did not receive mentoring).

The NYC DOE (Rockoff, 2008) followed most of the NTC components in its mentoring program, including assignment to mentors who were released from classroom duties and who received training for their new roles. Two important deviations from the NTC model that could have impacted the outcomes included a one-year mentoring program instead of the two-year program recommended by NTC, and a higher mentor-teacher ratio than the 12:1 ratio proposed by NTC. Data came from administrative records about teacher and mentor characteristics and assignments, a log of contact hours, a survey of teachers evaluating their mentor, and student achievement data. The standard deviation in the number of hours of mentoring received by teachers was quite large—fourteen hours in 2004–2005 and seventeen hours in 2005–2006—suggesting considerable variability in program implementation.

Rockoff (2008) found that teachers in their first year who received mentoring were 4.5 percent more likely to complete their first year than teachers who did not receive mentoring. There were no significant effects of mentoring on retention or student achievement. New teachers in the program were 4.3 percent more likely to remain in the district and 3.6 percent more likely to return to their school than teachers who did not receive mentoring, but neither of these results was significant. A mentor's previous experience working in the school where the new teacher was teaching positively and significantly increased the likelihood of the teacher returning to the same school by 10 percent. Rockoff (2008) also found that new teachers who had opportunities for common planning with colleagues were more likely to return for a second year.

Two important aspects of the study suggest caution when interpreting results: (a) problems with identifying and then assigning teachers who qualified to be mentored and (b) changes in characteristics of new teachers before and after implementation of the induction program. Identifying and assigning new teachers to mentors was complicated by the unavailability of data about novices at the beginning of the school year. For example, teachers who were hired late or midyear were less likely to receive a mentor, and decisions about who needed mentoring were based on placement on the salary scale which, at times, was inaccurate (Rockoff, 2008). Therefore, some teachers who may have needed mentoring did not receive it, and vice versa.

Studies of Multiple Induction Programs

A recent SRI study of teacher induction programs in Illinois and Ohio provided additional support regarding the relationship between mentoring and retention, although specific descriptions about induction components were limited (Humphrey et al., 2008). Data were collected during the 2005–2006 and 2006–2007 school years. They included case studies of eight Illinois and five Ohio programs, surveys of all induction participants in all of the Ohio programs and in half of the Illinois programs, and retention data for all programs in both states. The survey was composed of six different constructs related to teaching, with three to six statements representing each construct: the school environment; the availability of instructional materials and supplies; induction support for working with special student populations; institutional support for instructional preparation and planning; mentor support for working with special student populations; and support for instructional preparation and planning.

Humphrey et al. (2008) reported no significant difference between teachers who returned to their school the following year and those who did not in terms of the supports they received from mentors. This might be partly explained by the infrequency of the meetings between novices and their mentors. Whereas 60 percent reported meeting at least weekly with their mentors, one in five teachers reported only meeting with their mentor once a month or less. Although 91 percent reported that their mentor had observed them teaching and offered feedback, only 27 percent reported this occurring at least monthly, and only 7 percent of teachers reported monthly opportunities to observe the mentor in her own classroom or demonstrate lessons in the novice's classroom.

Although the impact of mentoring on retention of beginning teachers was weak, Humphrey et al. (2008) found a statistically significant relationship between retention and the school environment. Seventy-six percent of teachers who reported strong support from the school environment returned to teach at the school the following year compared to 64 percent of teachers who reported weak support from the school environment. The significant difference in school environment is noteworthy because one of the items that comprised this index asked teachers the extent to which they agreed with the statement, "Teachers use time together to discuss teaching and learning" (6). As noted above, Smith and Ingersoll (2004) identified regular opportunities for collaboration and instructional planning as a significant factor in reducing attrition.

Another recent study, the Consortium on Chicago School Research's (CCSR) *Keeping New Teachers: A First Look at the Influences of Induction in the Chicago Public Schools* (Kapadia, Coca, and Easton, 2007) investigated the supports offered among the induction programs and the outcomes they produced. In 2005, CCSR included items related to induction programs for new teachers in their biannual survey. A total of 1,735 teachers identified themselves as first- or second-year teachers in CPS with less than three years of cumulative experience (two-thirds were elementary school teachers, and one-third were high school teachers). Respondents represented participation in a total of six different induction programs.

Rather than contrasting each induction program, the study explored how different factors impacted teachers' assessments of the overall experience of teaching that year, whether they looked forward to teaching next year, and whether they planned to remain in the same school. Roughly four-fifths of the sample of new teachers in this study participated in one or more induction programs, with 20 percent of teachers indicating that they were not participating in an induction program even though it was required. A strong potential for selection bias limits interpretability of the results.

About one-third of novice CPS teachers in both elementary and high schools reported meeting with their mentor on a weekly basis; one-quarter reported daily interactions (Kapadia, Coca, and Easton, 2007). Over three-quarters of the beginning teachers in both elementary and high school reported receiving helpful support from their mentors who observed and discussed their teaching. Seventy-nine percent of elementary teachers and 72 percent of high school teachers reported receiving useful assistance for developing various teaching strategies. Although high school teachers were more likely than elementary teachers to report that mentoring influenced their decision to remain in teaching, none of the results were significant.

Mentoring did seem to be related to a teacher's decision to remain at their school. For elementary teachers, mentoring supports that significantly increased the likelihood of remaining at the school included help with developing various teaching and classroom management strategies, analyzing student work, and assessing student learning. In contrast, although high school teachers indicated that mentoring influenced their decision to stay at the school, only analyzing student work resulted in a significant difference (Kapadia, Coca, and Easton, 2007). This was also the area where both elementary and high school teachers were least likely to receive help, though those who did were 25 percent more likely to intend to stay than teachers who did not.

To examine the extent to which new teachers in CPS received other induction supports and the influence supports had on teachers' experiences and plans, teachers were asked to rate the helpfulness of different supports.

Support could be available through a formal program or as part of informal relationships or activities available to all teachers. This presented a challenge for understanding the impact that induction programs alone might have. Despite this limitation, 45 percent of both elementary and secondary teachers rated regular opportunities to collaborate with other teachers as very helpful.

This result was consistent with other studies (Humphrey et al., 2008; Kelley, 2004; Smith and Ingersoll, 2004) regarding the importance teachers place on collaborative activities. Further, teachers who reported having regular opportunities for collaboration were more likely to report plans to remain in teaching. Regular opportunities for collaboration were also associated with an increased likelihood of a teacher's plans to remain at the same school. Other components that yielded significant results for teachers' plans to remain in the same school included principal's encouragement, release time to observe teaching, and participation in a network of other teachers. Finally, elementary teachers regarded the assistance they received from the principal to be the third most helpful support they received; for secondary teachers, participation in a network of teachers was the third most helpful support (Kapadia, Coca, and Easton, 2007).

The first large-scale, randomized control trial of the effects of comprehensive induction on teacher retention released findings from the first year of the study in late 2008 and is discussed elsewhere in this volume (Glazerman, Dolfin, Bleeker, Johnson, Isenberg, Lugo-Gil, Grider, Britton, and Ali, 2008). The purpose was to evaluate the impact of comprehensive induction programs as compared to the current programs districts were offering. Comprehensive induction was defined to include programs that carefully selected and trained full-time mentors, provided structured support for new teachers, planned for weekly meetings with mentors, emphasized a focus on instruction and opportunities to observe experienced teachers, used formative assessment tools that allowed ongoing evaluation of practice, and offered outreach to district and school-based administrators to educate them about induction goals.

Mathematica Policy Research, Inc., (Glazerman et al., 2008) conducted the evaluation and selected the NTC of Santa Cruz, California, and the Educational Testing Service (ETS) of Princeton, New Jersey, to provide the induction programs to the participating districts. The intent of the study was to evaluate the effects of a comprehensive induction rather than the effects of the specific programs; therefore, results were pooled across districts.

To answer the research question about the effect of induction on classroom practice, data were collected from teachers who taught reading/language arts in a self-contained classroom. To answer the research question about the effect of induction on student test scores, data were collected from teachers who taught in a self-contained classroom in a tested grade and subject. A fall survey collected baseline information about the teachers; two additional surveys asked about the duration and intensity of induction activities in which teachers participated. In the spring, beginning teachers were observed for one to two hours while teaching a literacy unit (Glazerman et al., 2008).

School-level data included student records, a mobility survey, and student achievement data. The response rate for the surveys and teacher observation exceeded 85 percent. The evaluators used hierarchical linear modeling (HLM) to analyze the outcome data, which allowed them to correctly identify units of analysis and devise unbiased estimators in order to conduct hypothesis testing (Glazerman et al., 2008).

All mentors had a minimum of five years of teaching experience plus experience in providing professional development and were regarded as outstanding teachers. Mentors received training for their role before and during the school year. The ratio of teachers to mentors was intended to be 12:1, but the actual caseloads varied over the year (Glazerman et al., 2008). In addition to working with their mentor for two hours a week, beginning teachers in the treatment group also attended monthly professional development programs and had opportunities to observe veteran teachers during the year. Throughout all of these activities, the focus was on instruction and meeting the needs of beginning teachers.

Statistically significant differences were reported between the treatment and control groups in the amount, types, and content of induction support received, but not in outcomes. Treatment group teachers received more mentoring and were twice as likely to have a regular meeting time with their mentor during the school day. Although the frequency of meetings with mentors did not differ significantly between the two groups, teachers in the treatment group reported spending an average of twelve minutes more with their mentor than did teachers in the control group (Glazerman et al., 2008). Teachers in the treatment group were significantly more likely to attend professional development sessions focused on lesson planning, analyzing student work, and differentiated instruction.

According to the evaluators, no significant results were reported on the impact of induction on classroom practices or student standardized test scores. In addition, they observed no impact of participation in comprehensive induction programs on retention, defined as the percent of teachers who remained in their originally assigned school. Seventy-five percent of the treatment group was retained, as compared to 74.6 percent of the control group. There was less than a 3 percent difference in treatment and control groups for teachers who moved to a different school and less than 1 percent difference in teachers leaving the profession (Glazerman et al., 2008).

While the Mathematica study provided strong evidence that an externally designed, comprehensive induction program (such as those provided by NTC or ETS) was likely to be no more effective in reducing first-year turnover than the typical induction supports provided by districts, several caveats should be considered. First, the results generalize to elementary schools in high-poverty districts only, where 50 percent or more of the students receive free or reduced-price lunches. Second, the comparison was not to "no induction" or "no mentoring" but to whatever the district typically provided. As noted above, over 80 percent of the beginning teachers in the control group had mentors. Finally, the results only covered retention after the first year.

METHODOLOGICAL PROGRESS

More recent research on the impact of induction and mentoring has made significant strides toward improving methodological design, including the use of randomization (Glazerman et al., 2008), analysis of large, nationally representative data sets to improve generalizability (Hahs-Vaughn and Scherff, 2008; Smith and Ingersoll, 2004), and the use of statistical controls and other techniques to reduce the threat of selection bias (Glazerman et al., 2008; Humphrey et al., 2008, Rockoff, 2008; Smith and Ingersoll, 2004). Problems persist in analyzing natural variation in program participation and outcomes, however, where attempts to adjust for selection effects may not be completely effective (Humphrey et al., 2008; Kapadia Coca, and Easton, 2007; Kelley, 2004; Rockoff, 2008).

External validity may also be limited for studies focusing on induction programs in particular cities (Kelley, 2004) or states (Humphrey et al., 2008). Studies based on large, nationally representative samples (e.g., Hahs-Vaughn and Scherff, 2008; Smith and Ingersoll, 2004) are likely to improve generalizability of the results, although they are typically unable to investigate relationships between quality and impact of induction programs. Smaller qualitative studies can offer descriptive evidence about the qualities of induction programs and mentoring experiences, although the ability to make causal claims or generalize findings from these studies is extremely limited. Studies that make use of mixed methods, for example, combining random assignment, survey research, time logs, and classroom observation with in-depth interviewing, can offer more complete understanding about the impact of induction on beginning teacher retention.

FUTURE RESEARCH

Most of the research on increasing retention among beginning teachers has examined retention rates after only one year of teaching (Cheng and

Brown, 1992; Eberhard et al., 2000; Glazerman et al., 2008; Humphrey et al., 2008; Smith and Ingersoll, 2004). Longitudinal studies that track teachers for the first five years in the profession would give a better understanding of the lasting impact induction programs have on reducing attrition. Studies based on nationally representative samples, such as the Schools and Staffing, would be enhanced if retention patterns could be followed for more than just one year. In developing the sampling frame for the Teacher Follow-up Survey, the Schools and Staffing Survey is sent to school administrators to determine if teachers sampled in the base year are still teaching in the school, moved to another school, or left teaching.

Another hindrance to understanding the degree to which induction can mitigate attrition is the variability in the content of programs and the lack of clarity in the boundaries between different supports. Induction can consist of informal advice from a buddy teacher across the hall to comprehensive induction. Surveys that only ask about whether someone had a mentor or participated in various induction activities miss out on collecting important data that could be investigated to better understand the varied "packages" of induction supports as well as the degree to which different packages might differentially influence teacher outcomes. Further, although nationally representative survey data can provide a window into the types of support that teachers are receiving, randomized control trials where the variability in supports is intentionally manipulated is required to assess the causal impact of different components.

Clearer conceptions of induction and mentoring, specifically what induction programs include and do not include, would help to increase the comparability of results across studies. It is also clear that different forms and levels of support are likely to be needed for teachers in different schooling contexts (elementary versus secondary, high poverty versus low poverty, positive school climate versus negative school climate, teaching literacy versus science). One approach to induction is unlikely to fit the range of needs, and a stronger research base that spans different methods, different levels, different subjects, and different contexts is clearly required.

CONCLUSION

Definitive evidence regarding the impact of induction and mentoring on the retention of beginning teachers remains inconclusive. Results from Smith and Ingersoll (2004), Kelley (2004), and Kapadia, Coca, and Easton (2007) indicated support for induction programs in increasing retention, particularly when the intensity and frequency of supports are high. In all three studies, opportunities to collaborate and plan with colleagues were noted as connected to reducing attrition. In the Mathematica study, however, comprehensive induction programs were not more effective than the current support that high-poverty districts have in place for supporting beginning elementary teachers (Glazerman et al., 2008).

The SRI International study of induction programs in Ohio and Illinois returned more mixed results. Significant increases in retention were associated with a positive school environment, although not with mentoring supports emphasizing instructional preparation and planning (Humphrey et al., 2008). Intensive and comprehensive induction models seemed to have an impact on reducing attrition among beginning teachers (Smith and Ingersoll, 2004) in studies of natural variation, but not in experiments comparing comprehensive programs to what is currently in place. As district leaders and policy makers confront decisions about how to retain new teachers, more research is still needed to understand if sizeable investments of time and money in induction programs will have a lasting impact.

REFERENCES

Alliance for Excellent Education. 2004. *Tapping the potential: Retaining and developing high quality new teachers.* Washington, DC: Author.

Brown, J. G., and C. Wambach. 1987, February. *Using mentors to increase new teacher retention: The mentor teacher induction project.* Paper presenteed at the annual meeting of the American Association of Colleges for Teacher Education, Arlington, VA. (ERIC Document Reproduction Service No. ED 280816).

Cheng, M., and R. S. Brown. 1992. *A two-year evaluation of the peer support pilot project: 1990–1992.* Toronto, Canada: Toronto Board of Education, Research Department.

Eberhard, J. P., P. Reinhardt-Mondragon, and B. Stottlemyer. 2000. *Strategies for new teacher retention: Creating a climate of authentic professional development for teachers with three or less years of experience.* Corpus Christi: South Texas Research and Development Center, Texas A&M University.

Fuller, E. 2003. *Beginning teacher retention rates for TxBESS and Non-TxBESS teachers.* Unpublished manuscript, State Board for Educator Certification, Austin, TX.

Glazerman, S., S. Dolfin, M. Bleeker, A. Johnson, E. Isenberg, J. Lugo-Gil, M. Grider, E. Britton, and M. Ali. 2008. *Impacts of comprehensive teacher induction: Results from the first year of a randomized controlled study.* Washington, DC: U.S. Department of Education.

Gold, M. 1987. *Retired teachers as consultants to new teachers: A new inservice teacher training model. Final report.* Washington, DC: American Association of State Colleges and Universities, Washington, D.C.

Hahs-Vaughn, D., and L. Scherff. 2008. Beginning English teacher attrition, mobility and retention. *Journal of Experimental Education* 77(1):21–53.

Henke, R. R., X. Chen, and S. Geis. 2000. *Progress through the teacher pipeline: 1992–1993 colllege graduates and elementary/secondary school teaching as of 1997.* Washington, DC: National Center for Education Statistics.

Humphrey, D. C., M. E. Wechsler, K. R. Bosetti, J. Park, and J. Tiffany-Morales. 2008. *Teacher induction in Illinois and Ohio: Findings and recommendations.* Menlo Park, CA: SRI International.

Ingersoll, R. M. 2001. Teacher turnover and teacher shortages: An organizational analysis. *American Education Research Journal* 38(3):499–534.

———. 2000. The status of teaching as a profession. In *Schools and society: A sociological approach to education,* eds. J. H. Ballantine and J. Z. Spade, 102–18. Belmont, CA: Wadsworth Press, Ingersoll.

Ingersoll, R. M., and N. Alsalam. 1997. *Teacher professionalization and teacher committment: A multilevel analysis.* Washington, DC: National Center for Education Statistics.

Ingersoll, R. M., and J. M. Kralick. 2004. *The impact of mentoring on teacher retention: What the research says.* Denver: Education Commission of the States.

Ingersoll, R. M., and T. M. Smith. 2003. The wrong solution to the teacher shortage. *Educational Leadership* 60(8):30–33.

Kapadia, K., V. Coca, and J. Easton. 2007. *Keeping new teachers: A first look at the influences of induction in the Chicago public schools.* Chicago: Consortium on Chicago School Research, University of Chicago.

Kelley, L. M. 2004. Why induction matters. *Journal of Teacher Education* 55(5):438–48.

Lopez, A., A. Lash, M. Schaffner, P. Shields, and M. Wagner. 2004. *Review of the research on the impact of beginning teacher induction on teacher quality and retention.* Menlo Park, CA: SRI International.

Odell, S. J., and D. P. Ferraro. 1992. Teacher mentoring and teacher retention. *Journal of Teacher Education* 43(3):200–204.

Rockoff, J. 2008. *Does mentoring reduce turnover and improve skills of new employees? Evidence from teachers in New York City.* Unpublished manuscript, Columbia University, New York.

Serpell, Z., and L. A. Bozeman. 1999. *Beginning teacher induction: A report on beginning teacher effectiveness and retention.* Washington, DC: American Association of Colleges for Teacher Education.

Smith, T. M., and R. M. Ingersoll. 2004. What are the effects of induction and mentoring on beginning teacher turnover? *American Educational Research Journal* 41(3):681–714.

Spuhler, L., and A. Zetler. 1993, 1994, 1995. *Montana beginning teacher support program.* Helena: Montana State Board of Education.

8

Influence of Teacher Induction on Mentor Teachers

Susan G. Hanson, New Teacher Center

Many of the chapters in this volume document the growing number of investigations into the potential benefits of induction programs for novice teachers. In comparison, relatively few studies focus on the influence of induction programs on the mentors. It is important to understand the broad impact of induction and mentoring programs, especially the ways in which mentors may benefit professionally. Research regarding teacher mentors usually focuses on understanding the skills and knowledge necessary to support effective mentoring of beginning teachers (e.g., Athanases and Achinstein, 2003; Hall, Draper, Smith, and Bullough, 2008; Hobson, Ashby, Malderez, and Tomlison, 2009; Orland, 2001), rather than on what mentors personally gain from mentoring.

It was not until the mid-1980s that educators began to consider the evidence suggesting that mentors may benefit from mentoring (Huling and Resta, 2001). As a result, there have been few focused efforts to review the empirical research literature on the impact of mentoring on experienced teachers selected to be mentors of beginning teachers. This chapter summarizes the limited empirical evidence regarding the influence of mentor preparation on mentoring practice and on mentors as professionals. By reviewing the evidence of ways that induction programs influence mentors, this review contributes to our broader understanding of the potential power of well-conceived school-based induction programs and to the need for more research in this area.

METHOD FOR IDENTIFYING RELEVANT STUDIES

Manual searches of major education journals addressing teacher professional development and searches of electronic databases such as the Educational Resources Information Center and Google Scholar served as the starting point for this review. Empirical studies that focused on mentor teachers working as part of a district induction program and that documented outcomes for mentors were sorted into three broad categories. The first category comprised studies of mentor professional development and the act of mentoring on the mentors' learning and attitudes. The second category consisted of studies of impact on the mentor's own classroom teaching. The last category considered mentors' involvement in induction programs beyond mentoring and classroom teaching.

THE INFLUENCE OF MENTORING ON MENTORS

Huling and Resta (2001) reviewed papers written primarily from the 1990s through 2001 that reported on the benefits of mentoring to mentors, often as unanticipated or secondary positive effects within a larger study. As mentor teachers assisted novice teachers, they perceived that they were improving professional competency in such areas as reflective practice, cognitive coaching, exposure to new curriculum and teaching ideas, and rich collegial interactions. Their brief review did not distinguish between benefits for full-time mentors versus part-time mentors or between mentors who received training and those who did not.

Gilles and Wilson (2004) examined the growth and development of full-time mentors in focus group interviews with thirteen first-year mentors and nine second-year mentors. The study examined the mentors' perceptions of their own professional development. Learning to be a successful mentor, learning new ideas, working with adults, and reflection were most frequently mentioned. Mentors reported that the program impacted growth in professional confidence, access to professional networks, increased leadership abilities, and increased professional demeanor. Gilles and Wilson concluded that mentoring, like teaching, was developmental.

Hanson and Moir (2006) conducted a survey regarding the influence of full-time mentoring experience on the skills and attitudes of fifty veteran mentors who had completed their tenure of working as full-time mentors. Ninety-four percent reported that the mentor training and experience deepened their understanding of teaching and learning, and 90 percent reported that it increased their reflections on their own practice. Interviews with eighteen of the veteran mentors suggested that opportunities to meet regularly and work collaboratively in professional learning communities with other mentors helped them learn new teaching strategies, gain new ideas, and become more self-reflective.

As part of an evaluation of their school and university partnership at the University of Hong Kong, Lopez-Real and Kwan (2005) focused on how the mentoring process might simultaneously enhance mentors' professional development. A survey of 259 mentors working with a teacher education program for one to four years found that 70 percent of those who responded (45.5 percent) claimed that they had benefited professionally from mentoring. Follow-up interviews with eighteen of the mentors suggested that the impact of reflecting on teaching, explaining teaching methods to new teachers, and continuing to examine their own teaching approaches and attitudes in greater depth led to professional development.

These recent studies, as well as some initial studies that included mentors (Ackley and Gall, 1992; Ganser, 1996), supported a shift from a perspective of mentoring as a one-way process intended to benefit novice teachers to a more complex perspective in which mentors may also professionally benefit from the professional development and mentoring that they experience as induction program staff. Work in this field suggested that mentoring contributed to perceived professional growth of experienced teachers, particularly if they received sustained professional development and were full-time mentors.

The number of studies reporting the impact of professional development and mentoring on mentors who participated in formal induction programs is very small and relies on self-reporting. Most articles did not identify whether the mentors were fully or partially released from teaching. Details regarding the professional development activities in which mentors participated, including length, format, activities, facilitator backgrounds, and the extent to which mentors had opportunities to practice using their new skills and knowledge, were missing. It is one step to identify the new knowledge, skills, and perceptions that mentors reported, another to understand the conditions under which induction programs effectively helped mentor teachers gain knowledge and skills, and another to understand how mentors engaged in practice as a result of professional development. No studies documented mentors' actions or perceptions before and after professional development.

THE INFLUENCE OF MENTORING
ON THE MENTOR'S CLASSROOM TEACHING

This section reviews studies that considered the question of whether mentoring had an effect on the mentor's subsequent or concurrent classroom practice. Three studies of part-time mentors and two studies of full-time

mentors were reviewed to consider whether experienced teachers transferred the knowledge, skills, and practices learned as teacher mentors to
their own classroom teaching.

Clinard and Ariav (1998) explored the perceptions of 158 part-time mentor teachers at 55 schools in the United States and 21 mentors at one school
in Israel from 1991–1998. All of the mentors received similar mentor
training and ongoing support. The mentors reported that being reflective
more often in planning and implementing lessons had the biggest impact.
American mentors reported that they were able to benefit and channel their
new skills into their teaching more than the Israeli mentors.

Riggs and Sandlin (2002) examined the impact of a large induction
program on mentor teachers' perception of growth in their ability to
implement effective classroom instruction practices. These mentors had
participated in five days of summer training and five follow-up trainings
to prepare them to implement a formative assessment system with new
teachers. Some 348 mentors completed a Mentor Efficacy Scale developed
by Riggs (2000), along with a survey on changes they made in implementing effective teaching practices as described in the California Standards for
the Teaching Profession. Mentors reported positive changes, with the most
change occurring in the areas of classroom management, discipline, and
professionalism. There was a significant, but small, positive correlation between mentor self-efficacy and self-reported impact on teaching practice.

Hanson and Moir (2006) investigated twenty-nine mentors' perceptions
of growth after they had completed a three-year term serving as full-time
mentors. Over 80 percent of the teachers reported that mentoring had
greatly increased their ability to analyze student work, use student assessments to guide instruction, differentiate instruction for students with different needs, and increased their repertoire of teaching methods. As a set,
these three studies contributed to our knowledge by identifying areas in
which mentors believed induction influenced their classroom practice. The
studies relied on mentor perceptions and did not include observation of
mentors' actual teaching practice before and after mentoring.

Kline and Salzman (2006) published a comparative study designed to
investigate how the teaching practices of K–8 part-time mentors might differ from those of their nonmentoring colleagues. Participants for this study
consisted of fifteen pairs of experienced K–8 teachers who were matched
according to district, age, and number of years of teaching experience.
Eleven of the teachers taught at the same school. Data included observed
and documented teaching behaviors, in addition to teachers' discourse
about their practice. The researchers compared the practice of experienced
teachers who mentored with the practice of those who did not. No statistically significant differences in the professional practice of each mentor/
nonmentor pair were found. The results of the study raised concerns about

the mentors' ability to model high-quality, standards-based instruction for new teachers.

Tauer's (1996) case study of ten mentor teachers in two school districts found little evidence that the mentors had grown professionally from the experience as "evidenced by changes in thinking or practices related to teaching" (10). Based on four interviews with each mentor, she concluded that only two of the ten mentors exhibited professional growth.

These four studies, three of which relied on mentor perceptions, provided limited evidence on mentoring experience as a positive impact on the mentor's subsequent or concurrent classroom practice. Combining teaching with mentoring may have had a slightly positive impact on classroom teaching in terms of feeling more able to implement desired instructional practices and being more reflective in planning and implementing lessons. The one study comparing the practices of mentors with those of their non-mentoring colleagues had no statistically significant results.

None of the studies included observation of mentors' teaching practice before and after mentoring. The very limited number of studies on the influence of mentoring on teaching in different subject areas, grade levels, and school contexts prevents generalizing the limited research regarding the influence of mentoring on teaching.

IMPACT OF MENTORING ON LEADERSHIP DEVELOPMENT AND CAREER PATHS

The final group of studies summarized here considered the broader influence of mentoring on leadership development and career paths of teachers, who served as mentors. Susan Villani (1999, 2005) concluded that induction and mentoring programs had the potential, perhaps more than any other initiative, to both cultivate and provide teachers and their principals with opportunities to engage in collective action to build school capacity. She also described the personal benefits teacher mentors reported, including leadership development, rejuvenation, reduction of isolation, a sense of investment and membership in the school community, and new learning about schools and the process of change.

Focus groups with twenty-five first- and second-year mentors (Gilles and Wilson, 2004) and annual individual interviews with twenty-eight mentors over three years (Hanson and Moir, 2009) produced similar examples of leadership opportunities for mentors. These included facilitating professional development classes for new teachers, presenting at conferences, leading after-school inservice meetings, and assuming leadership roles at a local university. Third-year mentors in both studies also reported opportunities to mentor new mentors.

It is generally agreed that experienced teachers benefit professionally from serving as mentors, yet few studies have tracked mentors' activities or behaviors after mentoring. Freiberg, Zbikowski, and Ganser (1997) surveyed eighteen former mentors from an urban school district. Approximately one-third of the mentors returned to the classroom after mentoring. Interviews with five veteran mentors, who were offered unsolicited jobs outside of working in the classroom, indicated that the new jobs provided ways to build on what they had learned as mentors or combined elements of mentoring and teaching. The freedom and respect afforded them as mentors made it difficult for them to envision themselves back in a more controlled environment, especially one with a fixed schedule.

Moir and Bloom (2003) surveyed thirty-five mentors who had completed their tenure as full-time mentors with the Santa Cruz New Teacher Project. Seven of the veteran mentors were principals or assistant principals, fourteen were serving in professional development leadership roles, and fourteen were classroom teachers. The administrators and curriculum leaders reported that their "mentoring experience was the single most formative factor in their development" (60). To investigate how these mentor alumni differed from administrator colleagues with other backgrounds, they conducted interviews and made school observations. They concluded that former mentors had a deep understanding of teaching and learning, they knew how to help classroom teachers grow and how to create learning communities, and they were attuned to the needs of beginning teachers.

Subsequently, Hanson and Moir (2006, 2008) surveyed fifty former full-time mentors and interviewed a subsample to learn how the mentor experience influenced their professional careers, practices, and attitudes. Thirty-four percent (seventeen) returned to classroom teaching, 24 percent (twelve) were support teachers, 18 percent (nine) were principals or vice principals, and 6 percent (three) became college professors. The remaining 18 percent (nine) retired or consulted part-time. The administrators, support teachers, and college professors all had leadership roles, and together they made up almost half of the population.

The administrators unanimously reported that their experience as a mentor was very applicable to their current work. They all reported that their experience as an advisor greatly contributed to their ability to talk with teachers about their teaching and creating a learning environment. They also reported being able to act as a change agent at their school and to become a school leader more quickly.

The studies reviewed in this section provided insight into potential influences of full-time mentoring on leadership skills, which may lead to some mentors becoming school or district administrators. The studies also suggested that some mentors had a hard time going back to their classrooms. Very few studies went beyond a general list of benefits and provided no information on how leadership skills were actualized in practice. And, as with almost all studies in this review, the findings were based on the self-report.

CONCLUSION AND IMPLICATIONS

This summary of the extant literature suggested that mentoring contributed to mentors' perceived professional growth, especially if they participated in mentor training as part of an induction program. Areas of perceived growth included improved reflective thinking about their mentoring practices, newly developed ideas about teaching strategies, and opportunities for working with adult learners. It also suggested that mentors perceived a positive effect on their classroom teaching practice and enhanced mentors' leadership capacity and skills.

Most of the studies relied only on mentors' self-reports and provided little detail regarding mentors' backgrounds, training, or practice. There should be more studies in this area that investigate mentors' mentoring and teaching practices before and after their training. In addition, more information is needed on mentors' experiences in different kinds of schools and induction programs. Such studies will help us understand better the conditions under which induction programs enable mentor teachers to gain knowledge and skills in mentoring, teaching, and school leadership.

This summary also raises the possibility that schools and districts may ultimately benefit from the development and experience of teacher mentors. The knowledge and skills that experienced teachers acquire may not only assist new teachers to develop their teaching practice but also may help the mentors become even more effective in teaching their own students. With their enhanced skills, knowledge, and experience, mentors may be able to help leverage change in school systems by playing different kinds of leadership roles in schools and in districts.

In conclusion, there are not a sufficient number of studies examining the impact of mentoring—neither on mentors' learning nor on their practice as teachers or as mentors. There are even fewer studies on any long-term benefits of mentoring in terms of leadership within a building or a district. Many of the studies that do exist are conference presentations or more than ten years old. This means that while it may be intuitive to think that being a mentor is professionally or personally beneficial, the extent to which the claimed benefits translate to improved practice for students has yet to be documented. It is clear that this is a line of research that needs to be developed over the next ten years.

REFERENCES

Achinstein, B., and S. Athanases, eds. 2006. *Mentors in the making: Developing new leaders for new teachers*. New York: Teachers College Press.

Ackley, B., and M. D. Gall. 1992, April. *Skills, strategies and outcomes of successful mentor teachers.* Paper presented at the annual meeting of the American Educational Research Association, San Francisco, CA.

Athanases, S. Z., and B. Achinstein. 2003. Focusing new teachers on individual and low performing students: The centrality of formative assessment in the mentor's repertoire of practice. *Teachers College Record* 105(8):1486–1520.

Clinard, L. M., and T. Ariav. 1998. What mentoring does for mentors: A cross-cultural perspective. *European Journal of Teacher Education* 21(1):91–108.

Freiberg, M., J. Zbikowski, and T. Ganser. 1997. Promoting mid-career growth through mentoring. *Journal of Staff Development* 18(2):52–54.

Ganser, T. 1996. What do mentors say about mentoring? *Journal of Staff Development* 17(3):36–39.

Gilles, C., and J. Wilson. 2004. Receiving as well as giving: Mentors' perceptions of their professional development in one teacher induction program. *Mentoring and Tutoring* 12(1):87–106.

Hall, K., R. J. Draper, L. Smith, and L. Bullough. 2008. More than a place to teach: Exploring the perceptions of the roles and responsibilities of mentors. *Mentoring & Tutoring: Partnership in Learning* 16(3):328–45.

Hanson, S., and E. Moir. 2009, October. *Mentoring as a successful strategy to retain high quality educators.* Paper presented at the Kappan International Summit, Indianapolis, IN.

——. 2008. Beyond mentoring: Influencing the professional practice and careers of experienced teachers. *Phi Delta Kappan* 89(6):453–58.

——. 2006, April. *Beyond mentoring: The career paths of veteran mentors and how they use their new skills as teachers, leaders, and colleagues.* Paper presented at the annual meeting of the American Educational Research Association, San Francisco, CA.

Hobson, A., P. Ashby, A. Malderez, and P. Tomlinson. 2009. Mentoring beginning teachers: What we know and what we don't. *Teaching and Teacher Education* 25(1):207–16.

Huling, L., and V. Resta. 2001. *Teacher mentoring as professional development.* Washington, DC: ERIC Clearinghouse on Teaching and Teacher Education. (ERIC Document Reproduction Service No. ED460125).

Kline, L., and J. Salzman. 2006. Mentoring: A serendipitous professional development opportunity. In *Research on teacher induction: Teacher education yearbook XIV,* ed. J. R. Dangel, 169–92. Lanham, MD: Rowman & Littlefield.

Lopez-Real, F., and T. Kwan. 2005. Mentors' perceptions of their own professional development during mentoring. *Journal of Education for Teaching* 31(1):15–24.

Manthei, J. 1992, April. *The mentor teacher as leader: The motives, characteristics and needs of seventy-three experienced teachers who seek a new leadership role.* Paper presented at the annual meeting of the American Educational Research Association, San Francisco, CA.

Moir, E., and G. Bloom. 2003. Fostering leadership through mentoring. *Educational Leadership* 60(8):58–60.

Orland, L. 2001. Reading a mentoring situation: One aspect of learning to mentor. *Teaching and Teacher Education* 17(1):75–88.

Riggs, I. M. 2000. *The impact of training and induction activities upon mentors as indicated through measurement of mentor self-efficacy.* San Bernardino: California State University.

Riggs, I. M., and R. A. Sandlin. 2002, April. *Professional development of mentors within a beginning teacher induction program: How does the garden (mentors) grow?* Paper presented at the annual meeting of the American Educational Research Association, New Orleans, LA.

Tauer, S. M. 1996, April. *The mentor-protege relationship and its effects on the experienced teacher.* Paper presented at the annual meeting of the American Educational Research Association, New York.

Villani, S. 2005. Mentoring promotes teacher leadership. In *Teacher mentoring and induction: The state of the art and beyond,* ed. H. Portner, 169–211. Thousand Oaks, CA: Corwin Press.

———. 1999. Mentoring teachers: A good, strong anchor. In *Teaching: A career, a profession,* eds. M. F. Hayes and I. K. Zimmerman, 19–26. Wellesley: Massachusetts Association of Supervision and Curriculum Development.

9

Components of 1997–2008 Teacher Induction Programs

Reflections on Comprehensive Induction Systems

Ann L. Wood, California State University, Los Angeles
Randi Stanulis, Michigan State University

The goal of this chapter is to delineate common components of induction programs based on a review of the literature from 1997 through 2008. The literature documented a wide variation in what is meant by induction, and induction programs vary greatly in their complexity and intensity across states and even within the same states or school districts (Alliance for Excellent Education [AEE], 2004; Shields, Esch, Humphrey, Young, Gaston, and Hunt, 1999). Despite these variations, commonly accepted goals of induction have remained relatively consistent over time (Wood and Stanulis, 2009).

These include goals to (a) improve teacher quality, (b) increase novice teacher retention, (c) promote novice teachers' professional well-being and satisfaction, (d) provide a coherent system of teacher formative assessment, (e) satisfy mandated requirements related to induction, and (f) improve the teaching of diverse students. Many authors agreed that systematic comprehensive induction is a multifaceted, organized system of teacher professional development that consists of induction activities such as mentoring, reflective inquiry, and formative assessment for novice teachers in their first, second, or third year of teaching (AAE, 2004; Bartell, 2005; Horn, Sterling, Baliar, and Metler-Armijo, 2006; Ingersoll and Smith, 2004; Shields et al., 1999; Stanulis, Burrill, and Anes, 1997; and Wood and Stanulis, 2009). This concept of induction is grounded in the work of Feiman-Nemser's (2001a) continuum of learning to teach and Odell and Huling's (2000) mentoring framework for induction.

METHOD FOR REVIEW OF LITERATURE

Data sources for this review included Education Resources Information Center (ERIC), Dissertation Abstracts, Psychological Abstracts, and Sociological Abstracts. Keywords included combinations of the following terms: *teacher induction, beginning teacher induction, new teacher induction, novice teacher induction, teacher professional development, in-service education, teacher development,* and *teacher formative assessment.* The initial search yielded more than 260 documents. Selection criteria focused on studies that were conducted in the United States with first-, second-, or third-year K–12 classroom teachers. Studies that did not examine induction programs offering support and formative assessment were excluded. This reduced the number to 132 studies.

Case studies and studies that examined only mentor programs or mentors' learning were also excluded, as were studies that examined retention or cost-benefit. These criteria reduced the number of studies to 70. In the last step, we categorized theses studies as (a) quantitative studies, (b) qualitative studies, (c) program evaluations, (d) literature reviews, (e) conceptual studies, (f) policy reports, (g) program descriptions, (h) books, and (i) conference papers. Table 9.1 indicates the rating of publication for inclusion in the literature review and the number of documents in each category.

LIMITATIONS OF THE LITERATURE REVIEW

We selected studies based on a focus or emphasis on an induction component, and this may minimize the significance of other program components. The largest number of studies (20) was qualitative, and many of these had small sample sizes. Therefore, many of the findings may not be generalized beyond the context of the specific study. Several studies reported research on the author's own induction program, rather than external analysis, and

Table 9.1. Summary of Documents Evaluated (n = 70)

Rating of Publication for Inclusion in Literature Review	*Number of Documents*
Quantitative studies (large-scale and small-scale)	7
Qualitative studies	20
Program evaluations	3
Literature reviews	6
Conceptual studies	9
Policy studies	7
Program descriptions	4
Books	9
Conference papers	5

must be interpreted with caution. Specialized induction programs such as those designed for only special educators, science, mathematics, or other subject matter teachers were omitted from this study, so they might be studied separately and their components compared to general induction programs.

FINDINGS OF THE REVIEW

Based on our analysis of the 1997–2008 induction literature, we found nine key induction program components. We have organized this chapter based on the findings that appear in this literature. These include (a) educative mentors' preparation and mentoring of novice teachers, (b) systematic and structured observations, (c) formative assessment of novice teachers, (d) reflective inquiry and teaching practices, (e) developmentally appropriate professional development, (f) a supportive school culture for novice teachers, (g) administrators' active role in induction, (h) program evaluation, and (i) a shared vision of teaching and learning.

Educative Mentors' Preparation and Mentoring of Novice Teachers

According to the New Teacher Center (Moir and Bloom, 2003), mentors are the central agents of change in induction programs. They must have the ability to initiate new teachers into new school norms and best practices—ones that were not yet the status quo in schools. This can happen only when mentors' learning is aligned with the induction program's vision.

Mentoring was the most frequent subject of research studies (nineteen qualitative studies and four quantitative studies).

Mentoring practice included interacting regularly with novice teachers (Arends and Rigazio-DiGilio, 2000), conducting formative assessment observations (AEE, 2004; Olebe, 2001), collecting and discussing evidence of student learning with beginning teachers (Stanulis and Ames, 2009; Wood, 1999), and developing a plan to strengthen the novice's instruction and classroom learning environment in collaboration with the teacher (Feiman-Nemser, 2001a; Wood and Waarich-Fishman, 2006). These mentoring functions comprised *educative mentoring*, which relies on an explicit vision of quality teaching and of teacher learning that help novices learn from their practice by identifying problems, probing thinking, and focusing on students' learning (Feiman-Nemser, 2001a, 2001b).

Educative mentoring focused on helping novice teachers learn to teach using methods aligned with professional standards of teaching and learning (Olebe, 1999). Mentors were carefully selected and well matched to novice teachers by school-site location, grade level, and subject matter (Schwille, Nagel, and DeBolt, 2000).

To create educative mentoring that aligns with goals of comprehensive induction, mentor selection, incentives, release time, and preparation are factors that have been considered. Mentors' background knowledge, open-mindedness, and willingness to practice reflective teaching themselves can also impact the novice teachers' induction experiences. Similarly, mentors' understanding of the induction program's purpose and the role of reflection in teaching shapes the new teachers' experiences in the induction program (Gless, 2004; Spillane, 2002; Youngs, 2007).

Mentor incentives included professional development, release time, university course credit, and stipends. Incentives were an important part of acknowledging this professional work and may influence the quality of mentoring (Recruiting New Teachers, Inc., 1999; Villani, 2002). Mentoring can also be highly influenced by the model used to deliver mentoring services (full-release, partial, or no release), although no one service delivery model is deemed best (Meckel and Rolland, 2000). Mentors participated in ongoing professional development to help them learn content knowledge and strategies to use as they worked with novice teachers (Schwille and Dynak, 2000). Current induction research shows that mentors' preparation focuses on the elements illustrated in table 9.2.

Table 9.2. Foci of Mentor Preparation

Mentor Preparation Focus	Research
Defining a sound rationale for supporting new teachers	Feiman-Nemser, 2001b; Ingersoll and Smith, 2004; Odell and Huling, 2000
Understanding new teachers' concerns and learning needs	Costigan, 2004; Moir, 2003; Schwille and Dynak, 2000
Learning skills and techniques to meet new teachers' learning needs	Bartell, 2005; Feiman-Nemser, 2001a; Odell and Huling, 2000; Wang, Schwille, and Odell, 2008
Enhancing strategies for building a trusting mentoring relationship	Odell and Huling, 2000; Stanulis and Meloche 2008; Wang and Odell, 2002
Developing a repertoire of reflective, educative mentoring skills	Horn, Sterling, Blair, and Metler-Armijo, 2006; Stanulis, Burrill, and Ames, 2007
Developing observation and formative assessment feedback skills	Stanulis and Ames, 2009; Moir and Baron, 2002
Working with adult learners	Arends and Regazio-DiGilio, 2000; Johnson and Kardos, 2003
Analyzing student work to assess student learning	Ames, Stanulis, and VanZee, 2006; Stansbury and Zimmerman, 2000

Systematic and Structured Observations

Three qualitative induction studies addressed the systematic use of observations of novice teachers, a component of most twenty-first century induction programs (AEE, 2004; Fideler and Haselkorn, 1999; Wood, 2001). These observations were primarily conducted by mentors and were often grounded in state-mandated teaching standards (Fideler and Haselkorn, 1999; Stanulis, 2006) as well as academic content standards (Olebe, Jackson, and Danielson, 1999; Wood and Waarich-Fishman, 2006).

In the Launch into Teaching Program at Michigan State University, mentors learned specific ways to collect evidence of novice teacher and student talk and classroom action. Mentors then had data to use in conversations with the novice. Through conversations based on observations, mentors challenged novices to develop principled reasons for their teaching decisions and to consider ways to improve their teaching effectiveness (Stanulis et al., 2007).

Formative Assessment of Novice Teachers

Two program evaluations and nine qualitative studies delineated the role of formative assessment in induction programs. Formative assessment refers to a process of measuring a novice teacher's professional growth developmentally, not for purposes of evaluation as in summative assessment, but to provide feedback and foster continuing teacher development among novice educators.

The goals of formative assessment systems included helping novice teachers learn how to assess their own professional competence through organized and continuous reflective discussions about their teaching practices with their mentors (Olebe, 2001). Within many formative assessment systems, standards of practice were defined, demonstrated, and implemented (Moir and Baron, 2002; Olebe, 1999) and novice teachers were helped to identify their teaching strengths and areas for further professional development (Athanases and Achinstein, 2003).

Evidence of novice teachers' strengths and weaknesses was collected through mentor observations, team teaching, and novice teachers' analyses of student work in collaboration with their mentors. In some induction programs, such as the BEST program in Connecticut, new teachers participated in a culminating performance-based assessment across identified induction standards (Connecticut State Department of Education [CSDE], 1999). In other programs, novices shared growth portfolios that represented their progression in developing their knowledge, skills, and dispositions (Wood, 2000).

Some induction programs used the Pathwise System of Formative Assessment (Educational Testing Service [ETS], 2003), based on Danielson's

(1996) framework for professional practice. It provides a series of novice teacher classroom observations to be conducted by mentors trained to formatively assess novice practices across six developmental domains of teaching. Other programs use the California Formative Assessment and Support System for Teachers (CFAAAT) (Educational Testing Service, 2004) or the Formative Assessment System (FAS) designed by the New Teacher Center. FAS provides novice teachers with mentored assistance in conducting inquiries and learning activities focused on different teaching standards (Moir, 2003). A longitudinal, comparative study of Pathwise and FAS demonstrated that there was no significant difference between the effectiveness of these two formative assessment systems (Mathematica Policy Research, 2005).

Reflective Inquiry and Teaching Practices

Published induction program descriptions frequently mentioned reflective inquiry. In addition, four qualitative research studies investigated inquiry and reflective teaching processes. The ways in which reflective inquiry and habits of mind are fostered within an induction program can influence the kind of mentoring and novice teacher learning that occurs. Induction programs encourage deep reflections on novice teachers' daily teaching experiences by providing ongoing, classroom-based, structured inquiries of practice (Fideler and Haselkorn, 1999; Strong and Baron, 2004; Wood, 1999). Ball and Cohen (1999) described the importance of helping novice teachers learn in and from practice by studying authentic artifacts of practice in collaboration with other teachers.

In a quantitative study of the perceived effectiveness of induction practices, Perez, Swain, and Hartsough (1997) reported that novice teachers found activities that involved reflections about teaching (e.g., journal writing) were not as effective as reflections during actual teaching (e.g., team teaching and coaching).

In contrast, Kelley (2004) conducted a four-year study of ten cohorts of novice teachers (1,000) in the Partners in Education Program (PIE), an induction partnership involving the University of Colorado and six school districts. Grounded in the concept that classroom-based inquiry creates powerful ways to improve instruction and student learning, PIE teachers kept reflective dialogue journals with their mentors, took three graduate courses, and conducted a teacher-as-researcher project in their classrooms. Of the eight cohorts analyzed, 123 out of 124 novice teachers expressed appreciation of the inquiry-based graduate courses and identified the teacher-as-research project as the highlight of these requirements.

Youngs (2007) found that the kind of learning experiences provided to novice teachers in two different urban districts varied based on mentor selection, novice teachers' assignments, and the kinds of professional development experiences offered to novice teachers. In one district, mentors emphasized support through reflection, facilitated opportunities for novice teachers to analyze student work, examined specific curricular needs of their students, and helped novice teachers to understand the impact of their curricular decisions. In the other district, mentors did not emphasize helping novices develop reflective practices but focused more on classroom management techniques and psychological support for novice teachers rather than on content-specific knowledge and skills for gathering evidence of student learning.

Developmentally Appropriate Professional Development

Two qualitative research studies provided information on professional development based on novice teachers' differentiated needs. Induction programs that were more comprehensive offered more learning experiences for novice teachers provided activities that matched the different needs of first-, second-, and/or third-year teachers (Arends and Rigazio-DiGilio, 2000; Feiman-Nemser et al., 1999). Program activities focused on increasing the depth of understanding and complexity with which novice teachers approached their practice.

Grossman and colleagues found that in the second year of teaching, novices were more ready to think about concepts, ideas, and understandings that were not possible during the first year of teaching (Grossman, Valencia, Evans, Thompson, Martin, and Place, 2000). A study by Yopp and Young (1999) found that first-year novice teachers preferred release time more than second-year teachers. Second-year teachers preferred the time with their mentors more than release time.

Supportive School Culture for Novice Teachers

Based on the conceptual studies of Feiman-Nemser (2001a, 2001b) and Feiman-Nemser and Norman (2005), three qualitative studies (Horn et al., 2006; Pardo, 2006; Resta, Huling, White, and Matschek, 1997) emphasized the importance of creating a school culture that supported growth, satisfaction, and continued learning for novice teachers. Peterson (2005) documented that novice teachers were often given larger class sizes; more students with special needs or behavioral problems; classrooms with the least equipment, textbooks, and/or resources; multiple-grade assignments; roving or fleeting teachers' assignments with no classroom of their own; and many extracurricular duties. Peterson referred to these well-known school practices as "the hazing of new teachers."

In their 1999 policy study, Shields, et al. found that California induction programs rarely provided reduced duties for novice teachers and that this finding was consistent with national induction patterns, where reduced workloads for novice teachers were all but nonexistent (Fideler and Haselkorn, 1999). The Quartz and TEP Research Group (2003) reported that a negative school milieu often resulted in novice teachers becoming angry about these inequities and struggling with desires to quit teaching. Some studies posited that no induction component or system could make up for a nonsupportive school culture (Bartell, 2005; Johnson, 2004). The following three aspects of school culture have been identified in the literature as important elements for building a supportive culture.

Novice Teacher Orientation

Orientation can be an important learning experience that helps novice teachers learn key information to fit into the culture of school and to begin the work of teaching (Stanulis et al., 2007). Orientations varied greatly in length and substance across programs. Some offered a seminar or half-day program, while others sponsored a full week of orientation activities (Arends and Rigazio-DiGilio, 2000). Typical components of the orientation were an overview of the school's mission, mandated curricula, school/district policies and philosophy (Feiman-Nemser, 2001a), and time to meet their mentors for the first time (Stansbury and Zimmerman, 2000).

Sanctioned Time

Several studies pointed to the provision of regularly scheduled times for novice teachers to plan, reflect on, and develop instructional strategies (AEE, 2004; Bartell, 2005). Novice teachers were given time to observe other teachers, attend professional development seminars, and work with their mentors (Arends and Rigazio-DiGilio, 2000; Horn et al., 2006; Wood and Waarich-Fishman, 2006).

Collegial Interactions

Novice teachers were given time to interact with one another and build networks of support. Activities included groups of teachers who engaged in instructional planning, team planning, and discussing grade-level needs and assistance (Arends and Rigazio-DiGilio, 2000). Venues included novice teacher study groups, book clubs, Internet chat rooms, bulletin boards, or online mentored support (Feiman-Nemser, 2001b; Stansbury and Zimmerman, 2002).

Administrators' Active Role in Induction

Two qualitative studies addressed site administrators' roles in teacher induction. Successful implementation of the components of induction programs depended, to a large extent, upon site administrators' leadership and commitment to induction (Brock and Grady, 1997). In her research of a large urban district's induction program in California, Wood (2005) found that principals occupied several roles in induction programs. Four are discussed below.

Principal as New Teacher Recruiter

Wood (2005) found that principals often recruited teachers through district searches or job fairs at universities. This was positive for the novice teachers who accepted employment at the schools of the principals who had recruited them, if the principals stayed at the school for several years and worked to build collaborative interactions. There were long-term deleterious effects on novice teachers, however, when principals were subsequently transferred from the schools during the novices' first year.

Facilitator of Site-based Mentor Training and Services

Site administrators directly or indirectly facilitated the educative mentoring of novice teachers through approving and providing sanctioned times for mentor preparation, ongoing support, and services to novice teachers (AEE, 2004; Bartell, 2005). In contrast, administrators who disliked or disapproved of scheduled time for induction activities sabotaged induction programs by their lack of support (Arends and Rigazio-DiGilio, 2000).

New Teacher Advocate

Another role that site administrators played was that of being a novice teacher advocate (AEE, 2004; Brock and Grady, 2005; Wood, 2005). Novice teachers frequently and positively recalled principals who visited their classrooms regularly, talked to them about lessons, greeted them warmly, seemed interested in their progress, and gave them advice to prevent teacher burnout.

Builder of School Culture Supportive of Novice Teachers

For many novice teachers, their principal was more important to them than their mentor (Wood, 2005). The principal set the tone for accepting and integrating new teachers into the school community (American Federation of Teachers, 1998; Johnson, 2004). To build a supportive school culture for novice teachers, some site administrators participated in induction trainings, communicated regularly with district induction leaders and site mentors, and interacted regularly with novice teachers (Wood, 2005).

Program Evaluation

Two qualitative studies discussed the role of program evaluation in induction. Barnett, Hopkins-Thompson, and Hoke (2002) and Horn et al. (2006) stated that effective induction programs must have an ongoing program evaluation system that focuses on teacher retention (Fideler and Haselkorn, 1999), teacher quality, and increased student achievement (Darling-Hammond, 2000).

Davis, Resta, and Higdon (2001) described the program evaluation component of the Teacher Fellows Program (TFP), a school/university partnership program that provided first-year teachers with induction at the graduate level. During a fifteen-month period, novice teachers received a $14,000 fellowship, completed an induction program, and earned a master of education degree while they were being mentored by Faculty Exchange Teachers (mentors) in leadership skills. Program evaluation data found that 100 percent of two of the three cohorts were teaching and that district administrators had very positive perceptions of the program.

Runyan, White, Hazel, and Hedges (1998) described the formative evaluation of the Kansas Goals 2000 Early Career Professional Development Program. This Early Career program was a large, collaborative induction program among universities, the Southeast Education Service Center, and sixty-eight school districts. It provided differentiated support and formative assessment to novice teachers in their first three years of teaching. A Teacher Needs Assessment Questionnaire (TNAQ) obtained feedback on participants' satisfaction, needs, and learning. Based on Fuller and Bown's (1975) stages of teacher development, the TNAQ tracked teachers individually and as a group three times a year to show their quantitative professional progression through three stages of development.

A Shared Vision of Teaching and Learning

Several published program descriptions cited a shared view of learning and teaching as integral to their induction programs but offered no research on this program component. Only one program, the Launch into Teaching Induction Program (LIT), a Teachers for a New Era Project at Michigan State University, described this component as integral to its induction program (Stanulis and Floden, 2009). Feiman-Nemser (2001a) found that teachers who formulated their mentoring based on an explicit vision of quality teaching worked with novices in ways that fostered novice teachers' inquiry and continued learning.

In university and school induction programs, there is a possibility of a mismatch in purposes and practices if this explicit vision of teaching and learning is not discussed and developed together. For example, as researchers in a pilot induction program examined the challenges of shifting the focus of mentoring from a psychological and social support of to conversations about teaching and learning, they realized the importance of opening up discourse about the school context, school leadership, and teacher learning (Stanulis and Meloche, 2008).

CONCLUSION AND IMPLICATIONS

As we read the literature, it was difficult to find programs that encompassed all nine components; most induction programs contained the first two to five components. The literature revealed that induction programs offering multiple and varied induction activities are assessed as most effective by novice teachers and others (AAE, 2004; Horn et al., 2004; Shields et al., 2004). Ingersoll and Smith (2004) found that novice teachers who participated in multiple induction activities were less likely to move to other schools and less likely to leave the teaching profession.

Current research does not systematically study the effectiveness of individual induction components or sets of components. More rigorous, small-scale induction studies are needed to analyze empirical data and demonstrate the intricacies of program effects. Large quantitative studies such as Fletcher, Strong, and Villar's (2008) are needed to examine the connections between specific induction components and student learning. Studies are also needed to measure teacher and student learning through comparative and systematic research that provides ways to look within and across induction programs.

Researchers can also investigate each individual induction component by conducting systematic research that examines the effects of each component on novice teacher effectiveness and on first-, second-, and third-year teachers in induction programs. We need experimental studies that explore the effects of program components on teacher effectiveness across local and statewide induction programs. We also need more comparative studies of general induction programs versus specialized programs, ones targeted toward specific subject areas and grade levels to determine if these two types of induction programs differ in their combinations of components for comprehensive induction.

To conclude, an exploration of the literature between 1997 and 2008 yielded a collection of nine induction components. Current research does not yet answer the question of how each induction program component impacts novice teacher effectiveness or which combination of components improves the effectiveness of novice teachers in their first, second, and third induction years. Further study of this set of nine components across induction programs will bring us closer to answering these critical questions.

REFERENCES

Alliance for Excellent Education. 2004. *Tapping the potential: Retaining and developing high-quality new teachers*. Washington, DC: Author.

American Federation of Teachers. 1998. *Beginning teacher induction: The essential bridge*. (Policy Brief No. 13.). Washington, DC: Author.

Ames, K., R. N. Stanulis, and D. VanZee. 2006, December. *Moving beyond superficial conversations: Mentoring beginning teachers in literacy*. Paper presented at the annual meeting of the National Reading Conferences, Los Angeles, California.

Arends, R. I., and A. J. Rigazio-DiGilio. 2000, July. *Beginning teacher induction: Research and examples of contemporary practice*. Paper presented to the Japan–United States Teacher Education Consortium, Honolulu, HI.

Athanases, S., and B. Achinstein. 2003. Focusing new teachers on individual and low performing students: The centrality of formative assessment in the mentor's repertoire of practice. *Teachers College Record* 105(8):1486–1520.

Ball, D. L., and D. K. Cohen. 1999. Developing practice, developing practitioners: Toward a practice-based theory of professional education. In *Teaching as the learning profession: Handbook of policy and practice*, eds. L. Darling-Hammond and G. Sykes, 3–32. San Francisco: Jossey Bass.

Barnett, B., P. Hopkins-Thompson, and M. Hoke. 2002. *Assessing and supporting new teachers*. Chapel Hill, NC: Southeast Center for Teaching Quality.

Bartell, C. 2005. *Cultivating high-quality teaching through induction and mentoring*. Thousand Oaks, CA: Corwin.

Brock, B., and M. Grady. 2005. *Developing a teacher induction plan*. Thousand Oaks: CA, Corwin.

———. 1997. *From first-year to first-rate: Principals guiding beginning teachers*. Thousand Oaks, CA: Corwin.

Connecticut State Department of Education (CSDE). 1999. *A guide to the BEST program for teachers*. Hartford, CT: Author.

Costigan, A. 2004. Finding a name for what they want: A study of New York City's teaching fellows. *Teaching and Teacher Education* 20(2):129–43.

Danielson, C. 1996. *Enhancing professional practice: A framework for teaching*. Alexandria, VA: Association of Supervision and Curriculum Development.

Darling-Hammond, L. 2000. *Solving the dilemmas of teacher supply, demand, and standards: How we can ensure a competent, caring, and qualified teacher for every child*. New York: National Commission on Teaching and America's Future.

Davis, B., V. Resta, and K. Higdon. 2001. Teacher fellows: A graduate program for beginning teachers. *Action in Teacher Education* 23(2):43–49.

Educational Testing Service. 2003. *Pathwise*. Retrieved July 10, 2001, from http://www.ets.org/pathwise/index.html.

Educational Testing Service. 2004, August. Beginning Teachers' Engagement with BTSA/CFASST: Study of the Impact of the California Formative Assessment and Support System for Teachers. CFASST report 1: ETS RR-04-30.

Feiman-Nemser, S. 2001a. From preparation to practice: Designing a continuum to strengthen and sustain teaching. *Teachers College Record* 103(6):1013–55.

———. 2001b. Helping novices learn to teach. Lessons from an exemplary support teacher. *Journal of Teacher Education* 52(1):17–30.

Feiman-Nemser, S., S. Schwille, C. Carver, and B. Yusko. 1999. *A conceptual review of literature on new teacher induction.* Washington, DC: Office of Educational Research and Improvement (ERIC Document Reproduction Service No. ED 449147).

Fideler, E., and D. Haselkorn. 1999. *Learning the ropes: Urban teacher induction programs and practices in the United States.* Belmont, MA: Recruiting New Teachers.

Fletcher, S., M. Strong, and A. Villar. 2008. An investigation of the effects of variations in mentor-based induction on the performance of students in California. *Teachers College Record* 106(4):716–46.

Fuller, F. F., and O. H. Bown. 1975. Becoming a teacher. In *Teacher education: The 74th yearbook of the national society of education,* ed. K. Ryan, 25–52. Chicago: University of Chicago Press.

Gless, J. 2004. *Mentor teacher selection.* Santa Cruz: New Teacher Center at the University of California, Santa Cruz.

Grossman, P., S. Valencia, K. Evans, C. Thompson, S. Martin, and N. Place. 2000. Transitions into teaching: Learning to teach writing in teacher education and beyond. *Journal of Literacy Research* 32:631–62.

Horn, P. J., H. A. Sterling, H. C. Blair, and K. Metler-Armijo. 2006, January. *Induction strategies for future teachers.* Paper presented at the annual meeting of the American Association of Colleges for Teacher Education (AACTE), San Diego, CA.

Ingersoll, R. M., and T. M. Smith. 2004. Do teacher induction and mentoring matter? *NASSP Bulletin* 88(638):30–59.

Johnson, S. M. 2004. *Finders and keepers: Helping new teachers survive and thrive in our schools.* San Francisco: Jossey-Bass.

Kelley, L. 2004. Why induction matters. *Journal of Teacher Education* 55(5):438–48.

Johnson, S. M., and S. M. Kardos. 2004. Professional culture and the promise of colleagues. In S. M. Johnson, ed., *Finders and keepers: Helping new teachers survive and thrive in our schools.* San Francisco: Jossey-Bass.

Mathematica Policy Research. 2005. *Evaluation of the impact of teacher induction programs.* Washington, DC: Institute of Education Sciences, U.S. Department of Education.

Meckel, A., and L. Rolland. 2000. BTSA models for support provision. *Thrust for Educational Leadership* 29(3):18–20.

Moir, E. 2003. *Launching the next generation of teachers through quality induction.* Paper presented to the National Commission on Teaching and America's Future. 2003 Annual Commissioners and Partner States' Symposium, Racine, WI.

Moir, E., and W. Baron. 2002. Looking closely, every step of the way. Formative assessment helps to shape new professionals. *Journal of Staff Development* 23 (4).

Moir, E., and G. Bloom. 2003. Fostering leadership through mentoring. *Educational Leadership* 60(8):58–60.

Odell, S., and L. Huling, eds. 2000. *Quality mentoring for novice teachers.* Indianapolis, IN: Association of Teacher Educators and Kappa Delta Pi.

Olebe, M. 2001. A decade of policy support for California's new teachers: The beginning teacher support and assessment program. *Teacher Education Quarterly* 28(1):85–109.

——. 1999. California formative assessment and support system for teachers (CFASST): Investing in teachers' professional development. *Teaching and Change* 6(3):258–71.

Olebe, M., A. Jackson, and C. Danielson. 1999. Investing in beginning teachers: The California model. *Educational Leadership* 56(8):41–44.

Pardo, L. S. 2006. The role of context in learning to teach writing: What teacher educators need to know to support beginning urban teachers. *Journal of Teacher Education* 57(4):378–94.

Perez, K., C. Swain, and C. Hartsough. 1997. An analysis of practices used to support new teachers. *Teacher Education Quarterly* 24(2):41–51.

Peterson, M. 2005. Hazed! *Educational Leadership* 62(8):20–23.

Quartz, K., and TEP Research Group. 2003. "Too angry to leave": Supporting new teachers' commitment to transform urban schools. *Journal of Teacher Education* 54(2):99–111.

Recruiting New Teachers, Inc. 1999. *Learning the ropes: Urban teacher induction programs and practices in the United States.* Belmont, MA: Author.

Resta, V., L. Huling, S. White, and D. Matschek. 1997. The teacher fellows program: A year to grow. *Journal of Staff Development* 18(1):42–45.

Runyan, K., V. White, L. Hazel, and D. Hedges. 1998. *A seamless system of professional development from preservice to tenured teaching.* Paper presented at the annual meeting of the American Association of Colleges for Teacher Education (AACTE), New Orleans, LA.

Schwille, S. A., and J. Dynak. 2000. Mentor preparation and development. In *Quality mentoring for novice teachers*, eds. S. J. Odell and L. Huling, 67–76. Indianapolis, IN: Association of Teacher Educators and Kappa Delta Pi.

Schwille, S. A., A. L. Nagel, and G. P. DeBolt. 2000. Mentor selection and mentor/novice matching. In *Quality mentoring for novice teachers*, eds. S. J. Odell and L. Huling, 57–66. Indianapolis, IN: Association of Teacher Educators and Kappa Delta Pi.

Shields, P., C. Esch, D. Humphrey, V. Young, M. Gaston, and H. Hunt. 1999. *The status of the teaching profession: Research findings and policy recommendations. A report to the teaching and California's future task force.* Santa Cruz, CA: Center for the Future of Teaching and Learning.

Spillane, J. P. 2002. Local theories of educational change: The pedagogy of district policies and programs. *Teachers College Record* 104(3):377–420.

Stansbury, K., and J. Zimmerman. 2002. Smart induction programs become lifelines for the beginning teacher. *Journal of Staff Development* 23(4):10–17.

——. 2000. *Lifelines to classrooms: Designing support for beginning teachers. Knowledge brief.* San Francisco: West Ed. (ERIC Document Reproduction Service No. ED447104).

Stanulis, R. N. 2006, April. *Keeping content and context central: University-school comprehensive induction in the Michigan State University Teachers for a New Era Project.* Paper presented at the annual meeting of the American Educational Research Association, San Francisco, CA.

Stanulis, R. N. and K. Ames. 2009. Learning to mentor: Evidence and observation as tools in learning to teach. *The Professional Educator.* 33(1): 28–38.

Stanulis, R. N., G. Burrill, and K. Ames. 2007. Fitting in and learning to teach: Tensions in developing a vision for a university-based induction program. *Teacher Educator Quarterly* 34(3):135–47.

Stanulis, R. N., and R. Floden. 2009. Intensive mentoring as a way to help beginning teachers develop balanced instruction. *Journal of Teacher Education* 60(2):112–22.

Stanulis, R. N., and B. H. Meloche. 2008, March. *Challenges in developing, enacting, and analyzing mentoring that focuses on teaching and learning: A university-school collaboration.* Paper presented at the annual meeting of the American Educational Research Association, New York.

Strong, M., and W. Baron. 2004. An analysis of mentoring conversations with beginning teachers: Suggestions and responses. *Teaching and Teacher Education* 20(1):47–57.

Villani, S. 2002. *Mentoring programs for new teaches: Models of induction and support.* Thousand Oaks, CA: Corwin Press.

Wang, J., and S. Odell. 2002. Mentored learning to teach according to standards-based reform: A critical review. *Review of Educational Research* 72(3):481–546.

Wang, J., S. Schwille, and S. Odell. 2008. Effects of teacher induction on beginning teachers' teaching: A critical review of literature. *Journal of Teacher Education* 59(2):132–52.

Wood, A. 2005. The importance of principals: Site administrators' roles in novice teacher induction. *American Secondary Education* 33(2):39–62.

———. 2001. What does research say about teacher induction and IHE/LEA collaborative programs? *Issues in Teacher Education* 10(2):69–81.

———. 2000. Teaching portfolios: Tools for reflective teaching in inner-city teacher induction. In *Research on effective models for teacher education, teacher education yearbook viii,* eds. D. J. McIntyre and D. Byrd, 111–26. Thousand Oaks, CA: Corwin.

———. 1999. How can new teachers become the B.E.S.T.? In *A better beginning: Supporting and mentoring new teachers,* ed. M. Scherer, 116–23. Alexandria, VA: Association of Supervision and Curriculum Development.

Wood, A., and R. Stanulis. 2009. Quality induction: "Fourth-wave" (1996–2006) teacher induction programs. *New Educator* 5(1):1–23.

Wood, A., and N. Waarich-Fishman. 2006. Two induction models in one urban district: Transitioning to teacher credentialing. In *Research on teacher induction: Teacher education yearbook xiv,* ed. J. Dangel, 67–87. Published in partnership with the Association of Teacher Educators. Landham, MD: Rowman & Littlefield.

Yopp, R. H., and B. L. Young. 1999. A model for beginning teacher support and assessment. *Action in Teacher Education* 21(1):24–36.

Youngs, P. 2007. District induction policy and new teachers' experiences: An examination of local policy implementation in Connecticut. *Teachers College Record* 109(4):797–836.

10

Exploring the Potential of Internet-based Technology for Mentoring and Induction Programs[1]

Renée T. Clift, University of Arizona
Lara Hebert, Yu-Ming Cheng, University of Illinois at Urbana-Champaign
Julia Moore, Kennesaw State University
Nancy Clouse, University of Montana

The ubiquitous nature of Internet-based technologies has changed the ways individuals can communicate with one another through e-mail, chat, blogs, threaded conversations, and in communities such as Tapped In, Facebook, and MySpace. The number of preservice teacher education programs using e-mail, web-based courseware, and blogs to instruct and support prospective teachers has increased exponentially over the past few years. But at the same time, web-based support for beginning teachers is a notion that remains underdeveloped—a conclusion drawn by the coauthors of this paper who met while doing independent research on the nature and impact of electronic support for novice teachers. In this chapter we pool our knowledge to discuss eleven programs, each of which is in print, informed by data, and readily accessible.

IDENTIFYING PROGRAMS

To identify the programs using technology to support new teachers, three of the coauthors each conducted separate reviews of research publications connected to using technology in mentoring and induction programs as a part of their graduate work (Hebert) or dissertation research (Clouse, 2007; Cheng, 2008), concentrating primarily on dissertations, journal articles, and book chapters. Conference or other nonpublished presentations were excluded from this review with the knowledge that scholars across the country are studying this topic but have yet to publish their work. Therefore, we acknowledge that some existing programs may not have been identified in this article, but our intent is to provide a baseline analysis of programs using Internet-based mentoring or professional development for novice teachers.

MENTORING NEW TEACHERS VIA THE INTERNET

Proponents of using e-mail and electronic conferences to link mentors and novice teachers (commonly referred to as e-mentoring) argue that technology can be used to provide support in a timely manner, reduce isolation, provide content-based matches between mentors and novice teachers, and offer multiple perspectives on a given topic in group conversations. They also argue that, particularly for novice teachers in rural areas, e-mentoring can reduce time constraints because novices and mentors can meet online without having to drive long distances in order to meet face-to-face (DeWert, Babinski, and Jones, 2003; Klecka, Clift, and Cheng, 2005; Klecka, Clift, and Thomas, 2002).

Many schools have difficulties finding qualified mentors with the appropriate grade-level or content-area expertise within the school or even in nearby schools. Challenges of finding appropriate mentors impact rural and urban schools the most, but all districts experience this challenge in areas such as orchestra or Japanese because no other person may be teaching that subject within the district (Fulton, Yoon, and Lee, 2005). E-mentoring has the capability of recruiting mentors from multiple school districts and cities.

Although it is difficult to pinpoint exactly when electronic mentoring first started, it is probably safe to assume that informal e-mentoring occurred with the inception of e-mail among researchers and scientists using ARPANET, Usenet, and BITNET networks in the late 1970s and early 1980s. In 1985 America Online expanded the use of e-mail to the general public, and Katherine Merseth (1991) was one of the first educators to use e-mail to support new teachers through the Beginning Teacher Computer Network (BTCN) based at Harvard University. This program supported graduates from three different masters of education programs during their first year of classroom teaching.

Welcoming Interns and Novices
with Guidance and Support Online

Judi Harris, then at the University of Texas at Austin, developed the Electronic Emissary in 1993 to provide a matching service for curriculum-based, electronic exchanges among teachers, their students, and experts in the field (Harris, O'Bryan, and Rotenberg, 1996). Harris's project grew into a service for preservice and novice teachers called Welcoming Interns and Novices with Guidance and Support Online (WINGS), offering personalized mentoring. New teachers selected their own e-mentors from a database of practicing teachers who volunteered to fill this role. WINGS expanded its services to include a discussion forum and a "Hot Links for Teachers" database. The contents of this evolving, searchable database originated from specific questions asked by participants (and answered by WINGS staff) regarding teaching and learning.

Lighthouse Project

The Lighthouse Project began in 1997 in North Carolina. Program participants were trained in how to use the e-mail listserv and how to problem solve using a collaborative consultation model during an initial, face-to-face workshop. The problem-solving format included the following steps: (a) the beginning teacher described a problem he or she was struggling with, (b) the other participants helped to clarify the problem by offering alternative perspectives and discussing possible causes for the problem, (c) the group brainstormed possible solutions, (d) the group collaborated to generate an action plan, and finally (e) the teacher carried out the suggested plan and reported back to the group (DeWert, Babinski, and Jones, 2003). This program is no longer operational and was absent from the literature beyond its initial, pilot year.

Mathematics, Science, and Technology Project

In 1998 the School of Education at the University of North Carolina-Chapel Hill initiated the Mathematics, Science, and Technology Project (MaSTech). All participants were either enrolled in, graduated from, or were faculty in a middle-grades mathematics or science education degree program or had teaching experience in middle-grades mathematics or science (Friel, 2000). Like the Lighthouse Project, this program also used the collaborative consultation model of problem solving. The authors did not report on data pertaining solely to the beginning teachers, but they provided selected quotes from beginning teachers, indicating that the online support was helpful and maintained a connection with the campus and one another. The project did not last beyond one year because of problems with the technology and Internet access.

Novice Teacher Support Project

As one component of a support system for novice teachers in five counties in East Central Illinois, the Novice Teacher Support Project's (NTSP) electronic mentoring program began in 2000 (Klecka, Clift, and Thomas, 2002). The e-mentoring supplemented face-to-face professional development sessions offered regularly throughout the year. As a function of available funding, implementation strategies varied year-to-year, ranging from stipends provided for participation to purely voluntary participation. In 2007, a new program administrator decided not to continue the technology-based support.

In 2003–2004 the NTSP staff worked with Loyola University of Chicago, Northeastern Illinois University, and Governor's State University to enable them to use e-mentoring with their graduates. Each of the three sites designed their e-mentoring projects to fit their individual needs. Loyola University of Chicago's program began its support with first-year teachers and volunteer mentors who graduated from Loyola's program. Northeastern Illinois University's program served special education student teachers and graduates who went on to teach in high-needs schools. Governor's State University used e-mentoring to support the students (all full-time teachers) in their alternative certification program. These three programs were still in operation in 2007.

E-mentoring for Student Success

A partnership among the National Science Teachers Foundation, Montana State University, and the New Teacher Center at Santa Cruz, e-Mentoring for Student Success (eMSS) began in 2002 to provide mentoring for beginning science teachers and has now expanded to include other states. This online resource provides mentoring from experienced teachers in the same discipline, discussion forums for content and pedagogy, a just-in-time resource for when novice teachers need immediate answers, access to practicing scientists, mentor training, and vetted, relevant, online curriculum and teaching resources (Jaffe, Moir, Swanson, and Wheeler, 2006).

Table 10.1 provides a summary of all of the programs discussed above. From the table and the descriptions one can see that mentoring support has grown from e-mail exchanges to electronic conferencing using more sophisticated software than simple e-mail. Most of the projects are externally funded and based at universities. They use a variety of software packages and, therefore, the programs seem to have been developed independently from one another. The sites have become more sophisticated over time and include numerous resources for new teachers.

Table 10.1. Internet-based Mentoring Programs

Beginning Teacher Computer Network (1987–1990)

Participants
Secondary education graduates from three M.Ed. programs at Harvard University teaching in middle schools and high schools across the United States

Description
Graduates provided with a toll-free phone number for dial-up access to e-mail and public, content-specific bulletin boards.
Facilitated by a teacher education program coordinator and a graduate assistant who had previous teaching experience
Supported by Common Ground software

Research/Evaluation Results
Survey and interview data indicated:
- 22% of participants dialed in daily, 48% 1–3 times per week, and 30% 1–2 times per month. The greatest use was at the beginning of semesters.
- Site used mostly for moral support as opposed to technical assistance.
- Participation reduced feelings of isolation.
- Participants felt that they were able to have frank discussions due to confidentiality and relationships built during coursework.

Analysis of postings indicated:
- The professional exchanges were oriented to problem formulation and solution.
- The diversity of teaching contexts required participants to be excessively reflective about their individual teaching situations as related to the experiences of others.

Merseth (1991)

Lighthouse Project (1997–1998)

Participants
Pilot program included twelve beginning teachers, four experienced teachers, and eight education faculty.

Description
Started with communicating via e-mail list then moved to threaded discussions during last six weeks of pilot project

Research/Evaluation Results
Results of the pilot study conducted by program developers using analysis of online discussions, follow-up phone interviews, and survey of support group's effectiveness
- Online discussions provided teachers the opportunity to clarify thinking about complex educational issues and make more informed decisions regarding their practice.

(continued)

Table 10.1. *(Continued)*

- Beginning and experienced teachers were loaned laptops and provided university e-mail addresses and unlimited Internet access.
- Beginning teachers experienced decreased feelings of isolation; increased emotional support, confidence, and reflection; more enthusiasm for work; demonstrated ability to adopt a more critical perspective; and improved problem-solving skills.

DeWert et al. (2003)

Welcoming Interns and Novices with Guidance and Support Online (1993–present)

Participants

Participation limited to the last year of preservice preparation and to teachers who have graduated from the university

Description

Beginning teachers selected their own e-mentors from an online pool of experienced teachers for personalized one-on-one electronic mentoring interactions via e-mails or through discussion forums with a larger community of beginning teachers and e-mentors.

Research/Evaluation Results

Case studies of ten protégé-mentor pairs for one academic year using interviews, e-mail discussions, and original applications as data sources indicated:

- Beginning teachers received practical to general suggestions from mentors.
- Beginning teachers reported that mentors provided personal and emotional support.
- There were mutual reflective professional development exchanges between mentors and beginning teachers.

Abbott (2003)

Mathematics, Science, and Technology Project (February–May 1998)

Participants

Seven preservice teachers, four first-year beginning teachers, two graduate students who served as telementors, and four faculty members who served as university supervisors

Description

All teacher participants were given a laptop for this four-month study.

Preservice teachers were required to post three times a week. Beginning teachers were encouraged to do so, as well.

Research/Evaluation Results

Surveys of participants indicated:

- Participants appreciated a sense of belonging to the online community and the opportunity to be reflective.
- Facilitators reported that maintaining a delicate balance regarding control, structure, and freedom was a challenge.
- The online moderator's role was important for facilitating and synthesizing online postings, making sure questions are responded to, and summarizing and grouping themes to promote understanding.

Friel (2000)

Novice Teacher Support Project (2000–2007)

Participants
First-year to fourth-year teachers across all grade levels and disciplines and a group of experienced teachers who served as e-mentors

Description
Electronic conferences covering content-specific and general issues in curriculum, teaching and learning
• Linked with six Saturday professional development sessions
• Teacher participants and e-mentors met face to face twice a year
• Used Web Crossing Software

Research/Evaluation Results
Interviews with teachers and mentors indicated that
• Password-protected web gave participants a sense of anonymity and safety.
• Participants felt secure in discussing topics of concerns.
• Face-to-face interaction among and between teachers and e-mentors could enhance the online participation.
• Providing directions for the roles of e-mentors and teachers could enhance the mutual development of the online mentoring relationships.

Klecka, Clift, and Thomas (2002)
Analysis of two years of conversations indicated:
• Online discussions could be categorized into four domains: social, interactive (direct and indirect replies), cognitive (clarification, strategies sharing, value statements), and metacognitive (evaluation, reflected planning, regulation, and self-awareness).
• Tension between mentors' and mentees' expectations of e-mentoring, the availability of information, and the online status (experts versus novices) affected how knowledge was distributed online.
• Participants' perceived responsibility to contribute to e-mentoring also affected the level of participation.

Klecka (2004)

Very little research on the development or the impact of the projects has been published. Most of the data were based on self-report and were collected by staff affiliated with the project. Many of the studies do not appear to be grounded in communication theory, learning theory, or sociocultural theory, perhaps because most of the work is conducted for the purpose of formative evaluation. No cross-site research appears to be occurring, which may indicate that researchers external to the programs could not be given access to the data because of agreements with institutional review boards, something the coauthors have experienced in their own research. No study was found that investigated the impact of mentoring on classroom practice, although work is in progress that is attempting to do so.

The primary focus of the research is on participants' perceptions of the medium and self-reports on reasons for using or not using the technology. Rarely are actual conversations analyzed, but the few that exist suggest that using the technology might, indeed, reduce isolation and might promote reflection on teaching. At this time it is impossible to summarize across published studies for multiple reasons: because so few studies exist, because the studies are not addressing similar questions, and because researchers are not examining similar kinds of evidence.

PROFESSIONAL DEVELOPMENT FOR NEW TEACHERS VIA THE INTERNET

The body of evidence that mentoring, alone, is not sufficient to support and retain new teachers is growing. Smith and Ingersoll's (2004) analysis of national data from the Schools and Staffing Survey found that new teachers who participated in basic mentoring only programs were as likely to leave their schools (and teaching altogether) as those who had no mentors. Teachers who had mentors and collaborative opportunities with veteran colleagues in their schools showed significant differences in attrition rates. With the addition of a network of professional contacts and other resources such as a reduced teaching load or an aide, the attrition rate dropped even more.

Teachers Learning in Networked Communities Initiative

In 2003 the National Commission for Teaching and America's Future (NCTAF) began a project titled Teachers Learning in Networked Communities (TLINC). Working with four partner communities (Seattle, Washington; Memphis, Tennessee; and Denver and Jefferson counties, Colorado), they began to examine how networked professional learning communities might be incorporated into a district's professional development program with a particular focus on new teacher induction. Their goals were to reduce teacher isolation, provide increased support, and create a professional community that recognizes the process of improving practice as continual.

In Phase One, NCTAF (2005) identified several lessons they learned as they began to create professional learning communities across the sites. Although all four communities had some sort of mentoring system in place, they found the distinction between working in electronic learning communities and traditional mentoring difficult. In general, the university teacher education partners tended to be more experienced and sometimes more enthusiastic about the use of technology for learning community formation than their K–12 partners. District leaders who saw the potential of networked learning communities had for furthering important district goals were key to a project's success. Some of the districts, however, were inadequately prepared to implement networked communities due to their current technology infrastructures.

In January 2006 each site began using the already established online learning community for educators called Tapped In (www.tappedin.org). Each district structured its Tapped In interface to meet the specific needs of the district—complementing their existing mentoring and induction programs. The midyear evaluation report for year two of TLINC found that online interactions between spring 2006 and fall 2007 had broadened from experimentation and occasional program leadership meetings to include regular online group meetings that increased participation of preservice and novice teachers.

Common challenges across the sites included how to make online interactions beneficial and routine as opposed to yet another task for busy teachers to undertake and how to handle the dilemmas arising from the use of different online platforms by the various institutions involved. The researchers cautioned against the disjointedness of using varied tools for online networking that could create a silo effect, preventing cross-group interactions. Concerned about TLINC's ability to sustain itself beyond the two-year funding cycle, the evaluators recommended increased cross-site collaboration, sharing, and research (Metiri Group, 2007).

Milwaukee Public Schools

In fall 2001 the Harvard Graduate School of Education and the Educational Development Center began working with Milwaukee Public Schools (MPS) as codesigners and evaluators of the Milwaukee Professional Support Portal (Holland, Dede, and Onarheim, 2006). In 2002–2003, 150 new teachers agreed to participate in online communities in exchange for laptops and continuous technical support. Cadres of between eleven and twenty-six new teachers and two teacher-leader facilitators discussed video case-based induction modules produced by Teachscape (www.teachscape. com). The MPS site also included the Curriculum Design Assistant to be used as a collaborative, online environment for creating, posting, and finding lesson plans. This service is no longer available.

Table 10.2 provides more details about the TLINC and MPS initiatives along with a summary of research findings. Both offer professional development resources, such as lesson plan databases, and both provide tools for teachers.

The available evaluation data suggest that teachers are not turning to the sites as often as the developers had intended. And, as with the projects focusing on mentoring, much of the data are based on self-report. That having been said, both projects are to be commended for using an external evaluator and for providing valuable insight into what was and was not working within the initiatives.

TWO WORKS IN PROGRESS

The findings from the above initiatives parallel the experiences of two programs that three of the coauthors have recently begun implementing but have not yet reached the point of having documented research. The Illinois New Teacher Collaborative (INTC) (intc.education.illinois.edu) and University of Georgia's Building Resources: Induction and Development for Georgia Educators (BRIDGE) (www.teachersbridge.org) are both striving to provide statewide support for beginning teachers in the form of easily accessible, vetted resources and through the development of online professional community environments for networking and collaborative professional development. Both online platforms are open to all educators but maintain a specific focus on the needs within their home states.

The resources portion of BRIDGE allows new teachers to submit questions about curriculum and teaching and to receive answers from community members. Each resource is not only linked to the critical question asked but also to the Georgia Framework for Teaching. In the communities portion of BRIDGE educators are able to create or join learning communities. Three distinct groups, specifically new teachers from around the state, a group of math and science educators, and Pathways to Effective Teaching through Communities of Support (PETTCOS), are currently piloting these cross-career learning communities. The PETTCOS project began in 2006 as a pilot program to create learning communities among preservice teachers, teacher education professors, novice teachers, experienced teachers, and mentors through both face-to-face and online interactions.

Table 10.2. Professional Development Sites for Beginning Teachers

Teachers Learning in Networked Communities—Seattle, Washington

Participants Preservice teachers and teacher education faculty from the University of Washington, beginning teachers, and mentors	*Research/Evaluation Results* External-evaluator case study indicated: • Time needed to learn new software in order to be willing and able to use it. • Resistance to new technology a challenge. Metiri (2007)

Description
Staff Training Assistance and Review mentoring program with seven full-time release mentors serving eighteen mentees each (thirty-six new teachers on waiting list for a mentor)—three active Tapped In groups for new teachers (elementary, middle, and high school) "On Demand" source of resources online and use of SRI's Tapped In for mentor study groups focused on instructional dilemmas (one mentor and approximately five mentees). Each dilemma discussed as a three-week seminar.

Teachers Learning in Networked Communities—Memphis, Tennessee

Participants Beginning teachers, full-time mentors, and University of Memphis student teachers	*Research/Evaluation Results* District survey indicated: • New Teacher Center website was a good resource for new teachers and mentors. External evaluation indicated: • Difficult to recruit voluntary participants, despite incentives. • Online interactions primarily occurred among students enrolled in courses that used Tapped In for UM coursework. • Recruitment of new teachers difficult due to approval process for participation being slow. • Tapped In not approved by district administration. Metiri (2007)

Description
One-to-one mentoring used New Teacher Center model with primary online tools including a New Teacher website containing program forms and resources as well as e-mail communications and newsletters.
Tapped In used by University of Memphis preservice courses and alternative certification courses.

(continued)

Table 10.2. *(Continued)*

Teachers Learning in Networked Communities—Denver and Jefferson Counties, Colorado

Participants	Research/Evaluation Results
Beginning teachers, mentors, site coordinators, and preservice interns at PDS schools connected to the University of Colorado at Denver Health Sciences Center	External-evaluator conducted case study indicated: • Emergent Teacher Leaders community was most active • Working across two sites with increased number of site managers and strategy to encourage diverse implementation strategies made training and support difficult • Use of Tapped In possibly hindered due to already established use of online environments that differ by location • Concerns about confidentiality of discussions • Concerns about time necessary to participate in professional communities
Description	
Based upon statewide initiative *Linking for Learning and Leadership* and focused on building professional learning communities among educators with varied experience ranging from preservice through induction and leadership years	
Online facilitators planned an online induction activity with at least one discussion per month focused on a posted lesson plan. Participation by inductees was voluntary.	
Mentors from three buildings in Denver trained to run community rooms with an expectation of three scheduled synchronous chats per building.	
	Metiri (2007)

Milwaukee Public Schools Professional Support Portal

Participants

MPS teachers ranging in experience from novice to expert

Description

Cadres of eleven to twenty-six new teachers discussed video
cases of teaching practice with two experienced teacher
facilitators using Tapped In and face-to-face interactions.

Provided a novice teacher self-assessment tool.

Offered a searchable lesson plan database with over 2,000
reviewed lesson plans and provided the ability for teachers to
collaborate on lesson plan development.

A facilitator self-assessment tool used with the initial pilot cadres
provided strong, nonthreatening formative assessment for
planning future facilitator training. The tool was adapted by
building administrators to assess their own facilitation skills.

Used Plumtree commercial platform, which is now integrated into
Oracle Weblogic Portal.

Research/Evaluation Results

Survey of staff in twenty-five MPS schools indicated:

- 54% had never heard of or seen the PSP.
- Of those who had used the portal, 28% found it to be useful, and
  17% found it to be a useful means of connecting with colleagues.
  Holland et al. (2006)

Without administrative buy-in, use of the tools wasn't encouraged
and the sites floundered.
Holland et al. (2006)

Program coordinators reported challenges such as difficulties of
providing evolving content that was of interest to the users.
Holland et al. (2006)

Changes in school board and superintendent positions slowed
momentum due to need to reteach newcomers and convince of
benefits.
Dede and Nelson (2005)

The mission of INTC and of INTC Online differs from most other online support initiatives in that the intent is to provide support for beginning teachers as well as support for those focused on recruiting and retaining quality teachers. As a result, the resources, as well as the communities, focus on meeting the differing needs of preservice teachers, beginning teachers, mentors, induction program coordinators, administrators, teacher education faculty, and those interested in induction and mentoring research and policy. INTC Online contains a searchable "Resources-on-Demand" database that allows members to submit new resources and to rate the resources already available.

INTC has also begun to compile a listing of the various induction and mentoring programs offered around the state. This database provides a location for program coordinators to showcase their efforts and serves as a catalyst for new ideas and networking among new and continuing induction program leaders. The virtual communities encourage discussions of teaching and mentoring practice, but very few discussions are active. As with TLINC, Georgia's BRIDGE and INTC Online are in their infancy with no research published to date regarding either process or impact. However, as the developers and coordinators of these two initiatives, we empathize with the struggles documented by the programs reviewed above.

QUERYING THE FUTURE ROLE OF INTERNET-BASED TECHNOLOGY IN SUPPORTING NEW TEACHERS' LEARNING

While social networking sites are becoming increasingly popular (Boyd and Ellison, 2007), this review of the literature suggests that Internet-based, professional networking sites have not yet attracted a critical mass of new teachers and that program developers have not yet solved the question of how to encourage new teachers to think of the sites as valued and accepted program structures, as opposed to experimental projects. Considerable duplication of efforts occurs as different institutions, primarily universities, design and bring opportunities online. We found almost no cross-referencing of other programs or acknowledgment of ways in which programs learned from the success and failure of others, with the exception of the collaboration occurring between TLINC project developers.

This may be due to the nature of publications about the programs. While a few initiatives have been in operation for several years, little published information can be easily found about the design process, the ways in which the sites are used and by whom and for what purposes, or the impact of the programs on participants. For those projects that are no longer functioning, documentation that explains why this is the case rarely exists.

Most projects began with external funds, which leads us to speculate that one reason many projects are now off-line is because insufficient funding prevented them from continuing. Another reason is likely due to turnover in program administration or in the administrative positions that support the program administrator. Few of the projects have been incorporated into an existing, long-standing structure, with the possible exception of some TLINC projects. Even the TLINC projects, however, are experiencing challenges with implementing and sustaining their online components. Overall, these Internet-based induction supports seem to have begun as a good idea but were not embraced as an important and sustainable source of support for new teachers or mentors.

FACTORS PROMOTING OR INHIBITING SUCCESS

Based on the programs discussed above, five factors seemed to either promote or inhibit success, depending on how these factors played out over time. First, designs connected to an ongoing, institutionalized program that was already in existence appear to have longer life spans. WINGS is a good example of this because it began as an offspring of the already successful Electronic Emissary project, and it continues to supplement the well-established University of Texas teacher education program. Preservice teachers were introduced to this resource while enrolled in their teacher education program and then continued using this support mechanism as they moved into their own classrooms.

The second factor is that the program must be perceived as useful and important to a number of participants—it cannot just be the pet project of a faculty member, district administrator, or grant writer. It must be a value-added component of professional development for new teachers, not just another responsibility added to their already busy schedules. With a change in project leadership, online components may be removed from the program as with the Novice Teacher Support Project. In addition, we see evidence of challenges resulting from the lack of buy-in from school administration and other leadership hindering implementation in many of the initiatives discussed.

The third factor is that the new teachers must perceive that they are benefiting in some way and that they have a critical mass of people with whom to interact. In both the e-mentoring Expansion Initiative and Memphis' TLINC project, program developers found that just providing the online environments and activities did not result in instantaneous usage. Recruiting and maintaining participation has been difficult within all the sites where participation is voluntary.

A fourth factor, the quality of the online facilitators, appeared either within program design literature or within literature related to programs' formative assessments. eMSS provides extensive training for their facilitators, and feedback from external evaluators led eMSS to extend this training beyond just new mentors to include returning mentors, scientist participants, and eMSS project staff. Georgia's BRIDGE discussion facilitators also receive training, and other projects have found that the role of facilitator impacts the quality of discussions.

The fifth factor relates to external funding. All of the programs initially relied on external funds to support development, implementation, and extension. Funding, presumably, also supported research and evaluation. But with the exception of WINGS and the possible exception of the BRIDGE, no program has persisted beyond the duration of external funds. If developers cannot be sure that the project will continue, it is difficult to build widespread support—fiscally and philosophically—among administrators, colleagues, and new teachers. And, without longevity, it is difficult to study program impact.

CHALLENGES IN STUDYING ONLINE PROGRAMS

Without a more substantive body of research it is difficult to learn from the successes and challenges of others. And yet, allowing researchers access to the participants of other programs is problematic in that it may violate the confidentiality and anonymity that program developers feel is crucial for enabling honest conversations. People's rights to participate in a program without being obligated to participate in research has long been protected by institutional review boards, and this protection is especially important for new teachers. They need to feel that they can ask honest questions and share important issues without fear of judgment or reprisal. In a medium that is already underused, giving researchers permission to study interactions may function as another factor that inhibits participation.

Researchers must also consider that the sense of being "watched" may change the nature and the character of the conversations. If a mentor, a professional development provider, or a new teacher knows that their work is being analyzed, they may self-censor and only discuss topics that they perceive as being safe. In more traditional, face-to-face settings, qualitative researchers devote considerable time to establishing credibility and gaining acceptance from participants. Doing so in the online context may be considerably more difficult because interaction is often asynchronous and lacking visual cues to support text-based exchanges.

Finally, because teaching is completely context dependent, researchers need to design studies that go beyond surveys, interviews, and conversation analysis and move into the classroom. It is important to learn whether the impact of online support stops with new teachers experiencing decreased isolation, participating in reflective conversations, or accessing practical tips. Does participation in online induction and mentoring have an impact on teachers' practices? Does it make a difference in what children and adolescents know, understand, and accomplish? Researchers need to move study designs into the classroom to investigate questions such as these.

Programs are being built, but there is no long line of participants waiting excitedly for a chance to view and experience what these programs have to offer. We hope that in the next twelve years, programs and research on program impacts will triple; that strong, vibrant, long-lasting models of how to use technology effectively to support new teachers and to promote the continuous improvement of teaching quality have been developed; and that these models are found to be tried and true.

REFERENCES

Abbott, L. D. 2003. *Novice teachers' experiences of telementoring as learner-centered professional development.* Unpublished doctoral dissertation, University of Texas, Austin.

Boyd, D. M., and N. B. Ellison. 2007. Social network sites: Definition, history, and scholarship. *Journal of Computer-Mediated Communication* 13(1): article 11. Retrieved January 3, 2008, from http://jcmc.indiana.edu/vol13/issue1/boyd .ellison.html.

Cheng, Y. 2008. *Socio-cultural influences on face-to-face and electronic mentoring of new teachers learning to teach.* Unpublished doctoral dissertation, University of Illinois, Urbana-Champaign.

Clouse, N. K. 2007. *The leadership role in online support programs for beginning teachers.* Unpublished doctoral dissertation, University of Montana, Missoula.

Dede, C., and R. Nelson. 2005. Technology as proteus: Digital infrastructures that empower scaling up. In *Scaling up success: Lessons learned from technology-based educational improvement,* eds. C. Dede, J. Honan, and L. Peters, 110–32. New York: Jossey-Bass.

DeWert, M. H., L. M. Babinski, and B. D. Jones. 2003. Safe passages: Providing online support to beginning teachers. *Journal of Teacher Education* 54(4):311–20.

Friel, S. N. 2000. MaSTech: An on-line community to support preservice and new teachers of middle grades mathematics and science. *Educational Technology & Society* 3(3):273–85.

Fulton, K., I. Yoon, and C. Lee. 2005. *Induction into learning communities.* Washington, DC: National Commission on Teaching and America's Future. Retrieved November 19, 2005, from http://nctaf.org/documents/NCTAF_Induction _Paper_2005.pdf.

Harris, J., E. O'Bryan, and L. Rotenberg. 1996. It's a simple idea, but it's not easy to do: Practical lessons in telementoring. *Learning and Leading with Technology* 24(2):53–57. Retrieved March 30, 2004, from http://emissary.wm.edu/templates/content/publications/October96LLT.pdf.

Holland, I., C. Dede, and K. Onarheim. 2006. Processes supporting the regional evolution of effective professional development: Milwaukee's initiation of a professional support portal. In *Online professional development for teachers: Emerging models and methods*, ed. C. Dede, 213–36. Cambridge, MA: Harvard Education Press.

Jaffe, R., E. Moir, E. Swanson, and G. Wheeler. 2006. E-mentoring for Student Success: Online mentoring and professional development for new science teachers. In *Online professional development for teachers*, ed. C. Dede, 89–116. Cambridge, MA: Harvard Education Press.

Klecka, C. L. 2004. *Distributed mentoring: Developing electronic conferencing to support new teachers*. Unpublished doctoral dissertation, University of Illinois at Urbana-Champaign.

Klecka, C., R. T. Clift, and Y. Cheng. 2005. Are electronic conferences a solution in search of an urban problem? *Urban Education* 40(4):412–29.

Klecka, C., R. T. Clift, and A. T. Thomas. 2002. Proceed with caution: Introducing electronic conferencing in teacher education. *Critical Issues in Teacher Education* 9:28–36.

Merseth, K. K. 1991. Supporting beginning teachers with computer networks. *Journal of Teacher Education* 42:140–47.

Metiri Group. 2007. *Teachers Learning in Networked Communities (TLINC) year two midyear report*. Culver City, CA: Author. Retrieved May 15, 2007, from www.nctaf.org.

National Commission on Teaching and America's Future. 2005, August. *Teaching and learning in networked communities: Phase I evaluation report*. Retrieved November 28, 2005, from www.netaf.org/resources/research-and-reports/netaf-research-reports/index.

Smith, T. M., and R. M. Ingersoll. 2004. What are the effects of induction and mentoring on beginning teacher turnover? *American Educational Research Journal* 41(3):681–714.

NOTE

1. This material is based upon work supported by the State Farm Companies Foundation and the College of Education at the University of Illinois at Urbana-Champaign. Any opinions, findings, and conclusions or recommendations expressed in this publication are those of the authors and do not necessarily reflect the views of the State Farm Companies Foundation or the College of Education at the University of Illinois at Urbana-Champaign.

11

The University's Role in Supporting New Teachers

Glimpsing the Future by Examining the Past

Cynthia L. Carver, Michigan State University

Historically, the new teacher support baton has been passed from universities to school districts as teacher candidates become early career professionals. As a result the yeoman's work of supporting and developing new teachers has fallen on the shoulders of the districts and states that employ them, and not on the universities that were responsible for their preparation. Though convenient, this division of labor does little to foster the seamless transition from preparation to practice that reformers advocate, nor does it make good use of the university-based expertise and resources that could be of critical help during this early phase in learning to teach.

Given persistent teacher shortages in high-need areas, troubling retention rates among our newest teachers, and the increased pressure on teacher preparation programs to account for the quality of its graduates, it is a good time to ask: What role might a university or college play in induction programming and practice? To explore this question, I begin by looking to the literature for a discussion of the purposes commonly attributed to university-supported induction models.[1] Next, I describe and provide examples of three different approaches to university-supported induction. Finally, I look back across the review for insights into the university's role in induction. In closing I suggest that the best measure of a university's contribution to induction programming may well be the innovative practices it supports.

HIGHER EDUCATION'S ROLE IN INDUCTION

The question of whether and how universities might participate in the induction process has largely escaped conceptual or empirical exploration. In fact, reference to the university's role is often limited to a paragraph in a closing discussion. While passing reference lends credence to the importance of university involvement in induction, its overall lack of attention within the literature highlights the need for further study. Like the professional development school literature that it resembles, writings on the university's role in induction are scattered across a range of peer-review articles, books, chapters, and conference proceedings. That said, the literature remains a reasonable starting point for inquiry into this question.

In selecting literature I conducted a series of searches using various keywords: *beginning teachers, induction, mentoring, university-role,* and *school-university partnerships.* I started with peer-reviewed materials and added conference papers, chapters, and books when they described a university-supported induction model. Although many of these papers reported research outcomes, my interest was in how they described their programs. Also, I began the review with the 1980s reform era, a time during which many of these programs were initiated. Due to sheer volume, but also to the diffuse nature of these reports, the programs reviewed in this chapter are best considered illustrations of the varied ways that universities have understood and responded to the task of supporting new teachers.[2]

GROWING SUPPORT FOR A UNIVERSITY ROLE

The university's involvement in new teacher support reaches back at least as far as Conant's (1963) report on teacher education, which argued for stronger links between teacher preparation and schools and a new focus on the beginning teacher. However, it wasn't until the 1980s that the movement to include universities in the support of new teachers gained momentum. Ongoing efforts to articulate the purposes and features of school-university partnerships that took teacher learning seriously (Goodlad, 1990; Holmes Group, 1986) were critical in building a foundation for this work, as were positions espoused by reform groups interested in promoting a professional stance toward teachers' work and learning (Carnegie, 1986; NCTAF, 1996).

Within the teacher education community the National Council for the Accreditation of Teacher Education (NCATE) was urging teacher education programs to maintain contact with their graduates and assist first-year teachers on a need basis (Huling, 1990). In 1986 the Association of Teacher Educators (ATE) concluded that the development and administration of induction programs should draw on the collective resources of universities and schools (Huling, 1990). The following year the ATE Induction Commission published a monograph of their proceedings (Brooks, 1987), one chapter of which dealt with the university's role (Johnston and Kay, 1987).

A wide variety of small-scale university-based induction programs emerged in subsequent years, many of which were designed to provide first-year teachers with both mentored support and coursework toward a graduate degree (Auger and Odell, 1992; Kelley, 2004; McGlamery, Fluckiger, and Edick, 2002).

During this same time period a number of states drafted policies that mandated university involvement in induction, often as a partner in program design and delivery. Furtwengler (1995) reported that seven states had enacted legislation requiring university participation in induction. Within five years that number had doubled (Serpell, 2000). An example of this was California's Beginning Teacher Support and Assessment Project, which stipulated inclusion of a university partner. Alternately, states like Louisiana expected individual faculty members to serve with principals and mentors on new teacher support teams.

The structure and features of induction programs have evolved through the years with interest in the university's role continuing to grow through a variety of enhanced partnerships involving unions, accrediting bodies, and external funders (AFT, 2001; Fulton, Yoon, and Lee, 2005). An example of this is the Strengthening and Sustaining Teachers (SST) Project, which believes that improved teaching and teacher retention rests on strong relationships among schools, universities, and unions that begin during the preservice years and continues through induction (Sahling and Whitford, 2004).

Similarly, NCATE has been working with a set of urban school-university partnerships to design and pilot models for bringing existing professional development school (PDS) work to scale. To illustrate, the University of Colorado at Denver supplements graduate coursework with an "induction looping" model that connects beginning teachers to their preservice mentors through monthly roundtables, peer coaching, and inquiry-oriented study (Levine, 2004).

The Teachers for a New Era (TNE) project, sponsored by the Carnegie Corporation of New York, provides yet another example of how universities are partnering with schools to support new teachers. Select teacher preparation programs have been working to restructure their programs around three design principles: evidence-based decision making, effective engagement of arts and science faculty, and an emphasis on teaching as an academically taught clinical profession (Hinds, 2002). To address this third principle, each of the TNE sites has worked closely with K–12 partner schools to develop, implement, and test strategies for following graduates into the field. The goal is to create a seamless and supportive transition between preservice preparation and classroom teaching.

These initiatives demonstrate a sense of shared responsibility for teacher preparation and employment, as well as the belief that new teacher support is enhanced when the resources and commitments of multiple stakeholders are combined (Basinger, 2000; Lewis, 2001). Still, the number of such partnerships remains limited and the university's role within these partnerships remains ill defined.

PROBLEMS OF SCOPE, SCALE, AND PURPOSE

Literature-based accounts of university-led or sponsored induction tend to represent small-scale programs, serving targeted populations, which are largely shaped by the research interests of the participating university (Fideler and Haselkorn, 1999). Most descriptions lack details about how programs are funded, structured, staffed, and evaluated. Many are one-time accounts, compromising our ability to study how a program evolves over time.[3] While it is clear that a range of school-university induction partnerships exist, the lack of a robust literature hampers our ability to learn from them.

We are further challenged by their scattered presence in the field. Although there is growing sentiment around the belief that teacher preparation programs should follow their graduates into the field, few universities are engaged in providing sustained support to new teachers. Reasons frequently given for this situation include the lack of financing and inflexible faculty reward structures (Riggs and Sandlin, 2002; Serpell, 2000; Wolfe, Bartell, and DeBolt, 2000). Because university programming is primarily supported with tuition dollars, universities need to find alternative funding streams (outside of coursework) if they are to extend support to their graduates. Even with adequate funding, staffing such programs can be difficult if university faculty are not recognized and rewarded for field-based work.

Moreover, university-supported induction partnerships are wrought with questions: Who is most responsible for supporting new teachers: the employing district, or the certifying university? Are all teachers served, or only those who graduated from the host university? Questions surrounding scale are equally troublesome. Are small-scale experimental models ones to study and learn from, or should we design programs with an eye toward easy and cost-efficient replication? Then there is the issue of whether or not university-based programs, given their bias toward teacher inquiry and professionalism, can ever flourish within an accountability-driven, standards-based system (Fideler and Haselkorn, 1999).

Given these challenges of scope, scale, and purpose, it is not surprising that few partnerships exist. Nor is it surprising, given the nature of partnership work and its history within the academy, that the literature offers an incomplete accounting of this work. Still, reform-oriented groups and organizations continue to advocate for a university role in teacher induction and to see higher education's involvement in new teacher support as a "promising strategy" for improving the quality of teachers and teaching (Corcoran, 2007).

THE RATIONALE FOR
UNIVERSITY INVOLVEMENT IN INDUCTION

The literature suggests at least four reasons for involving universities in the induction process. First, universities bring expertise and leadership that add value to that offered by school districts. Second, by involving the university new teachers experience greater continuity and coherence between their preservice preparation and their beginning years in the field, making the transition into teaching less abrupt. Third, involving universities in induction is seen as another means of elevating and maintaining high standards of teacher quality. Finally, university involvement is advocated on the grounds that having faculty involved in the field is critical to improving teacher preparation more broadly.

Expertise, Resources, and Leadership

Greater collaboration between schools and universities is widely viewed as a strategy for improving the quality of teaching. By bringing institutional strengths to the shared task of new teacher support, universities and schools have an opportunity to develop partnerships that respect one another's uniqueness (Stanulis, Burrill, and Ames, 2007). As Feiman-Nemser (2001) notes: "No single institution has the expertise, authority or financial resources to create the necessary structures and learning opportunities. Schools, universities, teacher unions and the state all have an important part to play" (1037).

University faculty and staff specialists are uniquely positioned to inform the design and implementation of induction programming, as well as the evaluation of those efforts. For example, university-based subject-matter experts can work with their K–12 counterparts to offer training that is specially designed with local needs and priorities in mind. Universities can also offer various incentives for such work (graduate credit, access to content specialists, alumni networks, and resource banks) in exchange for participation in the induction program (Shulman and Bernhardt, 1990).

A well-regarded induction partnership between the University of New Mexico and the Albuquerque schools highlights the possibilities (Auger and Odell, 1992). In this program university faculty provided program leadership, selected and trained mentors, supervised K–12 teachers in clinical teaching roles, and formally studied their efforts. Through a no-cost exchange, select new teachers received intensive mentoring for one year as they taught full-time and worked toward a master's degree.

Universities can also contribute to induction programming through targeted training and services. The St. Paul (MN) schools partnered with Hamline University to train mentors in leading "Learning Circles," an approach to mentoring developed by a Hamline professor and used in their induction program (Villani, 2002). As an incentive, this course was offered for university credit to interested mentors and new teachers.

Because they are removed from the evaluative process, university faculty can offer "third party" neutrality that is confidential, objective, and non-evaluative (Johnston and Kay, 1987; Shulman and Bernhardt, 1990). These attributes can help school-based developers set reasonable expectations for induction programs and can be especially helpful to new teachers or mentors who may be uncomfortable disclosing concerns to district officials (Ganser, 2001).

This was the case in the Novice Teacher Support Project (NTSP), a partnership between the University of Illinois at Urbana-Champaign, two regional educational offices, and twenty-one school districts. In a study of new teachers' expressed needs, researchers found that participants were more likely to take advantage of induction-related support and develop as professionals when they reported feeling safe as learners. Thus, researchers concluded that induction programs aim for a combination of inside and outside of district resources, as outside sources "create[d] safe places to extend support and to help new teachers explore alternative methods of creating educational improvement" (Chubbuck, Clift, Allard, and Quinlan, 2001, 375).

In sum, through the provision of subject-area expertise and research skills, universities represent a value-added induction partner. University faculty can provide extra hands and ideas for moving projects forward as well as a helpful "outside" perspective. This is perhaps most true in small and rural districts where extra resources and leadership are essential to moving ideas off the drawing table (Ganser, 2001). For example, Montana State University invited all new area math and science teachers to join an electronic network for content-based mentoring (Villani, 2002). By creating a statewide network, Montana State faculty used their expertise and resources both to reduce teachers' physical isolation and to address an unmet local need for subject-specific mentoring.

Greater Continuity between Preservice and Induction

Given their expertise in teacher development, universities are well equipped to complement and extend district-provided support to new and experienced teachers (Gold, 1996). Such partnerships can help to blur the lines between teacher preparation and ongoing professional development, creating a more seamless continuum of professional learning where the responsibility for teacher development becomes shared (Moir and Gless, 2001). University involvement in induction further contributes to powerful and sustained learning opportunities for teachers at all experience levels from novice to veteran (Feiman-Nemser, 2001).

Just as induction no longer has to be the sole responsibility of schools and districts, teacher preparation no longer has to be the sole responsibility of universities. In today's changing educational context, teacher learning is seen as a lifelong endeavor that begins at the university and continues throughout one's teaching career. School-university induction partnerships are uniquely positioned to facilitate a more seamless transition between preservice teacher preparation and ongoing professional learning.

Shared Accountability for Quality

In addition to sharing resources and creating a more seamless continuum of professional learning, university participation in induction is also seen as a tool for ensuring high-quality standards. This perspective rests on the assumption that teacher preparation and development is a collaborative endeavor for which multiple stakeholders—states, districts, and teacher preparation programs—share responsibility (see AFT, 2001).

With the shared goal of improved student learning, each partner depends on the other. States set preparation standards with which universities must comply; universities prepare candidates to assume teaching jobs within a competitive marketplace; districts continue to employ teachers who maintain licensure guidelines established by states. Induction partnerships help to reinforce the importance of high standards and improve accountability across partners. As one set of researchers noted:

> The professional development that is facilitated by the opportunity to work with novice colleagues has become just as valued a project outcome as the benefits offered to beginning teachers. Pre-service education, life-long renewal, and continued learning need to be linked not only conceptually, but formally, through collaborative and well-articulated programs involving teachers, universities, districts, county offices, state agencies and professional organizations (Young and Yopp, 1999, 36).

Improved Teacher Preparation

University involvement in induction has the potential to help universities improve programming and create more responsive teacher preparation programs (Gold, 1996). In some cases induction partnerships have grown from strong field-based preparation programs, as happened in several districts affiliated with a large school-university partnership in North Carolina (Edelfelt, 2000). When university faculty are involved in the field they gain a valuable perspective on workplace conditions, including the daily challenges faced by candidates (Shulman and Bernhardt, 1990). Furthermore, they gain firsthand knowledge of the policies and programs that new teachers are likely to encounter (Riggs and Sandlin, 2002).

In what are commonly referred to as exchange models, K–12 teachers are released from classroom duties to teach at the university, further infusing preparation programs with practical experience and insight. To illustrate, teachers on loan from the Albuquerque schools co-taught methods courses with faculty from the University of New Mexico. As reported by program administrators, "The presence of clinical faculty drawn from the ranks of the district's classroom teachers has transformed undergraduate teacher preparation in the college" (Auger and Odell, 1992, 263). As these examples highlight, cross-institutional partnerships improve teacher preparation by creating a forum for dialogue around shared interests, concerns, and observations (Feiman-Nemser, 2001).

FROM PURPOSE TO STRUCTURE

How do these four purposes—added expertise and leadership, seamless transition from preparation to teaching, increased accountability, and improved teacher preparation—translate into formal induction programming? The literature suggests three approaches to university-supported induction. The most common are exchange models that feature intensive mentoring, graduate coursework for new teachers, and clinical teaching positions for mentors. Another approach combines alternative certification with induction. Seminars, study groups, and electronic mentoring emerge as a third means by which universities stay connected to graduates. Although there is overlap among the three, each serves a distinct population and varies according to the purpose of the partnership and the role played by university faculty.

Teacher Exchange Programs

Traditional exchange programs go by a variety of names, but they have in common the following components: a cadre of newly certified teachers who receive intensive mentoring for teaching full-time and work toward a master's degree in education; K–12 teachers who are released full-time to mentor these beginning teachers, assist with district-level reform initiatives, and teach in the preservice program; plus university faculty who serve in a variety of administrative, teaching, and research roles. Although mentors continue to receive their regular salary, the new teachers accepted into the program are typically offered reduced salaries plus tuition credit toward a master's degree.

A strength of exchange programs is the multilayered nature of support offered to new teachers. For example, at the University of Nebraska at Omaha, select new teachers received four to five hours each week of mentoring, attended monthly seminars led by mentors, and participated in a yearlong graduate seminar that concluded with an action research project. Mentors received ongoing training in topics that included cognitive coaching, communication skills, and national teaching standards (McGlamery, Fluckiger, Edick, 2002).

Within these exchange program sites, a variety of collaborative structures have been created to foster collegiality among university and school participants. New teachers participating in a University of Colorado at Boulder program were expected to participate in two monthly seminars: one with teacher fellows in their district and the other in cross-district teams (Kelley, 2004). At Southwest Texas State mentors joined teaching fellows for Saturday classes so they could better guide fellows in the development of semester-long research projects (Resta, Huling, White, and Matschek, 1997). Mentors at the University of Nebraska filled a similar role when they helped new teachers prepare a culminating portfolio that contained classroom video, samples of student work, and an action research project (McGlamery, Fluckiger, Edick, 2002).

The more recent TNE initiatives similarly promote cross-institution inquiry and dialogue. Through a TNE-sponsored program at California State University at Northridge, teachers in Los Angeles now have the option of working toward a master's degree as part of their participation in the state-mandated mentoring program (Eaton, Chong, Burnstein, Ericson, and Filbeck, 2006). Unlike earlier exchange models, however, these teachers pay full tuition to participate and university faculties assume the leadership for all support programming.

At the University of Virginia and at Michigan State University, the TNE initiative helped to support the design of mentoring programs in collaboration with local school districts (Alvarado, 2006; Stanulis, 2006). In the Michigan State program new teachers and mentors also participated in monthly role-alike study groups, whereas University of Virginia participants attended quarterly workshops. Unlike traditional exchange models, however, these programs were designed to reach all beginning teachers, regardless of where they were prepared.

Alternative Certification with Mentoring

As a close cousin to the exchange model, and an example of how induction is changing teacher preparation, a handful of partnerships have been formed specifically to address teacher shortages. In these cases universities have partnered with districts to increase the number of certified teachers in areas of high demand, including math, science, and special education. These programs combine coursework toward certification with sustained mentoring in the field, often for midcareer candidates, but also for teaching assistants and those on emergency permits.

In a program designed with midcareer entrants in mind, Wayne State University (MI) partnered with the Detroit schools to pilot a program that would increase the number of certified teachers for the district (Ilmer, Elliott, Snyder, Nahan, and Colombo, 2005). Program components included full-time teaching positions, tuition toward completion of a master's degree with certification (featuring online learning modules), plus weekly cohort meetings and the help of an in-school mentor. In a related program, faculty at the University of California at Berkeley teamed with the Lawrence Berkeley National Laboratory to pilot an on-site training and mentoring program for scientists who were teaching on emergency permits in the San Francisco schools (Diehl, Harris, Barrios, O'Connor, and Fong, 2000).

The Career Development Program at the University of New Mexico was designed to fast-track teaching assistants in the Albuquerque schools into full-time teaching positions (Auger and Odell, 1992). In this seventeen-month licensure program, participants completed coursework and an initial field experience in the spring semester, followed by intensive coursework over the summer, a paired internship in the fall, and a solo internship in the spring. Courses were co-taught by university faculty and exchange teachers who served as field-based mentors to participants.

In a similar program at Southwest Texas State University, participants began with a semester of intensive coursework followed by a semester of student teaching (Huling, Resta, and Rainwater, 2001). At this point, participants were placed into full-time teaching positions where they received two years of intensive mentoring. Like the Career Development Program described above, mentors were carefully selected, trained, and supported in their work with new teachers so as to provide a "comprehensive, accelerated, customer-oriented teacher preparation program, coupled with an intensive induction support system" (Huling, Resta, and Rainwater, 2001, 326).

From these examples, two alternative certification models emerge: one that immediately places candidates into teaching positions and another that provides a more gradual immersion into the field. Both approaches, however, feature sustained on-site induction support coupled with graduate-level coursework—program components that are enhanced by university involvement.

Study Groups, Seminars, and E-Mentoring

Although there is a financial incentive for universities to link induction support to graduate-level coursework, doing so is not always feasible or responsive. A third way in which teacher preparation programs have stayed connected to their graduates is through study groups, seminars, and electronic networks. Sometimes these efforts represent a joint endeavor with area schools; other times they operate independently. Importantly, a number of these programs reach a large geographic area.

Included among these programs are efforts to support teachers' subject-specific learning. In the Alternative Support for Induction Science Teachers project (Luft and Patterson, 2002; Roehrig and Luft, 2004), project developers teamed with mentors and graduate students to offer a series of Saturday workshops designed to support inquiry-based science teaching. The program also featured monthly visits by project staff and participation by novices in an online community. Williams and Williamson (1996) have described a similar project with physical education teachers in the Chicago area.

A different approach was taken in designing the New Teachers' Network (NTC) at Hofstra University. This project intentionally bypassed local schools, reaching out directly to program graduates who were teaching in urban and suburban "ethnic minority" school districts in the New York City area (Hines, Murphy, Pezone, Singer, and Stacki, 2003). Program components included regular support group meetings, peer mentoring, and professional conferences. As the authors suggested, the NTC "provide[d] a safe, yet sometimes confrontational, forum that successfully engage[d] new teachers in conversations and activities that rejuvenate[d] them in their efforts to make a difference in urban and minority schools" (Hines et al., 2003, 301).

Still other universities have used new technologies to create electronic networks for new teachers. The University of Illinois used e-mentoring to reach new teachers in all twenty-one districts associated with the New Teacher Support Project (Cheng, Clift, and Klecka, 2004). In another context DeWert, Babinski, and Jones (2003) designed, implemented, and tested a statewide network to provide beginning teachers with "problem-solving assistance and peer support in an on-line collaborative community" (312). As these examples suggest, electronic networks have the advantage of serving large numbers of individuals at a relatively low cost.

Finally, all four of the original TNE sites used technology to create virtual professional development centers as a means of supplementing existing induction programming and reaching out to alumni who were no longer within commuting distance. Despite different formats and platforms, program graduates could access these sites at any time of day or night to find downloadable resources, discussion groups, and mentoring options. This was a particularly attractive option for Bank Street College whose graduates already had master's degrees and were scattered across a three-state area (Stern, Snyder, and Lit, 2006).

As this summary highlights, the university's role in induction varies from one program to the next. Still, several features unique to the university's involvement stand out. First, there is a clear emphasis across programs on using university-specific resources, such as graduate-level coursework and access to subject matter experts, to enhance induction programming. Second, university faculties bring an understanding of research-based practices and resourcefulness when studying these practices in new contexts. Third, university partners play a critical leadership role in the areas of visioning, advocacy, program administration, evaluation, and grant writing. Finally, university program developers have taken great care to design programs that uniquely match local resources with local needs.

BUILDING UPON STRENGTHS: LEADERSHIP FOR CHANGE

Having reviewed the literature, a clearer picture emerges for how the university might play a role in the development, implementation, and evaluation of induction programs. Although formal systems of support are likely to remain the primary responsibility of employing school districts, universities can play a meaningful and distinct role in induction. When the university is involved the novice is likely to feel greater continuity between the goals of preservice preparation and ongoing professional learning. For new teachers who switch jobs or who initially find themselves in a temporary position, this continuity can be critical. Universities also bring valuable and needed resources to the induction enterprise.

Among the induction-related activities reported by universities in this review, program development and evaluation were most common. In both areas higher education faculties were uniquely poised to bring theoretical and technical expertise, as well as resources and leadership, to the school-based setting. When university faculty are involved in program implementation it is often in the areas of mentor training and topic-specific consulting, although many programs have also incorporated graduate-level study and/or seminars purposefully designed for the novice teacher. Increasingly, university-led induction programs are incorporating new technologies to reach a wider audience with their services.

Universities can also provide valuable human resources in the form of subject specialists, grant writers, mentors, and trainers. Financial resources come in the form of grants and diverted dollars, including those targeted for masters' coursework. When shared across districts, these resources help to equalize support efforts across a region. When employed over time, these resources help to build institutional capacity for high-quality induction practices.

Universities bring more than resources, however. Embedded in the examples reported here is a clear conception of the type of teacher the program aspires to support. This teacher knows her content and how to teach it to her diverse students. She is reflective about her practice and attentive to individual students and their learning. Her instruction is informed by standards, and she is growing as a teacher leader. Similar observations can be made for the kind of instruction-focused, classroom-based mentoring desired by university-supported programs. Universities are naturally poised to bring the best of what is known to the practice of new teacher support.

Still, university-supported induction continues to be the exception, rather than the norm. Programs are geographically scattered with limited reach to the new teachers who need them. Most operate on a small scale. Given the inherent challenges these programs face—identifying new funding streams, revisiting faculty reward structures, forging new and collaborative partnerships around a shared purpose, working within existing policy contexts—this should not surprise or deter us. Universities have a unique and special place in induction; they provide protected places to imagine, develop, and test new practices.

By way of broad overview, higher education's unique role in induction may be simultaneously to spur, support, enhance, and examine induction programming as a complement to existing efforts by schools and districts. Universities can do this in multiple ways, from designing and delivering face-to-face induction programs to providing long-distance e-mentoring and resource support, from creating responsive master's degree coursework on campus, to delivering content expertise in the field. Implicit in all of these variations, however, is a close working partnership between those who prepare teachers and those who receive them, as well as a commitment to ensuring that the story behind these partnerships becomes part of the public record. It may well be that the university's greatest contribution will be to serve as an incubation center for teacher development, incrementally building capacity for change at a local level.

REFERENCES

Alvarado, A. 2006. *The induction program at the University of Virginia.* Paper presented at the annual meeting of the American Educational Research Association, San Francisco.

American Federation of Teachers (AFT). 2001. Beginning teacher induction: The essential bridge. *Educational Issues Policy Brief* 13. Washington, DC: Author.

Auger, F. K., and S. J. Odell. 1992. Three school-university partnerships for teacher development. *Journal of Teacher Education* 43(4):262–68.

Basinger, J. 2000. Teacher education extends its reach. *Chronicle of Higher Education* 46(35):A18.

Brooks, D. M. 1987. *Teacher induction: A new beginning.* Reston, VA: Association of Teacher Educators.

Carnegie Forum on Education and the Economy. 1986. *A nation prepared: Teachers for the 21st century.* New York: Author.

Cheng, Y., R. T. Clift, and C. L. Klecka. 2004. Exploring the potential of electronic mentoring. *Action in Teacher Education* 26(3):2–9.

Chubbuck, S. M., R. T. Clift, J. Allard, and J. Quinlan. 2001. Playing it safe as a novice teacher: Implications for programs for new teachers. *Journal of Teacher Education* 52(5):365–76.

Conant, J. B. 1963. *The education of America's teachers.* New York: McGraw Hill.

Corcoran, T. B. 2007. Teaching matters: How state and local policymakers can improve the quality of teachers and teaching. *CPRE policy brief,* RB-48. Pennsylvania: University of Pennsylvania, Graduate School of Education.

DeWert, M. H., L. M. Babinski, and B. D. Jones. 2003. Safe passages: Providing online support to beginning teachers. *Journal of Teacher Education* 54(4):311–20.

Diehl, C., J. Harris, D. Barrios, H. O'Connor, and J. Fong. 2000, April. *Teachers training teachers: Four perspectives on an innovative mentoring program for intern science teachers.* Paper presented at the annual meeting of the American Educational Research Association, New Orleans.

Eaton, A. J., S. B. Chong, N. Burstein, B. Ericson, and M. Filbeck. 2006, April. *New directions in teacher induction: Emerging strategies from the TNE initiative.* Paper presented at the annual meeting of the American Educational Research Association, San Francisco.

Edelfelt, R. 2000. *Second-year progress report: University-school teacher education partnerships.* Chapel Hill, NC: University of North Carolina.

Feiman-Nemser, S. 2001. From preparation to practice: Designing a continuum to strengthen and sustain teaching. *Teachers College Record* 103(6):1013–55.

Fideler, E., and D. Haselkorn. 1999. *Learning the ropes: Urban teacher induction programs and practices in the United States.* Belmont, MA: Recruiting New Teachers.

Fulton, K., I. Yoon, and C. Lee. 2005. *Induction into learning communities.* Washington, DC: National Commission on Teaching and America's Future.

Furtwengler, C. B. 1995. Beginning teacher programs: Analysis of state actions during the reform era. *Education Policy Analysis Archives* 3(3):1–22. Available at http://olam.ed.asu.edu/epaa/v3n3.html.

Ganser, T. 2001, February. *Building the capacity of school districts to design, implement, and evaluate new teacher mentor programs.* Paper presented at the American Association of Colleges of Teacher Education, Washington, D.C.

Gold, Y. 1996. Beginning teacher support: Attrition, mentoring and induction. In *Handbook of research on teacher education,* 2nd ed., eds. J. Sikula, T. J. Buttery, and E. Guyton, 548–94. New York: Macmillan.

Goodlad, J. I. 1990. *Teachers for our nation's schools.* San Francisco: Jossey-Bass.

Hinds, M. D. 2002. *Teaching as a clinical profession: A new challenge for education.* New York: Carnegie Corporation.

Hines, S. M., M. Murphy, M. Pezone, A. Singer, and S. L. Stacki. 2003. New teachers' network: A university-based support system for educators in urban and suburban "ethnic minority" school districts. *Equity & Excellence in Education* 36(4):300–307.

Holmes Group. 1986. *Tomorrow's teachers.* East Lansing, MI: Author.

Huling, L. 1990. Teacher induction programs and internships. In *Handbook of research on teacher education,* eds. W. R. Houston, M. Haberman, and J. Sikula, 535–48. New York: Macmillan.

Huling, L., V. Resta, and N. Rainwater. 2001. The case for a third alternative: One university's trip. *Journal of Teacher Education* 52(4):326–38.

Ilmer, S., S. Elliott, J. Snyder, N. Nahan, and M. Colombo. 2005. Analysis of urban teachers' first-year experiences in an alternative certification program. *Action in Teacher Education* 27(1):3–14.

Johnston, J. M., and R. Kay. 1987. The role of institutions of higher education in professional teacher induction. In *Teacher induction: A new beginning,* ed. D. M. Brooks, 45–60. Reston, VA: Association of Teacher Educators.

Kelly, L. M. 2004. Why induction matters. *Journal of Teacher Education* 55(5):438–48.

Levine, M. 2004. Going to scale with professional development schools in urban districts. *NCATE Newsletter* (Spring 2004):4–5, 7. Washington, DC: National Council for Accreditation of Teacher Education.

Lewis, A. 2001. *To create a profession. Report of the AASCU task force on professional development for teachers.* Washington, DC: American Association of State Colleges and Universities.

Luft, J. A., and N. C. Patterson. 2002. Bridging the gap: Supporting beginning science teachers. *Journal of Science Teacher Education* 13(4):287–313.

McGlamery, S., J. Fluckiger, and N. Edick. 2002. Omaha induction keeps one foot in the university. *National Staff Development Council* 23(4):37–40.

Moir, E., and J. Gless. 2001. Quality induction: An investment in teachers. *Teacher Education Quarterly* 29(1):109–14.

National Commission on Teaching and America's Future (NCTAF). 1996. *What matters most: Teaching for America's future.* Washington, DC: Author.

Riggs, I. M., and R. A. Sandlin. 2002, February. *Accountability for teacher education through participation in teacher induction.* Paper presented at the annual meeting of the American Association of Colleges of Teacher Education, New York City.

Resta, V., L. Huling, S. White, and D. Matschek. 1997. The teacher fellows program: A year to grow. *Journal of Staff Development* 18:42–45.

Roehrig, G. H., and J. A. Luft. 2004. Constraints experienced by beginning secondary science teachers in implementing scientific inquiry lessons. *International Journal of Science Education* 26(1):3–24.

Sahling, N. J., and B. L. Whitford. 2004. An early look at SST: Spawning communities of interest. In *The teaching career,* eds. J. I. Goodlad and T. J. McMannon, 157–83. New York: Teachers College Press.

Serpell, Z. 2000. *Beginning teacher induction: A review of the literature.* Washington, DC: American Association of Colleges for Teacher Education.

Shulman, J. H., and V. L. Bernhardt. 1990. The role of the university in new teacher programs. In *Designing programs for new teachers: The California experience*, eds. A. I. Morey and D. S. Murphy. San Francisco: Far West Laboratory for Educational Research and Development.

Stanulis, R. N. 2006, April. *Keeping content and context central: District-based comprehensive induction in the Michigan State University/teachers for a new era induction program.* Paper presented at the annual meeting of the American Educational Research Association, San Francisco.

Stanulis, R. N., G. Burrill, and K. T. Ames. 2007. Fitting in and learning to teach: Tensions in developing a vision for a university-based induction program for beginning teachers. *Teacher Education Quarterly* 34(3):135–47.

Stern, B., J. Snyder, and I. Lit. 2006, April. *Bank Street College of Education TNE induction model.* Paper presented at the annual meeting of the American Educational Research Association, San Francisco.

Villani, S. 2002. *Mentoring programs for new teachers: Models of induction and support.* Thousand Oaks, CA: Corwin Press.

Williams, J., and K. M. Williamson. 1996. University support for novice teachers: Successes, struggles and limitations. *Education* 116:366–71.

Wolfe, M. P., C. A. Bartell, and G. P. DeBolt. 2000. School district and university culture and responsibilities. In *Quality mentoring for novice teachers*, eds. S. J. Odell and L. Huling, 47–56. Indianapolis, IN: Kappa Delta Pi.

Young, B. L., and R. H. Yopp. 1999. A model for beginning teacher support and assessment. *Action in Teacher Education* 21(1):24–36.

NOTES

1. I use the terms *university, college,* and *higher education* interchangeably in this review.

2. To provide the reader with useful illustrations of practice, I describe a wide variety of induction partnerships in this review. Many of these programs have changed over time to address shifting priorities and resources. Thus, these descriptions should be viewed as illustrations that represent a single point in time.

3. Exceptions include programs at the University of New Mexico, the University of Wisconsin at Whitewater, Southwest Texas State, and the University of Colorado, Boulder.

III

EXAMPLE STUDIES ON TEACHER INDUCTION AND ITS EFFECTS

12

Mentoring for Equity

Focusing New Teachers on English Language Learners

Betty Achinstein, University of California, Santa Cruz
Steven Z. Athanases, University of California, Davis

U.S. teachers report being underprepared to meet the needs of English language learners (ELLs) (Darling-Hammond, Chung, and Frelow, 2002; Gándara, Maxwell-Jolly, and Driscoll, 2005). Focusing new teachers on ELLs is a particular challenge given a predominant cultural and linguistic mismatch between teachers and students and limited instructional repertoires focused on ELLs. Induction and mentoring programs hold promise for this work, but they often do not hold robust ideas about teacher knowledge, students, or change (Feiman-Nemser, Schwille, Carver, and Yusko, 1998), much less about ELL issues and equity. There also is a problematic assumption that new teacher mentors come ready-made, needing only technical tips, rather than situating mentoring in a complex knowledge base within diverse contexts where issues collide and compete (Achinstein and Athanases, 2006). Little research has addressed what mentors need to know and be able to do to help novice teachers focus on equity and ELLs. In this chapter, we shine a light on ways mentoring can guide novices to teach ELLs effectively.

FRAMEWORK: MENTORING FOR EQUITY AND ELLS

This chapter investigates what mentors need to know and be able to do to help new teachers focus on equity and meet ELLs' needs. Equity means addressing persistent patterns of difference in educational opportunities and achievement among students due to historical barriers to access, racism and other forms of bias, linguistic challenges, and poverty. Equity refers to a state in which gaps are eliminated and where achievement of all is raised. It includes providing differentiated supports for learners; using cultural competence; challenging inequitable practices to transform schools into more socially just systems; knowing how structural inequities persist in larger societal contexts; and knowing how race, ethnicity, language, and class impact teaching, learning, and schooling (Haycock, 2001; Ladson-Billings, 2001; Sleeter and Grant, 1999).

While much focus on equity has been on race/ethnicity, we highlight linguistic diversity. Issues of equity arise with the achievement gap and differential dropout rates between ELLs and English-speaking counterparts (Ruiz de Velasco and Fix, 2000). Addressing ELL needs requires knowledge and skills regarding language needs, cultural variation, techniques for second-language development, differentiated instruction, connections with families, language self-esteem, high expectations, and language as a resource instead of a deficit (de Oliveira and Athanases, 2007; Garcia, 1996). Linguistically responsive teaching includes learning students' linguistic and academic backgrounds, diagnosing linguistic demands of learning tasks, and scaffolding strategically (Lucas, Villegas, and Freedson-Gonzalez, 2008).

Teacher education has been slow to make substantive changes targeting ELLs (Lucas and Grinberg, 2008); urgent attention is needed during induction years as well. Yet, providing ELL-focused induction support is underconceptualized and lacking in implementation. For example, though required by California law to participate in ELL-focused induction to progress toward a clear credential, only half of new teachers surveyed for one study had done so (Gándara, Maxwell-Jolly and Driscoll, 2005).

TOWARD A MENTOR KNOWLEDGE BASE

Our work is framed by assumptions that mentors are not born but developed and that a clearly articulated knowledge base is needed for such development. Some direction for understanding mentors' knowledge to focus new teachers on equity and ELLs is provided by the knowledge base for teaching, with one synthesis identifying categories of learners and learning, contexts and purposes, and curriculum and teaching (Darling-Hammond, Wise, and Klein, 1999). However, mapping mentors' knowledge bases requires knowledge of both student *and* teacher learners; student, classroom, and community contexts *and* professional contexts; and knowledge of teaching related to students *and* mentoring new teachers. Previous work offered broad categories of a knowledge base for mentoring and mentor cases (Achinstein and Athanases, 2006; Feiman-Nemser, 2001; Wang and Odell, 2002).

Athanases and Achinstein (2003) found mentors could focus novices on individual students' learning, especially those underperforming, highlighting mentors' multilayered knowledge/abilities in several assessment domains. Achinstein and Barrett (2004) found mentors helped reframe novices' thinking about culturally/linguistically diverse learners and challenges of practice, extending novices beyond managerial frames focused on control, and offering a political frame identifying inequities and a human relations frame. While these studies identify aspects of effective mentors' knowledge, the present study extends the field by targeting what mentors need to know to focus new teachers on equity and ELLs.

METHODS

This study asked: How do experienced mentors and induction leaders characterize what mentors need to know and be able to do to focus new teachers on equity, with attention to ELLs? What does equity-focused mentoring targeting new teachers and their ELLs look like in actual practice of mentoring? How often do mentors and mentees converse about equity and ELLs, and on what do they focus? What complexities arise in mentoring for equity and ELLs?

To answer the first question, we examined wisdom of practice of expert practitioners (Shulman, 1983) in a network of teacher induction leaders who taught, mentored, organized mentors, and conducted inquiry on their practice. The Leadership Network for Teacher Induction (LNTI) is a reform network of induction leaders who support 2,750 novices in sixty Northern California districts. LNTI is a prime site for examining wisdom of practice of mentors supporting equity and ELLs. These leaders work in a context where California's students are 70 percent youth of color, 48 percent Hispanic, and 25 percent ELLs (CDE, 2002, 2006).

California has a funded induction program, and LNTI members had extensive experiences in teaching, mentoring, and induction leadership in varied contexts. LNTI also taps and develops members' wisdom of practice through collaborative inquiry projects. A limitation is that participants reflect the broader profession (primarily white, monolingual women). However, participants included several Latino, African American, and Asian American educators; and most participants provided perspectives of urban districts of mostly students from nondominant cultural/linguistic communities. Equity emerged as a LNTI focus; members engaged in professional development, action research, and ongoing discussions on equity.

We examined questionnaire responses of thirty-seven LNTI members to open-ended items: (1) What do mentors need to know and be able to do to help new teachers focus on issues of diversity and equity in teaching? (2) Select one of the things identified for question 1 and provide an example from your practice. Three researchers constructed categories to analyze response patterns in the preponderance of questionnaire data (Merriam, 1998). We used participants' own language to derive categories, but analysis also was informed by literature on the knowledge base for effective teaching (e.g., Grossman, 1990; Hollins, 1996; Shulman, 1987).

Categories were refined with attention to subthemes until a model was constructed to capture all relevant ideas. We conducted interrater reliability checks on categorization, refining categories until we reached at least 90 percent agreement. Participant-elaborated illustrations were used to delineate categories fully.

To answer the second set of research questions about mentoring in practice, we drew on data from a study of one of the network's induction programs, a highly regarded program representing a university, county office, and district consortium. The program involved two years of on-site weekly mentoring and monthly novice seminars.Mentors were selected through rigorous interviewing and participated weekly in professional development. We examined fifteen new teacher-mentor pairs. Teachers taught grades two through six and included four women of color, eleven white women, and two white men. Mentors were eleven white women, each with fifteen+ years of teaching. Full-time released mentors had caseloads of fifteen novices and ranged in experience from one to four years in the study's first year. We studied novices in their first two years of teaching. The twelve schools represented were in predominantly medium-sized districts with a range of ELL populations and SES levels, though schools had predominantly lower income, high Latino, and medium to high ELL populations.

We reviewed fifteen cases, including a series of interviews with novices and mentors conducted over two years, and audiotaped "reflecting conferences" after a mentor observed a literacy lesson. We analyzed spring conferences from the first year of teaching; we hoped transitioning issues would not dominate, yet chose first year to see what equity/ELL-focused mentoring was possible early in a career.

We analyzed cases for patterns identified in questionnaire results and to provide depth and contrast on ELL issues. We examined percentage of time in conferences focused on ELLs and equity, then coded for content of conversations, examining mentor focal areas related to ELLs, and equity and explored variation in practice. While many mentoring moves described may be used more generically, we coded only instances when ELLs "language minority students" or "target students" in language minority classrooms were explicitly identified. Finally, after reviewing and analyzing cases for cross-cutting themes, we selected a case vignette to highlight mentoring approaches and complexities related to ELLs.

FINDINGS: MENTORING FOR EQUITY

A Bilevel Knowledge Base for Equity-Focused Mentoring, with Attention to ELLs

From analysis of participants' responses, we found professional knowledge for effective equity-focused mentoring has a bilevel nature focused on new teachers (table 12.1, top row) and students (bottom). This involves a *bifocal perspective*: through one lens, the mentor focuses on the new teacher, what s/he knows and can do and needs to learn to more effectively promote equity; through a second, the mentor views the big picture—students with diverse learning strengths and needs, cultural and linguistic resources, and patterns of performance.

In participants' reporting, mentoring teachers for work with ELLs was a frequent equity focus. A bilevel perspective for ELLs means mentors observe and assess *novice teachers' efforts to engage ELLs* productively in learning— through support for language development, strategic reading, differentiated instruction, grouping strategies, and auditory/visual supports. Mentors also need *knowledge of ELLs* in classrooms, observing engagement and responses to instruction.

Bilevel Pedagogical Knowledge Needed to Mentor for Equity, with Attention to ELLs

Participants overwhelmingly identified pedagogical knowledge as most essential in mentoring for equity (table 12.1, 92 percent). This bilevel pedagogy includes (a) ways to *teach diverse youth*, including ELLs, and (b) ways to *guide teachers* during mentoring sessions to promote equitable learning for ELLs and other culturally/linguistically diverse youth.

With *pedagogy for academic development of ELLs*, mentors need research-informed practice, including what one participant called "an understanding of the stages of language development and other second language theories and what students are capable of doing at each stage so that teachers can differentiate." This includes approaches to support language instruction and academic literacy development (e.g., Specially Designed Academic Instruction in English techniques). Respondents noted mentors need to know participant structures to support ELLs' achievement, including language development in cooperative learning groups; adequate wait

Table 12.1. A Bilevel Knowledge Base for Equity-Focused Mentoring of Novices

Knowledge Domain and Number and % of Respondents Reporting (n = 37)

	Pedagogy 34 (92%)	Context 16 (43%)	Learner 10 (27%)	Self 10 (27%)
Focused on New Teachers	Wide repertoire of mentoring strategies and stances for observation, assessment, questioning, feedback, and critique to guide equity-focused teaching and reform	Embedded professional contexts; broader social contexts of schooling and teaching; leadership and change agency	Assessment of novice assets and needs on issues of equity; new teacher as adult learner; novice knowledge base, strategies, and cultural competence; novice's reflectivity level and receptivity to change	Focusing the novice on own identity vis-à-vis student diversity; mentor's focus on self regarding new teachers and their development
Focused on Students	Wide repertoire of strategies to serve all learners (especially culturally/linguistically diverse youth) and to promote equity	Local school culture: Student, parent, community; broader social and structural issues of inequity and discrimination	Assessment of students' funds of knowledge and challenges to deficit views; learning theory and culturally responsive learning theory	Mentor's knowledge of self related to student diversity and equity; awareness of own biases, stances, interactions with students

Adapted from Achinstein and Athanases (2005, 2006).

time; heterogeneous grouping for conversation with more fluent English-speaking peers; and equity cards or other tactics to promote ELLs' participation. One participant said many novices have been exposed to such a "tool box" and "mentors need to know this too."

The bifocal perspective also highlights *pedagogy of mentoring sessions* as strategic sites to guide equity-minded and ELL-focused instruction. The work begins with attending to individual students' learning and continues with attention to equity and diversity. This involves embedding such work in weekly conversations and using observational data to help teachers analyze equitable learning opportunities during instruction and documenting ELL engagement and achievement. A participant noted: "Always look for who is left out and who benefits. Don't be afraid to gently name the dynamics you see." Participants noted mentors need a repertoire of supports for novices, including attending to teachers' individuality and "ability to listen to teacher reflection and move that into a conversation that assists the teacher to look at a practice in a new way."

A frequent concern for the new teacher is tension between content coverage and scaffolding of text comprehension, vocabulary support, and language development needed by many ELLs. Effective mentors shift focus between these student needs and a novice's level of knowledge and skill. This involves knowing when a teacher is stuck and being able to change "from a consultant stance to a collaborative stance" as fellow lesson designer and strategist. The mentor also can use data to prod a resistant teacher to be more reflective about equity work with ELLs.

Support from Other Knowledge Domains in Mentoring for Equity, with Attention to ELLs

Mentoring for equity with ELLs requires other knowledge, including nested *contexts* (e.g., professional, community, policy, sociopolitical, institutional) within which a novice works. This includes knowing how contexts shape inequitable schooling opportunities and how to use this knowledge to advocate for change. This also means knowing how to help novices read, navigate, and advocate within political contexts of schooling, including tracking, instructional restrictions, testing practices, or language policies that undermine ELLs (Achinstein, 2006). The effective mentor knows ways to use "funds of knowledge," accessing information about local cultural, linguistic, and professional contexts, including district documents, community agencies, and human and material resources (Moll and Gonzalez, 2004).

Learner knowledge for equity-focused mentoring includes knowing how novices develop and diagnosing how teachers view students and their out-of-school lives, particularly when there is a cultural/linguistic gap between teacher and ELLs. Mentors can promote connecting with individuals, monitor viewing ELL students through deficit lenses or a failure to look deeper than surface behaviors such as "discipline problems," and "present data and work with novices on solutions." It may require probing about students' lives and links to academic performance, always grounded in the belief that "all students . . . culturally/linguistically diverse . . . are capable, gifted and talented children." Knowledge of learners includes the value of guiding teachers to models, including effective teachers with diverse students.

Participants reported that many novices are unprepared or unwilling to take on equity issues in instruction. This requires analyzing a teacher's *knowledge of self* related to equity and language development, assessing a novice's capacity and receptivity to address equity and ELL issues, and working to support and/or challenge the novice. Mentoring for equity involves knowing how to move a resistant teacher past racial or linguistic bias and "an attitude awareness shift without lecturing and/or pointing out that the novice's existing stance and values may be unexamined and limited." Participants noted mentors need to have engaged in self-reflection regarding educational inequities and biases they bring to mentoring ("It's important to keep your own house in order before helping others"), with attention to attitudes about bilingualism and about extra scaffolding for ELLs of diverse English proficiency levels.

MENTORS FOCUSING NOVICES ON EQUITY AND ELLS

Our second set of research questions concerned what ELL- and equity-focused mentoring looked like in practice in terms of time, focal areas, and complexities.

Time on Focus of ELLs

Mentoring conferences varied in length, from twenty to ninety minutes, yielding 4.5 to 20 pages of single-spaced transcripts. Mentors spent significant amounts of time focused explicitly on needs of ELLs. An average of 22 percent of conference time was focused on ELLs (with a range of 0 to 55 percent). Six of fifteen cases spent 28 to 55 percent of conference time on ELL needs. Those mentors working in contexts with high percentages of ELLs (61 to 100 percent) exhibited more time on ELL concerns than those in low or medium ELL contexts (table 12.2), an issue addressed later.

Mentor Focal Areas about ELLs and Equity

Table 12.3 shows mentoring conversations featured three focal areas. In thirteen of fifteen cases, mentors focused the novice on identifying the need

Table 12.2. Percentage Conference Time on ELL Issues by Classroom ELL Percentage

Teacher ID#	Low ELL (0–30%)					Medium ELL (31–60%)					High ELL (61–100%)				
	1	2	3	4	5	6	7	8	9	10	11	12	13	14	15
% English language learners in class	0	4	7	13	18	31	32	40	50	50	67	91	100	100	100
% Conference time on equity/ELL	0	0	3	6	29	17	28	3	20	18	25	55	44	28	53

for and *developing differentiated instructional strategies* for ELLs. Mentors assessed novices' understandings and practices in differentiating instruction and expanded mentees' repertoires.

In nine cases, mentors asked questions about and introduced strategies to treat individuals and subgroups of students differently based on language, cultural, and learning needs. Novices began to realize they needed to move from whole-group instruction to address needs of different learners through grouping and differentiated practices. Nine cases involved mentors assessing novices' use of guided instruction and scaffolding strategies (e.g.,

Table 12.3. Mentor Focal Areas on ELLs and Equity during Mentoring Conversations in Fifteen Mentor-Mentee Cases

	Number of Mentor-New Teacher Cases (n = 15)
Developing Differentiated Instruction	13
Identify differences in learners and how to address in instruction	9
Scaffolding strategies such as modeling and visuals	9
Academic language development/strategies	8
Grouping practices	4
High expectations	2
Assessing Individual Learners	9
Assessing individual student's understanding and gaps	7
Analysis of student work	4
Identifying positive individual success/reframing deficit	4
Prior knowledge, linguistic/cultural assets, ways of learning	2
Identifying Inequities of Participation	6
Equity of participation strategies and safe climate	6
Assessing student engagement and language access	3
Identifying and naming inequities in participation	2

visual cues, graphic organizers) to assist ELLs. In eight cases, mentors assessed novices' understandings and use of academic language development strategies, sharing observation data and scripted notes of teachers' language that promoted language acquisition. For example, this mentoring exchange identified visual scaffolds (M = Mentor; T = Teacher):

> M: I wonder if there was . . . a strategy you could have used to make the leap even more accessible for ELLs. You said it verbally, but what we know is often kids that aren't auditory learners also need to see it visually.

> T: Maybe put . . . my example on the overhead for the ELLs.

> M: . . . You see how that might have helped the ELLs. . . . They're really engaged. Then you [can] put a paragraph on the overhead, which is great for ELLs, and for kids that learn differently.

Another mentor extended differentiation to groups, describing how analysis of student work "could give you a sense of how to approach the groups, and . . . how to group [students]."

Nine of fifteen cases involved *assessment of individual learners* with explicit attention to ELL needs. Seven cases assessed teachers' knowledge of and strategies for student understanding, discussed strategies to check understanding, shared data on scripts of ELL students that demonstrated their (mis)understandings, or supported adjusting teaching midstream. Four cases involved mentors and teachers reviewing and analyzing students' written work. Four cases demonstrated how mentors identified successes and reframed novices' thinking about learners, moving from deficit to assets, through awareness of students' understanding and growth. Mentors used data and critical questions that challenged conceptions of learners. For example, one focused a novice on individual ELL student learning:

> M: What about kids like your ELLs, like Jésus . . . ? How are you going to make sure that they have success? What kind of thinking can you do around that?

> T: Checking in with them . . . [about] their progress to see that they understand it. . . . before the day it's due, looking at their work and seeing what they've done, so you can see if they understand it, . . . ask questions to see if they understand what's expected. If there is some disconnect with them, you need to work with them.

> M: Have you had the students work in a partnership . . . ? It could be that they do their own work and have their own product, but they work through the text together. . . . What might that look like? Could that give students like Jésus some support?

The exchange on grouping practices based on assessed student needs helped the novice see how different ELLs require different scaffolding and that peer grouping practices matter. The mentor ended by bringing the discussion back to the target student, Jésus, identifying how such approaches would support him and other ELLs.

In six cases, mentors *identified inequities of participation* through use of observation data. Mentors explored a repertoire of participation strategies to support ELLs, including practicing language in small groups before larger settings, partnering strategies, "participation sticks," "think-pair-share," and wait time. Three cases included a mentor's assessment of student engagement and language access. Mentors created participation charts identifying who spoke and who didn't, using them to address student engagement and safe climate needed for ELLs. In one example, a mentor focused on how to support ELLs by charting participation:

> M: I put these arrows to show how many hands went up immediately and then after these a few more went up, but it was generally the same talkative people.
>
> T: I remember . . . the back group, I was just begging them to please [participate].
>
> M: You said, "How about someone from the back table? I'll come back."
>
> T: . . . I was thinking about different ways to get those kids engaged more. I know it's their timidities, their English . . . and they're embarrassed to talk in front of peers. I notice that if they weren't up front, they really didn't want to say anything. . . .
>
> M: Can you think of any ways you might do it differently next time?

The two then discussed pulling popsicle sticks with kids' names and having group projects and other cooperative structures to increase participation.

Variation in Practice

Finally, we found that mentors who worked with teachers with higher percentages of ELLs not only spent more time talking about ELL issues but also addressed more focal areas than those with fewer ELLs. There was an average of addressing seven subdomains of focal areas in conversations about classrooms with 61 to 100 percent ELLs, and an average of addressing one in conversations about classrooms with 0 to 30 percent ELLs. Mentors varied in development of ELL issues within conversations. Some engaged issues in unelaborated, more perfunctory ways, while others elaborated conceptual *and* practical tools.

While it is predictable that conferences with novices who had more ELLs included more time on an ELL focus and concerning more ELL topics, the pattern raises questions about the degree to which novices with few ELLs receive breadth and depth of mentoring to serve their ELLs who are a small but important minority in class. If ELLs must be enrolled in classes with a critical mass of ELLs to ensure their teachers receive extensive mentoring to support their learning, equity questions arise.

ELL-FOCUSED MENTORING: A CASE VIGNETTE

This vignette demonstrates much of the knowledge base described by induction leaders' questionnaire responses as well as challenges mentors face in focusing novices on equitable learning for ELLs. The mentor was identified by the induction program's leaders as expert on equity and ELLs. A white woman in her forties, Sonya[1] was in her fourth year of mentoring. She articulated her knowledge of self related to equity: "I feel as a teacher and a mentor if you are not consistently challenging the system, you're furthering it."

Maggie, a white woman in her twenties, was a new teacher at Lake School (K–5, 96 percent Latino, 66 percent low income, 55 percent ELLs). Maggie's grade-level colleagues drew straws to decide who would work with each group. Maggie drew the short straw and received the "low" language ability–tracked fourth graders. Her more experienced colleagues drew "highs" and "middles."

Sonya described this inequity: "It doesn't make any sense to decide who gets the most challenged reading group by drawing straws and leaving that to the new teacher." Maggie was confronted with a class full of ELLs and students with different skills, six identified as "nonreaders."

An equity-focused problem Sonya addressed concerned Maggie's beliefs and practices related to ELLs and her capacity to differentiate instruction. Sonya explained Maggie tended "to keep on the lowest common denominator," shifting instruction downward, and not recognizing different student needs. Sonya tapped her knowledge of classroom pedagogy for equity in articulating high expectations for *all* students and the importance of differentiating instruction among ELLs.

Sonya also used knowledge of school/policy contexts when she found Maggie's district piloting a new reading series that focused on decoding and grammar over comprehension and the school keenly focusing on improving standardized test scores. Sonya identified this combination as problematic for ELLs because teachers were teaching rote, lower-order grammatical skills out of context as a way to prepare for tests. But it was her knowledge of contexts about broad social issues of inequity (labeling "low learners" in a context of inequitable school practices) that enabled her to bring a larger equity lens to the interaction: "There is a culture among teachers who've accepted that these kids are of 'limited intelligences,' designated as 'low learners.' . . . It's totally humiliating their intelligence and what they are capable of doing. You would never see that in a white, middle-class school."

Sonya used mentoring conferences to push Maggie's thinking, demonstrating pedagogical knowledge for diverse learners in identifying varied needs of ELLs. Sonya was concerned that Maggie was creating "dependence" among ELLs, as she tended to read aloud and rarely asked students to develop their own reading or comprehension abilities. Also, she wanted to help Maggie differentiate instruction, address students' different stages of language development, and not teach to the lowest common denominator.

Sonya's vignette demonstrates pedagogical knowledge for equity that targets the teacher. Sonya started with Maggie's stated concerns yet challenged her to move to more equitable ELL practices. Sonya found an opening when Maggie said she didn't know what her ELL students could do independently and that she was scaffolding so much. Sonya seized the opportunity to focus Maggie on developing her students' independence and higher-order capacities.

> *M:* How does differentiation look given that it's a whole group activity and [it's] quite a diverse group since you've got the six who are not comprehending independently yet.
>
> *T:* The only differentiation would be, for the lower kids, reading it out loud, they're following along . . .
>
> *M:* I'm wondering about . . . your whole thing you started out with, "How do I know what they can do on their own" and "How do I give them the maximum opportunity to do what they can do on their own." I'm wondering if you're not depriving the other seventeen [ELL] students of a chance to see what they can get on their own before you read it to them.

Sonya then explained a variety of ways to differentiate, with more intensive vocabulary work for some while pushing for independent comprehension from others. She was careful not to sound too directive:

> *M:* I don't want to take over. . . . [You might consider] not letting the differentiation for the very beginners keep the others from trying to get it on their own first. . . . Some of the kids who wind up in these so-called "low intensive groups," . . . [an issue] is they become more teacher dependent.

Sonya demonstrated her pedagogical knowledge of focusing novices on equity when she assessed Maggie's approaches that underserved many ELLs and supported novice changes. Sonya was respectful to keep pace with the novice (starting with Maggie's own concern), yet helped Maggie move toward more equitable practices. On one hand, Sonya highlighted her knowledge of student learners: examining needs of very different ELLs (differentiating the six from the seventeen), assessing the novice's challenges, and confronting Maggie about "depriving students of a chance to see what they can get on their own" and "pushing students away from feeling dependent."

On the other hand, Sonya respected Maggie's needs as an adult learner, careful to maintain a nondirective stance: "I was constantly . . . searching for an opportunity in the discussion. I kept coming back to that these people are capable of reading for themselves. . . . Every one of them, even if they are low. I have to find an opening for her to find that."

Sonya used observational data that described what students were doing and saying in order to challenge Maggie's thinking. Sonya interjected pushing questions and prompts: "I can't tell for sure where the students got this information from, you reading it or reading it themselves" and "Is there an opportunity for students to recheck their predictions?" Sonya said to Maggie that there was almost "no higher-level thinking in all of the lesson" and that assessing predictions would contribute to higher-level thinking.

By the end of these conferences, Maggie was beginning to rethink ideas about students and practice: "I know next time I would do things differently. . . . A real aha I had from the observation and feedback process is about giving them a chance to do more on their own so that I can get to know their independent comprehension level." She identified growth over the year in learning to differentiate instruction and meet the needs of all learners.

Sonya's mentoring highlights tensions between sensitivities to adult learners and knowledge of broader social inequities for student learners. Sonya chose not to confront Maggie with a critique of school inequities:

> My goal in the political sense is not something I can hit head on with her . . . about how there is a whole cultural-social thing that allows a whole group of teachers to look down on kids and expect less of them without even realizing they are doing it. That's not some place I would go with her.

Sonya was also careful in her critique: "If you tell [some teachers] what you think, they feel criticized and then shut down. Maggie is like that. It's a cross between giving her information that she is lacking, but not doing it in [a] blaming way." Sonya's nonconfrontational stance is one among several a mentor might take.

Sonya exhibited knowledge of professional contexts in relation to equity, identifying that she was working against both Maggie's resistance and the status quo of the school: "I'm working pretty much against everyone around her. I think I'm the only one who would bring that point of view in . . . and she was a little bit resistant to hearing it from me." Sonya reported that the ELL equity work would challenge Maggie's relationships at school: "She is going to have to think critically about her peers and the principal when she does that."

At times Sonya saw her role as activist in the school, reaching out to several educators over the four years she worked there: "I have to impact higher-level things that I know are not good for kids. . . . It's an activist role [to] get them to question academic tracking and work with a number of teachers and the principal to encourage them to question the system." The vignette reveals challenges of this work and how one mentor taps a knowledge base for equity- and ELL-focused mentoring, using it judiciously to enact change with a novice.

DISCUSSION

New teachers need support to address varied needs of their culturally and linguistically diverse students. Mentoring is one means to provide this support. However, mentoring often falls short of these goals, in part because the profession needs a stronger conceptual understanding of mentoring for equity and ELLs. This study contributes to such an understanding by analyzing practitioners' wisdom of practice, articulating a knowledge base for focusing novices on equity and ELLs, and identifying complexities in mentoring practice.

This knowledge base uses a bifocal perspective across four knowledge domains (pedagogy, context, learner, self), especially pedagogy that involves assessing and guiding a novice as the primary client of mentoring, but using a second set of lenses to focus on ELLs in novices' classrooms, their learning potential, linguistic and cultural resources, and diverse learning needs. In mentoring conversations in fifteen case studies, we found mentors spent significant amounts of time focused explicitly on ELLs' needs by developing differentiated instruction, assessing individual learners, and identifying and remedying inequities of participation. Mentors did this work with varying degrees of elaboration and complexity. Our vignette illustrated the work in a delicate balance of challenging the novice teacher's lowered expectations of ELLs while supporting and not blaming the teacher.

Our analyses advance theoretical understanding of a knowledge base for effective mentoring, particularly related to diverse learners and ELLs. Mentors need an instructional repertoire informed by understandings of social, cultural, and linguistic contexts that shape educational inequities. Effective mentors use a repertoire of assessing students' understandings and differentiating and scaffolding strategies specific to different developmental phases of ELLs. Mentors also need to understand new teachers as learners—their needs and competencies, receptivity to change, consciousness of equity concerns—and organizational contexts in which they work. Such knowledge informs pedagogical decisions mentors make.

Our research highlights the need for mentor development that addresses the complex knowledge base effective mentors use—so they can generate a repertoire of responses in varied contexts for ELLs. Current approaches to teacher induction policy and professional development may not suffice. Programs that merely recruit expert teachers and do not foster mentor development in supporting novices to focus on ELLs and equity will leave mentors ill equipped.

Mentor leaders in our study were engaged in ongoing professional development and inquiry in a community of practice that included an explicit equity focus, with expert outsiders, resources, examination and critique of practice, and construction of new knowledge as part of the learning enterprise. Developing mentors' knowledge and expertise no doubt benefits from such activity.

Our research points to needed work to understand which ELL-related topics in mentoring conversations get taken up by novices more readily, which have the greatest impact on ELL student learning, and how mentoring conversations can maintain focus on ELLs when there is not a critical mass of ELLs in a class. Our vignette highlights how mentoring for equity and ELLs may necessitate critiquing individual assumptions and institutional arrangements in classrooms and schools.

Mentors must, at times, confront a new teacher's resistance and "dysconscious" assumptions (King, 1991) about linguistically/culturally diverse students. Mentors can help novices see culturally/linguistically diverse learners' assets, as well as needs. Mentors who engage in a critique of institutional arrangements that undermine ELLs may struggle with tensions of easing the transition of novices into the culture of their school while challenging/changing the way things are done in schools. Finally, if mentors hold a key to supporting new teachers in addressing needs of ELLs, then mentors too will need advocates, as well as organizational arrangements that promote development of the mentors' knowledge, equity commitments, and capacities to foster change.

REFERENCES

Achinstein, B. 2006. New teacher and mentor political literacy: Reading, navigating and transforming induction contexts. *Teachers and Teaching: Theory and Practice* 12(2):123–38.

Achinstein, B., and S. Z. Athanases, eds. 2006. *Mentors in the making: Developing new leaders for new teachers.* New York: Teachers College Press.

———. 2005. Focusing new teachers on diversity and equity: Toward a knowledge base for mentors. *Teaching and Teacher Education* 21(7):843–62.

Achinstein, B., and A. Barrett. 2004. (Re)Framing classroom contexts: How new teachers and mentors view diverse learners and challenges of practice. *Teachers College Record* 106(4):716–14.

Athanases, S. Z., and B. Achinstein. 2003. Focusing new teachers on individual and low performing students: The centrality of formative assessment in the mentor's repertoire of practice. *Teachers College Record* 105(8):1486–1520.

California Department of Education (CDE). 2006. Public School Summary Statistics 2005–2006. Retrieved October 10, 2008, from http://www.cde.ca.gov/ds/sd/cb/sums05.asp.

———. 2002. English Learners as a Percent of Enrollment 1993 to 2002. Retrieved October 10, 2008, from http://www.cde.ca.gov/ds/sd/lc/elprct.asp.

Darling-Hammond, L., R. Chung, and F. Frelow. 2002. Variation in teacher preparation: How well do different pathways prepare teachers to teach? *Journal of Teacher Education* 53:286–302.

Darling-Hammond, L., A. E. Wise, and S. P. Klein. 1999. *A license to teach: Raising standards for teaching.* San Francisco: Jossey-Bass.

de Oliveira, L. C., and S. Z. Athanases. 2007. Graduates' reports of advocating for English language learners. *Journal of Teacher Education* 58(3):181–202.

Feiman-Nemser, S. 2001. Helping novices learn to teach: Lessons from an exemplary support teacher. *Journal of Teacher Education* 52(1):17–30.

Feiman-Nemser, S., S. Schwille, C. Carver, and B. Yusko. 1998. *A conceptual analysis of literature on beginning teacher induction.* A work product of the National Partnership on Excellence and Accountability in Education Report. Washington, DC: U.S. Department of Education.

Gándara, P., J. Maxwell-Jolly, and A. Driscoll. 2005. *Listening to teachers of English language learners: A survey of California's teachers' challenges, experiences, and professional development needs.* Santa Cruz, CA: Center for the Future of Teaching and Learning.

Garcia, E. E. 1996. Preparing instructional professionals for linguistically and culturally diverse students. In *Handbook of research on teacher education*, 2nd ed., eds. J. Sikula, T. J. Buttery, and E. Guyton, 802–13. New York: Simon & Shuster Macmillan.

Grossman, P. L. 1990. *The making of a teacher.* New York: Teachers College Press.

Haycock, K. 2001. Closing the achievement gap. *Educational Leadership* 58(6):6–11.

Hollins, E. R. 1996. *Culture in school learning: Revealing the deep meaning.* Mahwah, NJ: Lawrence Erlbaum.

King, J. 1991. Dysconscious racism: Ideology, identity, and the miseducation of teachers. *Journal of Negro Education* 60(2):133–46.

Ladson-Billings, G. 2001. *Crossing over to Canaan: The journey of new teachers in diverse classrooms.* San Francisco: Jossey-Bass.

Lucas, T., and J. Grinberg. 2008. Responding to the linguistic reality of the mainstream classroom: Preparing classroom teachers to teach English language learners. In *Handbook of research on teacher education: Enduring questions in changing contexts*, eds. M. Cochran-Smith, S. Feiman-Nemser, and J. McIntyre, 606–36. Mahwah, NJ: Lawrence Erlbaum.

Lucas, T., A. M. Villegas, and M. Freedson-Gonzalez. 2008. Linguistically responsive teacher education: Preparing classroom teachers to teach English language learners. *Journal of Teacher Education* 59(4):361–73.

Merriam, S. B. 1998. *Qualitative research and case study applications in education.* San Francisco: Jossey-Bass.

Moll, L., and L. Gonzalez. 2004. Engaging life: A funds of knowledge approach to multicultural education. Pp. 669–715 in *Handbook of research on multicultural education,* J. Banks and C. McGee Banks, eds. New York: Jossey-Bass.

Ruiz de Velasco, J., and M. Fix. 2000. *Overlooked and underserved: Immigrant students in U.S. secondary schools.* Washington, DC: Urban Institute.

Shulman, L. S. 1987. Knowledge and teaching: Foundations of the new reform. *Harvard Education Review* 57(1):1–22.

———. 1983. Autonomy and obligation: The remote control of teaching. In *Handbook of teaching and policy,* eds. L. S. Shulman and G. Sykes, 484–504. New York: Longman.

Sleeter, C. E., and C. A. Grant. 1999. *Making choices for multicultural education: Five approaches to race, class, and gender.* Upper Saddle River, NJ: Prentice-Hall.

Wang, J., and S. Odell. 2002. Mentored learning to teach according to standards-based reform. A critical review. *Review of Educational Research* 72(3):481–546.

ACKNOWLEDGMENTS

Portions of this chapter were adapted from B. Achinstein and S. Z. Athanases. 2005. Focusing new teachers on diversity and equity: Toward a knowledge based for mentors. Teaching and Teacher Education 21(7):843–62; and B. Achinstein and S. Z. Athanases. 2006. Mentors' knowledge of equity and diversity: Maintaining a bifocal perspective on new teachers. Pp. 38–54 in *Mentors in the making: Developing new leaders for new teachers,* B. Achinstein and S. Z. Athases, eds. New York: Teachers College Press.

NOTE

1. Individual's and school names are pseudonyms.

13

Bringing Content into Induction Programs

Examples from Science[1]

Julie A. Luft, Arizona State University, Tempe, AZ
Jennifer J. Neakrase, New Mexico State University, Las Cruces, NM
Krista L. Adams and Jonah Firestone, Arizona State University, Tempe, AZ
EunJin Bang, Iowa State University, Ames, IA

Induction programs generally strive to meet the needs of all teachers in a school or district. The programs often include meetings prior to the start of the school year, thus orienting teachers to procedures and policies that are unique to the school and the district. Around this time, teachers are also assigned a mentor who is familiar with their content area but who may not teach the same grade or academic topic. Throughout the school year, new teachers and their mentors may meet with one another to discuss instruction, logistics, and other matters related to instruction or the life of the new teacher. Most educators who discuss the configuration of these programs, such as Wong (2002), emphasized the basic needs of all beginning teachers.

For content specialists, this model of induction falls short and may even contradict the intent of many initial certification programs for secondary teachers. Options to learn about how to teach content may be more readily available in a teacher's later years, but by this time their skills or pedagogical knowledge may be at odds with the reform-based practices fostered during an initial certification program (Weiss, Pasley, Smith, Banilower, and Heck, 2003). The lack of a content focus during an induction program can easily lead new teachers to focus on the general mechanics of teaching and not the instructional strategies advocated in their content area (Luft, Roehrig, and Patterson, 2003).

There is an increasing interest in content-specific induction programs that support a seamless transition from a teacher's initial certification program through his or her first years in the classroom. To be successful, this type of program requires the involvement of experienced teachers, beginning teachers, teacher educators, and administrators. Collectively, these individuals continue the discussion related to teaching in a content area. Our work in this area focuses on secondary science teachers.

In the following sections, we share our rationale, give a brief overview of our research, and suggest roles and responsibilities for those involved in content-specific induction programs. We realize that this type of work challenges the typical norms of induction, but the evidence we have collected strongly suggests that this approach needs to be considered by those who work with beginning teachers.

NEW TEACHERS IN SCIENCE

An important goal of science instruction is to engage students in "science as inquiry." The *National Science Education Standards* [*NSES*] (National Research Council [NRC], 1996) articulated a vision for this approach to science that emphasizes students posing questions about phenomena, collecting and analyzing data, and conveying new insights to teachers and peers. Even though the inquiry-based approach is now considered critical to scientific learning, teachers find it difficult to implement. Experienced teachers are more likely to achieve inquiry instruction in their classes, whereas new or beginning science teachers struggle (Luft, 2001). The reasons for the difference in implementation are varied and include a lack of understanding of inquiry, limited content knowledge, developing beliefs, or a limited repertoire in this area (Luft, 2001; Smith et al., 2007). This difference in implementation has caught the eye of the teacher education community because new teachers are often products of an educational system that supports an inquiry approach in the classroom.

The current dialogue about early career science teachers reveals a complex process of learning to teach science (e.g., Bianchini, Johnston, Oram, and Cavazos, 2003; Davis, Petish, and Smithey, 2006; Luft, 2001; Simmons et al., 1999; Trumbull, 1999). These studies described how new science teachers modified their practices and knowledge during their initial years in ways that had not been understood previously.

For example, Trumbull's beginning teacher narratives, which covered several years, showed the need for beginning teachers to enhance their subject matter knowledge and also showed how the environment experienced by beginning teachers ultimately constrained their instructional intentions. Similarly, Simmons et al. (1999) found that most beginning science and mathematics teachers' beliefs and practices fluctuated between positions that focused on students and positions that focused on their instruction, and that beginning science and mathematics teachers held beliefs and practices that were often inconsistent with one another. Only after a few years in the classroom did their beliefs and practices stabilize and align toward a position that sought to build a student's knowledge or a position that primarily transmitted knowledge to the student.

Science teacher educators have addressed this problem by developing induction programs that reinforce the importance of content knowledge and instructional practices unique to beginning content-area teachers. Areas of emphasis would include teaching science with inquiry and illustrating the complex process of knowledge creation in science (see *NSES* [NRC, 1996]). One such program was developed by Luft, an author of this chapter.

This induction program was available to secondary science teachers who graduated from the local university or who worked in the local schools. In addition to emphasizing the teaching of science as articulated in the *NSES* (NRC, 1996), the program supported the new science teachers with the help of mentors from local schools, university science education faculty, and graduate students. A thorough description of the conceptualization and enactment of this program can be found in Luft and Patterson (2002). The early studies of the teachers who participated in this program revealed that a content-specific induction program could impact and support the learning trajectory of beginning science teachers (Luft et al., 2003).

Research about the impact of induction programs for science teachers is just emerging (Davis, Petish, and Smithey, 2006), as is our understanding about how content knowledge should be included in an induction program. The individuals involved in developing and implementing induction programs do recognize that new elementary and secondary teachers are not all the same and that secondary teachers in content areas need induction programs that support their development of practices and knowledge aligned with their content areas. Simply put, new secondary teachers need to experience induction programs that are as content focused as their initial certification programs.

FEIMAN-NEMSER REVISITED: LEARNING TO TEACH FOR CONTENT SPECIALISTS

In order to expand our understanding of the development of new teachers who are content specialists, we drew upon a significant paper published by Feiman-Nemser (2001) in which she explored the professional development process of educators from their preservice years through their early career professional development activities. We drew upon the central tasks for learning to teach as suggested by Feiman-Nemser and added additional tasks that would be important to teachers in content areas. We recognized that Feiman-Nemser acknowledged content in teaching, but we felt compelled to move content to a more central position during induction and early professional development experiences. A modified version of the Feiman-Nemser discussion of central tasks in teaching can be found in table 13.1.

In this modification, we are reinforcing the importance of building instructional competence by emphasizing one's ability to teach a subject. In our view, beginning content specialists who are exploring how to teach in a content area need ongoing support in order to enact sound subject matter instruction. It is not enough to have strong pedagogical knowledge or sound content knowledge. There must be a consistent focus on helping the beginning teacher to translate content into subject matter instruction.

Table 13.1.   Central Tasks for Early Career Professional Development[a]

Preservice	Induction/Newly Qualified	Early Professional Development
1. Examine beliefs critically in relation to vision of good teaching	1. Confront and revise/ refine beliefs in relationship to good practice	1. Expand and fortify beliefs
2. Develop subject-matter knowledge	2. Reinforce subject-matter instruction	2. Extend and deepen subject-matter knowledge
3. Develop an understanding of learners, learning, and issues of diversity	3. Examine student learning in the content area	3. Expand the ability to examine learning and teaching in the classroom, school, or community
4. Develop skills to study and improve teaching	4. Strengthen skills and dispositions to study and improve teaching	4. Expand and refine the repertoire for subject-matter instruction
5. Develop a beginning identity	5. Build and enact a beginning repertoire	5. Expand professional capacity and/or develop leadership skills
6. Develop the tools and dispositions develop leadership for professional development	6. Develop a professional repertoire	6. Develop an instructional practice that focuses on student learning
7. Transition from studenting to teaching		

[a]Adapted from Feiman-Nemser (2001).

LEARNING TO TEACH SCIENCE: EXPLORATIONS WITHIN THE FEIMAN-NEMSER FRAMEWORK

To illustrate the importance of inducting early career subject specialists, we drew upon the revised Feiman-Nemser (2001) framework and our own research on beginning secondary science teachers. Topics have been selected from table 13.1 and will be highlighted with the research we have conducted over the years. These overviews are meant to be informative and brief and to give insights into the first years of teaching and the advantage of a content-specific induction program. More comprehensive discussions of these studies are found in Luft et al. (2008) and Luft (2007; 2009).

SUBJECT-MATTER INSTRUCTION AND EXAMINING STUDENT LEARNING

In this first study, we acknowledged that it was important for teachers to understand the content knowledge they would teach. Content knowledge is not assessed by examining a teacher's major or minor in a discipline; rather, it should be evaluated based on how well a teacher understands the boundaries and the process by which the content knowledge advances. Without this knowledge, which Schwab (1978) discussed, a teacher may misrepresent both the content and the nature of the discipline. The content of science often includes topics such as facts, definitions, and models that are within the different disciplines. The "nature of the discipline" refers to an understanding of how science progresses as a field and includes the understanding that science is tentative, that theories inform exploration, and that all modes of investigation rely on evidence.

The teacher's ability to translate his/her content knowledge into classroom practice is referred to as pedagogical content knowledge (PCK) (Shulman, 1986). This unique knowledge draws upon content knowledge and general pedagogical knowledge (PK) and results in instruction that represents the content area to students. Van Driel, Beijaard, and Verloop (2001) expanded on the composition of PCK in science by stating that this knowledge consists of (a) instructional strategies that incorporate representations and (b) an understanding of student difficulties and/or misconceptions with topics related to the content that is taught.

In this study, we were interested in the PCK of in-field and out-of-field first-year secondary science teachers. By documenting the PCK of beginning teachers over the course of a year, we hoped to determine if content knowledge at the discipline level made a difference in terms of teaching a subject. By understanding the development of PCK, we can create better initial certification and induction programs.

Methods

The participants in this study were thirty-five beginning secondary science teachers, who were located primarily in two different regions in the United States, the West and the Midwest. All of the teachers participated in different induction programs. Of the teachers in this study, twenty-two were classified as in-field teachers because they had a major in the area they were teaching.

The data consisted of two semistructured interviews that were conducted with the participants before and after their first year of teaching. The first interview included a set of general questions that related specifically to teaching. The second interview covered PCK and followed the guidelines of Lee, Brown, Luft, and Roehrig (2007). This interview focused on how teachers planned their lessons and accounted for the knowledge of their students; it typically lasted between one and two hours. All of the interviews were audiorecorded. The analysis of the PCK interview was done by coding the responses of all teachers in two broad categories:

> 1. *Knowledge of student learning.* This category addressed the teachers' consideration of students when planning a lesson and when teaching. The category was further divided into three subcategories: students' prior knowledge, different levels of understanding among students, and students' difficulties with specific science concepts.
> 2. *Knowledge of instructional strategies, including science-specific strategies and topic-specific strategies.* This knowledge contributed to teachers' flexibility in adjusting their lesson plans to classroom situations. It included two areas: the quality of the inquiry in the teacher's lessons and how the phenomenon was represented in the classroom.

Responses were given a numerical value of 1, 2, or 3 in each category, corresponding to a limited, basic, or proficient level of PCK, with total scores between 5 and 15. In order to arrive at the value in each category, two different researchers coded each question set and discrepant codes were resolved by discussion. A discussion of the interview and analysis process can be found in Lee et al. (2007).

Findings

The beginning secondary science teachers showed a positive change in their PCK mean score over the first year of teaching (see table 13.2). The scores moved from just above a "limited" level of PCK toward a "basic" level. A limited score represented little or no use of the knowledge about student learning in science, little use of inquiry, and few representations during instruction. A basic level of PCK indicated that teachers were starting

Table 13.2. Means, Standard Deviations, and Statistics for Beginning Physical Science Teachers using the Lee et al. (2007) PCK Numerical Codes

PCK Category	Pre		Post		Post-Pre		
	M	SD	M	SD	t	p	MD
All	7.26	2.01	9.20	1.86	−4.89	<0.05[a]	1.94
In-field	7.00	1.54	9.41	1.76	−6.61	<0.05[a]	2.41
Out-of-field	7.75	2.73	8.75	2.09	7.75	0.297	1.00

[a]Significance at 0.05.

to develop lessons that accommodated the students' learning and that used some representations to convey science concepts.

A paired sample *t*-test was conducted to evaluate whether the mean total score from the second interview was significantly different than the mean from the first interview for the in-field/out-of-field groups of teachers. Overall, the prescores and postscores were significantly different at the 0.05 level among all of the teachers. A follow-up paired sample *t*-test was conducted to determine whether the in-field or out-of-field groups' PCK score changed significantly over the first year of teaching. A significant difference was found for the in-field group, but not for the out-of-field group. Table 13.2 reports these analyses.

In a follow-up examination, the individual categories that comprised an overall PCK score were examined. The in-field teachers showed significant change in all categories except scientific inquiry, whereas the out-of-field teachers only showed a significant change in the representations category. These data can be found in tables 13.3 and 13.4, respectively.

Conclusion and Discussion

In this study, there were two findings related to the PCK of beginning teachers. First, in-field teachers were more likely to be impacted by their understanding of students, which was a subcategory of PCK. Out-of-field teachers, on the other hand, were not impacted by their students and were more likely to use general instructional practices. Content, in the case of the in-field teacher, was important in allowing the new teacher to build his/her PCK. In the absence of this knowledge, the teacher focused on general tasks that were transferable between different content areas.

Second, and more importantly, there appeared to be a quantity and quality issue when discussing the PCK of in-field and out-of-field teachers. For teachers who had a major in their teaching field, the PCK they initially held allowed them to adapt their instruction to better meet the needs of their students and to adjust their instruction to represent science to their students

Table 13.3. Means, Standard Deviations, and Statistics for In-field Beginning Science Teachers in Individual Categories using the Lee et al. (2007) Coding Rubric

PCK Category	Pre		Post		Pre-Post		
	M	SD	M	SD	t	p	MD
Attention to prior knowledge	1.20	0.422	1.70	0.483	−3.00	0.015[a]	0.500
Attention to 0 variations in student learning	1.40	0.516	2.20	0.632	−4.00	0.003[a]	0.800
Attention to student misconceptions	1.20	0.422	1.60	0.516	−2.45	0.037[a]	0.400
Use of scientific inquiry	1.70	0.823	2.10	0.568	−1.31	0.223	0.400
Use of representations	1.70	0.483	2.20	0.422	−3.00	0.015[a]	0.500

[a]Significance at 0.05.

Table 13.4. Means, Standard Deviations, and Statistics for Out-of-field Beginning Science Teachers in Individual Categories using the Lee et al. (2007) Coding Rubric

PCK Category	Pre		Post		Pre-Post		
	M	SD	M	SD	t	p	MD
Attention to prior knowledge	1.33	0.500	1.67	0.707	−1.00	0.347	0.330
Attention to variations in student learning	1.78	0.441	1.67	0.877	316	0.760[a]	0.110
Attention to student misconceptions	1.44	0.527	1.67	0.500	−0.800	0.447	0.220
Use of scientific inquiry	1.56	0.527	1.89	0.782	−1.16	0.282	0.330
Use of representations	1.67	0.500	2.11	0.333	−2.53	0.035[a]	0.440

[a]Significance at 0.05.

in ways that were conducive to their learning. For these teachers, a major in the area they were teaching seemed to contribute to the quality of the PCK they formed. For the out-of-field teachers, their PCK was initially higher but ultimately only expanded into a few areas. The PCK of these teachers had a limited ability to change and did not modify as readily as their in-field peers. The lack of change could be attributed to the quality of PCK they held, which did not have a strong content-knowledge component.

Implications

Examining the differences in PCK of in-field and out-of-field beginning science teachers is important when considering the type of support necessary for the success of a new teacher. If research continues to show differences in the knowledge for teaching of in-field and out-of-field beginning teachers, induction programs will need to be configured to meet the needs of content specialists. By embedding content into induction programs, in-field and out-of-field teachers can be better supported to develop their PCK, which can impact student learning.

Building and Enacting a Beginning Repertoire and Content-focused Induction

This study followed the recommendations of two significant documents about science education in the United States, *Before It's Too Late* (National Commission on Mathematics and Science Teaching for the 21st Century, 2000) and *Educating Teachers of Science, Mathematics, and Technology: New Practices for the New Millennium* (Committee on Science and Mathematics Teacher Preparation, 2000). These documents emphasized the development of induction programs but offered few details on their configuration. Ideally, such programs would "strengthen and sustain" the reform-based practices and philosophies cultivated in science teachers during their pre-service programs.

Science education researchers have sought to understand the learning and practices of beginning content specialists in the midst of their first year. Bianchini and Cavazos (2007) and McGinnis, Parker, and Graeber (2004), for example, found that the first years of a teacher's career can be influenced by the teacher's background and associated support communities. However, these and other studies have not focused on how induction programs can impact the practices of beginning secondary science teachers.

In the present study, beginning science teachers experienced one of four different types of induction programs: (a) e-mentoring programs offered by universities and national associations to a large number of science teachers,

(b) general programs offered by school districts for all of their teachers, (c) university programs that worked with local districts to support secondary science teachers in particular, or (d) internship programs that offered certification while one was learning to teach science. All of the programs were described generally in Luft (2009), and the university program for secondary science teachers was thoroughly described in Luft and Patterson (2002).

Methods

Some 114 secondary science teachers were followed during their first year of teaching. Most of the teachers entered teaching with a bachelor's degree and worked in a high school in an urban setting. They taught an average class size of twenty-three students in an average school size of 1,350 students. About one-third of the teachers worked in schools in which at least 30 percent of the students qualified for free or reduced-price meals. The demographics of the teachers can be found in table 13.5.

The data collected included four observations and eight interviews with the first-year teachers during specific two-week periods. The observations were of one class period, and the interviews covered a week of instruction. During an observation or interview, we drew upon the Collaboratives for Excellence in Teacher Preparation protocol (Lawrenz, Huffman, Appeldoorn, and Sun, 2002) to capture the instruction (e.g., lecture, lecture with discussion, modeling, or hands-on activity) and the grouping of the students (whole group, individual, or small groups). A second set of instructional codes was noted, when possible, to capture unique aspects of science instruction.

For example, hands-on activities were also coded at a scale representing the type of activity, such as guided inquiry, verification laboratory, or process laboratory. At the end of each observation, the quality of the lesson was evaluated with the Oregon Teacher Observation Protocol (OTOP) developed by Wainwright, Flick, and Morrell (2003). This instrument was developed to assess science lessons based upon the *NSES* (NRC, 1996) and included pedagogical characteristics such as ideas are challenged, ideas are posed, students are involved in relevant projects, and a variety of materials are used to illustrate a concept. All of these data were entered into a spreadsheet and analyzed using an ANOVA (analysis of variance) statistic.

Findings

Although all of the teachers tended to use bell work to start class, the teachers in the general induction group used bell work significantly more than did teachers in the e-mentoring induction group, $F(3, 105) = 3.51$, p

Table 13.5. Demographics of Beginning Teachers (n = 114)

	General	e-Mentoring	University Program	Internship
Total	31	31	30	22
Male	12	8	16	6
Female	19	23	14	16
Type of school				
Urban	13	20	18	18
Suburban	9	4	11	4
RuraL	9	7	1	0
Middle	9	10	9	6
High	20	17	20	7
>30% ELL[a]	0	2	4	7
>30% FRL[b]	11	7	11	16
Academic preparation				
BS/BA	20	22	23	19
MA/MS	11	8	7	2
PhD	0	1	0	1
Courses to prepare				
1	15	12	13	7
2	13	14	13	10
3	2	1	2	2
4+	1	4	2	3
Teaching in content area				
In-field	17	15	19	7
Out-of-field[c]	14	16	11	15

[a]English Language Learners (ELL).
[b]Free and Reduced Lunch (FRL).
[c]Teaching out of field >50% of the time.

= .02. Bell work is a technique that gives teachers a few minutes to take attendance and orients students to the upcoming lesson. Teachers in the university science-specific induction group used discussion significantly more than did the teachers in the general induction group, $F(3, 105) = 3.12$, p = 0.03. Class discussions often resulted in students sharing their experiences and explaining their findings. These teachers (university group) also reviewed homework in class significantly more than did the teachers in the general induction group, $F(3, 105) = 2.79$, p = 0.04. This practice provided students with an opportunity to discuss their answers and conclusions to enhance their abilities and knowledge in science.

The teachers in the university induction group generally implemented more guided, direct, verification, and process laboratories than did their peers, whereas the internship group used the least number of laboratories in these areas. The statistical analysis revealed differences in terms of the laboratories the teachers enacted in class. In terms of guided inquiry, in which students developed a process to answer the question, the e-mentoring group implemented more laboratories than did the internship group, $F(3, 105) = 3.34$, $p = 0.02$. In terms of directed inquiry, when students were told how to answer the question, the university group implemented more laboratories than did the internship group, $F(3, 105) = 2.71$, $p = 0.05$.

A more general assessment of teachers' practices with the OTOP (Wainwright et al., 2003) revealed that the groups performed equally over the year. Nevertheless, the university induction group demonstrated more reform-based tendencies than did the general induction group, $F(3, 97) = 3.83$, $p = 0.01$. These were characterized by, for example, having students working collaboratively, teachers and students discussing concepts, teachers assessing the prior knowledge of students, and students reflecting on their learning. Again, the differences between these two groups were consistent from the first observation to the last.

Conclusion and Discussion

From these findings, it was evident that there were differences in the classroom practices of the beginning teachers at the induction program level. The classrooms of the university and e-mentoring program teachers (science-focused programs) were different than the classrooms of the other groups of teachers. The teachers in the science-focused programs were creating interactive environments that resulted in students discussing and exploring their newfound knowledge, and there were more guided, directed, verification, or process laboratories than in their general or internship counterparts.

Based on the conclusions offered by Luft et al. (2003) it appeared that science-focused induction programs did make a difference in performance when you took into account groups of teachers who did not have access to these types of programs. The university and e-mentored teachers were in programs that supported their practices in ways that were aligned with the *NSES* (NRC, 1996). This resulted in classrooms that were more interactive and had more opportunities for students to engage in inquiry science. It seems likely that these two groups of teachers had the opportunity to interact with science education specialists, which may have contributed to their selective accessing of resources to enhance their instruction.

In order to influence a beginning science teachers' performance, induction programs should focus on content. These types of programs draw upon the knowledge in the field of early career teachers to support their growth as professionals. A variety of models exist for this type of induction program, with new models developed regularly, but they all should be examined in order to determine the capacity of their impact on teachers who were content specialists and the feasibility of their implementation.

BRINGING CONTENT INTO INDUCTION PROGRAMS

When induction programs offer specialized support for content specialists, they offer a way for all teachers to strengthen and sustain their practice. In this chapter, we have touched on the inclusion of science in an induction program. But all educators who conceptualize and implement induction programs should consider how content is included in their programs. From our standpoint, it's not enough to have an assigned mentor. In addition, there needs to be an ongoing focus on the content and process of the subject area. This emphasis on content area often transcends the support that mentors provide to new teachers.

As educators develop induction programs that are content specific, there will be new roles and responsibilities for faculty in higher education, administrators, staff development specialists who work with induction teachers, mentors, and beginning teachers. Rhoton and Bowers (2003) acknowledged that administrators, colleagues, and mentors were essential in the socialization and mentoring processes of beginning science teachers. But it is also essential to have the new teachers and faculty/staff who are involved in their preparation engaged in the induction experience. An added advantage of involving additional personnel in the induction of new teachers is that more people will be invested in their development and performance. Table 13.6 highlights these new roles and responsibilities.

In table 13.6, each member of an induction team has a responsibility to support new teachers. By including faculty/staff from institutions of higher education in the induction process, it is possible to create a more seamless transition from initial certification programs through the beginning years of teaching. Faculty and staff can play an important role in establishing the initial dispositions and knowledge bases that will guide the beginning teacher and can help beginning teachers translate that content knowledge into instruction that supports student learning.

Adding content to induction programs will not be a simple task nor will it be without expense. But not adding content to induction programs will be costly in terms of the time that teachers invest in returning to the original positions that were cultivated during initial teacher certification. It will be costly, too, in terms of financial resources used to support experienced teachers in their use of reform-based practices. More importantly, it will be

Table 13.6. Responsibilities of Those Involved in the Induction of Subject Specialists

University/ College Faculty	Mentors	Beginning Teachers	Administrators/Staff Development Specialists
1. Knowledgeable of the local schools and committed to working in them	1. Knowledgeable of the new teachers' initial teacher preparation program	1. Ask for assistance early on and frequently	1. Support instruction that aligns with content instruction
2. Understand robust content instruction	2. Commitment and demonstrated ability to mentor a content specialist	2. Strengthen skills and dispositions to study and improve teaching	2. Physically place new teachers in one classroom close to the mentor teacher
3. Understand preservice learning to teach in a content area	3. Commitment to working with the faculty from preservice teacher preparation programs	3. Participate in professional organizations	3. Knowledgeable about the local program that supplies and supports teachers
4. Understand emerging methods that can support beginning teachers	4. Expertise in teaching the discipline and reflecting on one's own practice	4. Focus on student learning	4. Encourage and support professional activity
5. Knowledgeable about resources in the community that can assist beginning teachers	5. Knowledge of resources in the content area		5. Visit new teacher periodically
6. Commitment to following teachers from preservice through induction programs	6. Knowledgeable of the school and district		6. Support mentor in working with new teacher
7. Ongoing examination of preservice and instruction methods			7. Understand the various ways to teach the different content areas

costly for students who are disadvantaged by not having teachers who are fully supported to enact their content knowledge in the classroom.

Although most would consider a mentor in a content area to be adequate, we suggest that a more comprehensive view of induction support should be adopted. This type of support immerses new teachers in the ongoing development of their content knowledge. It provides rich discussions about teaching a content area at different levels and ensures that new teachers continue to consider how they translate content into practice. Ultimately, the rich support that is provided to the new teachers will ensure that they are contemplating how their content knowledge is shared with their students. Moreover, this type of support encourages reform-based practices, which put the student in the center of the schooling experience.

REFERENCES

Bianchini, J. A., and L. Cavazos. 2007. Learning from students, inquiry into practice, and participation in professional communities: Beginning teachers' uneven progress toward equitable science teaching. *Journal of Research in Science Teaching* 44(4):586–612.

Bianchini, J. A., C. Johnston, S. Oram, and L. Cavazos. 2003. Learning to teach science in contemporary and equitable ways: The successes and struggles of first-year science teachers. *Science Education* 87(3):419–43.

Committee on Science and Mathematics Teacher Preparation. 2000. *Educating teachers of science, mathematics, and technology: New practices for the new millennium.* Washington, DC: National Academy Press.

Davis, E., D. Petish, and J. Smithey. 2006. Challenges new science teachers face. *Review of Educational Research* 76(4):607–51.

Feiman-Nemser, S. 2001. From preparation to practice: Designing a continuum to strengthen and sustain teaching. *Teachers College Record* 103(6):1013–55.

Lawrenz, F., D. Huffman, K. Appeldoorn, and T. Sun. 2002. *CETP core evaluation, classroom observation handbook.* Minneapolis, MN: CAREI.

Lee, E., M. N. Brown, J. A. Luft, and G. H. Roehrig. 2007. Assessing beginning secondary science teachers' PCK: Pilot year results. *School Science and Mathematics* 107(2):52–60.

Luft, J. A. 2009. Beginning secondary science teachers in different induction programs: Findings from year 1. *International Journal of Science Education* 31(17): 2355–84.

———. 2007, October. *Beginning secondary science teachers in induction programs: Considering instructional performance and persistence.* Paper presented at the National Commission on Teaching and America's Future Conference on the Induction of Science and Mathematics Teachers into Professional Learning Communities, Racine, WI.

———. 2001. Changing inquiry practice and beliefs? The impact of a one-year inquiry-based professional development program on secondary science teachers. *International Journal of Science Education* 23(5):517–34.

Luft, J. A., K. Adams, E. J. Bang, S. Guskey, S. Hick, J. Firestone et al. 2008, March–April. *Building a continuum of practice: First year secondary science teachers.* Paper presented at the annual meeting of the National Association for Research in Science Teaching, Baltimore, MD.

Luft, J. A., and N. C. Patterson. 2002. Bridging the gap: Supporting beginning science teachers. *Journal of Science Teacher Education* 13(4):287–313.

Luft, J. A., G. H. Roehrig, and N. C. Patterson. 2003. Contrasting landscapes: A comparison of the impact of different induction programs on beginning secondary science teachers' practices, beliefs, and experiences. *Journal of Research in Science Teaching* 40(1):77–97.

McGinnis, J. R., C. Parker, and A. O. Graeber. 2004. A cultural perspective of the induction of five reform-minded beginning mathematics and science teachers. *Journal of Research in Science Teaching* 41(7):720–47.

National Commission on Mathematics and Science Teaching for the 21st Century. 2000. *Before it's too late*. Washington, DC: U.S. Department of Education.

National Research Council. 1996. *National science education standards (NSES)*. Washington, DC: National Academy Press.

Rhoton, J., and P. Bowers. 2003. *Science teacher retention: Mentoring and renewal*. Arlington, VA: National Science Teachers Association.

Schwab, J. J. 1978. Education and the structure of disciplines. In *Science, curriculum, and liberal education: Selected essays*, eds. I. Westbury and N. J. Wilkof, 229–72. Chicago: University of Chicago Press.

Shulman, L. 1986. Those who understand: Knowledge growth in teaching. *Educational Researcher* 15(2):4–14.

Simmons, P. E., A. Emory, T. Carter, T. Coker, B. Finnegan, D. Crockett et al. 1999. Beginning teachers: Beliefs and classroom actions. *Journal of Research in Science Teaching* 36(8):930–54.

Smith, T. M., L. M. Desimone, T. L. Zeidner, A. C. Dunn, M. Bhatt, and N. L. Rumyantseva. 2007. Inquiry-oriented instruction in science: Who teaches that way? *Educational Evaluation and Policy Analysis* 29(3):169–99.

Trumbull, D. J. 1999. *The new science teacher: Cultivating a good practice*. New York: Teachers College Press.

Van Driel, J. H., D. Beijaard, and N. Verloop. 2001. Professional development and reform in science education: The role of teachers' practical knowledge. *Journal of Research in Science Teaching* 38(2):137–58.

Wainwright, C., L. Flick, and P. Morrell. 2003. The development of instruments for assessment of instructional practices in standards-based teaching. *Journal of Mathematics and Science: Collaborative Explorations* 61(1):21–46.

Weiss, I. R., J. D. Pasley, P. S. Smith, E. R. Banilower, and D. J. Heck. 2003. *Highlights report, looking inside the classroom: A study of K–12 mathematics and science education in the United States*. Chapel Hill, NC: Horizon Research.

Wong, H. K. 2002. Induction: The best form of professional development. *Educational Leadership* 59(6):52–55.

NOTE

1. This study was made possible by NSF grant 0550847. The results herein represent the findings of the authors and do not necessarily represent the view of personnel affiliated with the National Science Foundation.

14

Linking Induction to Student Achievement

Eric Isenberg, Steven Glazerman, Amy Johnson, Sarah Dolfin, and Martha Bleeker,[1] *Mathematica Policy Research, Inc.*

We pose three interrelated questions about the link between teacher induction and student test scores:

1. What is the causal effect of an intensive and structured program of "comprehensive" teacher induction on student test scores after the first year of the program?
2. How do individual components measuring the types and intensity of teacher induction affect student test scores?
3. What explanations do teachers offer on how teacher induction programs affected their performance in the classroom?

Each question requires a different set of analytic methods. To answer the first question, we used a randomized controlled trial to estimate the impact of a package of comprehensive teacher induction supports on student achievement relative to a less formal set of induction supports. To answer the second, we conducted a correlational analysis to estimate the relationships between student achievement and the individual components and intensity of teacher induction programs. For the third, we conducted focus groups to elicit teacher perspectives on the effectiveness of induction.

Despite increased support for teacher induction programs at the state and local levels (Smith and Ingersoll, 2004) and policy emphasis on student test scores since passage of the No Child Left Behind (NCLB) Act, little empirical evidence is available on the relationship between teacher induction and student achievement. Thompson, Paek, Goe, and Ponte (2004, 2005) studied the California Beginning Teacher Support and Assessment (BTSA) program. Given that California implemented the program simultaneously throughout the state, the authors were unable to compare a treatment group of teachers who participated in the BTSA program to a control group of teachers who did not participate.

Instead, the authors compared test scores in math and reading/English Language Arts (ELA) for students of teachers who received strong induction support under BTSA to test scores for students of teachers who received weak induction support under BTSA, using teacher surveys to distinguish weak from strong support. The authors report positive but statistically insignificant differences in student test scores between the weak and strong induction groups.

Rockoff (2008) evaluated the effect of the New Teacher Center (NTC) induction program in New York City on test scores. Similar to California's BTSA implementation, New York City introduced the program simultaneously throughout the city. Rockoff followed two strategies. First, Rockoff compared outcomes for beginning teachers in New York City who participated in the mentoring program to those who, because of imperfect implementation of the program, did not participate. Second, Rockoff compared outcomes among mentored teachers who received varying levels of support. The results were ambiguous. Rockoff found that participants in the mentoring program were no more successful in improving student test scores than nonparticipants. Within the group of participants, however, student test scores improved with more hours of teacher mentoring.

Both the Thompson and Rockoff studies relied on comparisons between groups of teachers who may differ in ways not easily observed by the researcher. These unobserved differences might be confounded with effects of induction and produce misleading results. Thompson et al. used teachers' own reports of engagement with the BTSA program to determine the groups that received strong and weak induction support. If teachers who were more motivated to seek out extra induction support were also intrinsically better teachers, the results would confound selection and program effects.

Rockoff seeks to circumvent this problem by using the average number of hours spent by other teachers who shared a mentor with a given teacher as an instrumental variable to predict the time that the mentor spent with the given teacher. This approach assumes that a mentor's time allocation is not affected in reverse—from the "given teacher" to other teachers mentored. A mentor who is attentive to the needs of individual teachers may, however, spend more time with a particular teacher, reducing the amount of time available to spend with all other teachers.

The new results presented here come from a large-scale, federally funded randomized controlled study to evaluate the impact of comprehensive teacher induction programs relative to prevailing practice. Random assignment ensures that the differences in outcomes between the two groups (treatment and control) are attributable to differences in the interventions to which the groups were assigned and not to other factors.

The main results discussed here are designed to answer our first research question. We found no impact of teacher induction programs on test scores in the first year. We conducted a nonexperimental analysis to address the second question. The analysis suggested that content-oriented components of induction programs might help raise student achievement, although our nonexperimental findings carry the same caveat applied to the Thompson et al. (2004) and Rockoff (2008) studies.

Finally, we address the third question by reporting results from teacher focus groups, which suggest why we may have generated the findings that we did. Although focus groups are even less systematic than observational survey data, they can be more useful for generating hypotheses than closed-ended questioning techniques. Combining all three approaches is the best way to gain a full understanding of the relationship between induction and student achievement.

STUDY DESIGN

Selection of Program Providers, Districts, Schools, and Teachers

We selected two providers to implement comprehensive teacher induction during the 2005–2006 school year: Educational Testing Service (ETS) of Princeton, New Jersey, and the NTC at the University of California, Santa Cruz. Both ETS and NTC had experience implementing induction programs in authentic educational settings, although they modified their interventions to meet the study's needs. For study purposes, we required the programs to adapt their models for delivery in one year.

Both ETS and NTC, along with a technical working group of induction experts provided input on the study design. ETS and NTC cooperated with the researchers throughout the study.

We selected seventeen school districts in thirteen states to participate in the study on the basis of district size, poverty, and prevailing induction supports. Specifically, we sought districts that would have at least forty-eight beginning teachers at the elementary level, the minimum feasible scale for the study. We also sought districts with at least 50 percent of elementary students eligible for free or reduced-price lunch, thus ensuring that the schools were serving low-income students. We excluded districts in which significant resources had already been invested in comprehensive teacher induction programs. We assigned each participating district to either ETS or NTC based primarily on district preferences.

Schools were eligible to participate in the study if they hired new teachers who started in the 2005–2006 school year. Teachers were eligible for the intervention if they taught kindergarten through grade six, were new to the profession, and were not already receiving comprehensive induction support from a teacher preparation or certification program. District staff were allowed to interpret the teacher eligibility criteria in a manner consistent with local policies.

For the experimental components of the study, we randomly assigned each study school within the seventeen participating districts to either a treatment group, which received comprehensive teacher induction from ETS or NTC (as chosen by the district), or to a control group, which took part in the district's usual teacher induction program. For the student achievement analysis, we used data on approximately 250 teachers who taught reading or math in grades three through six in sixteen districts that provided test score data for their grade. (All sample sizes are rounded to the nearest 10 to comply with regulations of the National Center for Education Statistics, which granted the license to use the data.)

We used a cluster random assignment design; that is, study teachers in a school were either all exposed or all not exposed to treatment, depending on whether the school was assigned to the treatment or control group (Bloom, Bos, and Lee, 1999). This design was necessary because varying the types of induction services available in the same school building would be disruptive and controversial and could result in contamination of the control group. All eligible teachers were assigned to treatment or control status based on the school in which they were expected to teach at the time of random assignment. Because schools typically had one, two, or three eligible beginning teachers, the clustering of teachers within schools did not substantially reduce the power of the study design.

The Intervention

The comprehensive induction programs carefully selected and trained full-time mentors. The programs sought mentors with a minimum of five years teaching experience in elementary school, recognition as an exemplary teacher, and experience in providing professional development or mentoring to other teachers (particularly beginning teachers). Thirty-eight of the forty-four mentors (86 percent) held a master's degree, and 55 percent were certified in more than one area. They averaged eighteen years of teaching experience, and 14 percent were National Board–certified. Seventy-seven percent had previous mentoring experience, and 74 percent reported previous training to become a mentor.

The study aimed to assign each mentor to twelve beginning teachers, though mentor caseloads ranged from eight to fourteen teachers over the course of the year. Mentors served teachers across a set of schools and served many who taught a grade or subject different from their own experience. ETS provided the mentors with ten days of training; NTC provided twelve days of training. The training was conducted in four sessions, with the first session held during the summer before the induction program was implemented in the schools. The mentor trainings focused on improving beginning teachers' instruction, including the use of forms and processes, and mentoring skills for working with beginning teachers.

Both ETS and NTC used a curriculum of intensive and structured support for beginning teachers that included an orientation, professional development opportunities, and weekly meetings with mentors. The ETS program derives its content from Danielson (1996). The content of the NTC program is based on California Standards for the Teaching Professional (California Commission on Teacher Credentialing, 1997) and Continuum of Teacher Development (New Teacher Center, 2002). Both programs provided opportunities for novice teachers to observe experienced teachers and used formative assessment tools that permitted evaluation of practice on an ongoing basis and required observations and feedback. ETS also offered monthly study groups—mentor-facilitated peer support meetings for beginning teachers. In addition, both programs coordinated outreach to administrators to educate them about program goals and garner their support for the program. At the end of the school year, beginning teachers in treatment schools in both ETS and NTC districts participated in a colloquium celebrating the year's successes and teachers' professional growth.

Teachers and principals are expected but not required to attend induction events and they varied in their degree of participation. Average attendance by beginning teachers was 72 percent at monthly professional development sessions, 69 percent at study groups, and 87 percent at end-of-year colloquia. Attendance varied further by district; for example, average district attendance at monthly professional development sessions varied from a low of 56 percent to a high of 92 percent.

All treatment teachers were assigned to a full-time release mentor, but 89 percent of treatment teachers reported working with such a mentor. While the comprehensive induction programs offered principals an orientation and invited them to attend professional development sessions, 2 percent of treatment school principals actively resisted the program and initially made it difficult for beginning teachers to participate in the induction activities. District coordinators for the programs as well as mentors and program staff intervened to reduce such resistance.

DATA AND METHODS

Data

We collected data from a variety of sources. Participating school districts provided student records data at the end of the 2005–2006 school year, including pretest data from the previous year. We administered a baseline teacher survey in fall 2005 and surveyed teachers twice during the 2005–2006 school year (once in the fall and once in the spring) on the induction activities in which they participated. Response rates on the teacher surveys and observations exceeded 85 percent. Although some districts provided student records data for the students of teachers who taught grades one and two, we have limited our analysis of student achievement to grades three through six, which are subject to the NCLB Act. The tests that districts provided for grades three through six were generally the NCLB tests.

Random assignment produced groups that were similar on a wide variety of student and teacher characteristics. The top two panels of table 14.1 list the means and standard deviations of the student demographic and teacher control variables by treatment and control groups, along with the minimum and maximum values for the combined sample. Given that the unit of analysis is the student, teacher characteristics are a weighted average, with the implicit weight the number of students in the estimation sample for each teacher.

The bottom panel of table 14.1 shows the means and standard deviations for the induction measures, which are averaged over the spring and fall administrations of the induction activities survey. Treatment teachers generally received a higher level of induction services than control teachers. Far from receiving no services, however, 75 percent of control teachers had an assigned mentor and spent an average of more than 1.5 hours each week with a mentor.

Estimating the Impact of Comprehensive Teacher Induction on Student Test Scores

We used a mix of quantitative and qualitative methods to answer the three research questions. To address the first question, we estimated the effect of comprehensive teacher induction on student test scores relative to the test scores that would have been observed had there been no comprehensive induction program. To that end, we examined whether student achievement for teachers in schools randomly assigned to receive comprehensive induction services differed from student achievement for teachers in schools assigned to the control group.

We use a model-based approach to estimate program impacts. The statistical model is a value-added model of student achievement: $Y_{ijk,t} = \mu + \delta T_k +$

Table 14.1. Sample Characteristics by Treatment Status

| | Treatment Group | | Control Group | | | |
	Mean	Standard Deviation	Mean	Standard Deviation	Min	Max
Student Variables						
Female	0.50	0.50	0.49	0.50	0	1
African American	0.47	0.50	0.49	0.50	0	1
Hispanic/Latino	0.26	0.44	0.21	0.41	0	1
Asian	0.03	0.16	0.01	0.12	0	1
Native American	0.01	0.09	0.02	0.13	0	1
Multiracial	0.02	0.14	0.02	0.13	0	1
Special education	0.14	0.35	0.13	0.34	0	1
English language learner	0.09	0.29	0.07	0.25	0	1
Overage for grade	0.04	0.15	0.05	0.18	0	1
Receives free/reduced-price lunch	0.79	0.40	0.73	0.43	0	1
Teacher Variables						
Age in 2005	28.87	7.70	29.29	7.21	22	59
Male	0.12	0.32	0.18	0.37	0	1
Teacher race						
African American	0.27	0.44	0.18	0.36	0	1
Hispanic/Latino	0.12	0.32	0.14	0.33	0	1
Other race/ethnicity	0.06	0.24	0.03	0.15		
Teacher race matches majority						
of students	0.50	0.50	0.40	0.47	0	1
Master's degree	0.21	0.41	0.29	0.44	0	1
Associate's degree	0.01	0.09	0.00	0.06	0	1
Degree in education field	0.69	0.46	0.79	0.39	0	1
Irregular certification status						
Probationary	0.07	0.24	0.21	0.38	0	1
Additional requirements	0.19	0.39	0.19	0.37	0	1
Emergency	0.04	0.20	0.03	0.14	0	1
Other	0.04	0.19	0.03	0.14	0	1
Route into Teaching Not by						
Four-Year Program						
Postbaccalaureate	0.16	0.36	0.22	0.40	0	1
Teach for America	0.02	0.15	0.01	0.10	0	1
Other	0.22	0.40	0.18	0.36	0	1
Not a beginning teacher	0.11	0.31	0.14	0.33	0	1
Months of relevant teaching						
experience	4.10	11.25	9.67	34.26	0	
288						
Hired after school year began	0.09	0.29	0.07	0.25	0	
1						
Attended a competitive college	0.28	0.45	0.32	0.45	0	
1						
Held nonteaching job for five						
or more years	0.15	0.36	0.13	0.32	0	1
Sample Size (Student and Teacher						

Table 14.1. *(Continued)*

	Treatment Group		Control Group			
	Mean	Standard Deviation	Mean	Standard Deviation	Min	Max
Induction Variables						
Comprehensive teacher induction	1.00	0.00	0.00	0.00	0	1
BT was assigned a mentor	0.95	0.17	0.77	0.38	0	1
BT met with a literacy or math coach	0.79	0.32	0.81	0.31	0	1
BT received guidance in math content	0.45	0.42	0.31	0.41	0	1
BT received guidance in literacy content	0.61	0.39	0.38	0.42	0	1
BT worked with a study group	0.79	0.32	0.48	0.42	0	1
BT observed others teaching	0.75	0.31	0.66	0.36	0	1
Time BT spent in mentoring sessions (hours per week)	1.86	1.45	1.41	2.19	0	15
Time mentor spent observing teacher (hours per week)	0.54	0.42	0.19	0.37	0	2
BT received feedback on teaching (number of times)	4.77	2.30	3.63	2.20	0	12
Sample Size (Induction Variables)						
Students	2,150		1,620			
Teachers	120		90			

Notes: Students are included in this table if they have a math and/or reading pretest. Sample sizes for student and teacher variables differ from sample sizes for induction variables due to nonresponse to First and Second Induction Activities Surveys. Sample sizes vary across induction variables; modal sample sizes are presented. Sample sizes have been rounded to the nearest ten.
BT = Beginning Teacher.
Source: Data from 2005–2006 provided by participating school districts; Mathematica Teacher Background Survey administered in 2005–2006 to all study teachers; First and Second Induction Activities Surveys administered in fall/winter 2005–2006 and spring 2006 to all study teachers.

$\theta'Y_{ijk,t-1} + \alpha'W_{ijk} + \beta'X_{jk} + \gamma'Z_k + [u_k + e_{ijk}]$, where $Y_{ijk,t}$ is an outcome measured for student i of teacher j in school k at time t (posttest); T_k is an indicator variable equal to 1 if the teacher's school (k) was assigned to treatment; $Y_{ijk,t-1}$ is the student pretest variable; W_{ijk} is a vector of student characteristics serving as control variables; X_{jk} is a vector of teacher characteristics; and Z_k is a vector of district-grade fixed effects. The error term u_k represents unobserved school effects and e_{ijk} represents unobserved student effects. The parameters μ θ, α, β, and γ are ancillary intercepts and coefficients.

The main object of interest is δ, the treatment effect. Given the random assignment design, T is uncorrelated with every other independent variable in the model such that the estimated treatment effect is unbiased.

In estimating the model, we note that the error term has both a student and school component; therefore, the composite random error term in braces is not independently and identically distributed across students as is usually assumed in Ordinary Least Squares regression models. All analyses account for the correlation of outcomes for students in the same school by using robust standard errors (Huber, 1967; White, 1980).

We control for student and teacher characteristics (W_{ijk} and X_{jk}) to increase the precision of the estimates of treatment effects. In addition to the student pretest score, we control for the student and teacher characteristics listed in the top two panels of table 14.1 and district-by-grade fixed effects (Z). The fixed effects ensure that all comparisons of student test scores are made between treatment and control teachers in the same district and grade with students who take the same test. In cases without overlap in a district-grade between treatment and control teachers, we dropped all teachers from the analysis.

To facilitate aggregation by grade and district, we converted all test scores to a common metric called a z-score, which is obtained by calculating the mean and standard deviation for each test (that is, for all students in a district-grade), subtracting the district-grade mean from each student test score, and dividing by the district-grade standard deviation. The resulting score may be interpreted as the distance from the average score as a fraction of a standard deviation; a z-score of –0.5, for example, means that the score was one-half of a standard deviation below the mean. To reduce the impact of outliers on the regression analysis, all values above 3.5 in absolute value are set to positive or negative 3.5 (that is, a value of –4.7 would be set to –3.5).

Estimating the Relationship between Induction Components and Test Scores

We use two types of models to examine how variation in the type and intensity of teacher supports is related to outcome measures. The models exploit variation within as well as between the treatment and control groups. The first type of model mimics the experimental analysis by using the same dependent variable and control variables; however, in place of assignment to treatment status (which was randomly determined), we insert each of the nine key explanatory variables one at a time. Each variable measures services received (a "component"). In the second type of nonexperimental model, several induction components are entered simultaneously. Because the exposure to particular components of induction is not determined by the experimental design, we refer to this analysis as correlational or non-experimental.

The nine measures of teacher induction support are divided into measures of types of teacher induction and measures of the intensity of teacher induction. The first group lists key components of a teacher induction program, starting with assignment to a mentor. The next three measures are content-oriented induction supports: meeting with a literacy or math coach, receiving guidance in math content, and receiving guidance in literacy content. The final two types of induction support are group-oriented induction services: working with a study group and observing others teaching. The second broad group lists three alternate means of measuring the intensity of teacher induction services—the total time the beginning teacher spent each week in mentoring sessions, the total time the mentor spent each week observing the teacher, and the number of times within a three-month period that the teacher received feedback from the mentor.

Eliciting Teacher Perspectives

We conducted eight focus groups at the end of the teachers' second year of teaching, in summer 2007—separate focus groups with treatment and control teachers in each of four districts. The focus groups included sixty-six teachers (thirty-five treatment and thirty-one control). The focus groups provide insight into possible explanations for the study's experimental findings, although the informants are not statistically representative of the study sample.

FINDINGS

Experimental Analysis

The impact estimates on math and reading achievement are statistically indistinguishable from zero in the first year of teaching, suggesting that comprehensive teacher induction over and above the usual induction support has no impact on student test scores in the first year of teaching. Students would have performed just as well if their teachers received the prevailing levels of teacher induction support. This finding is documented in table 14.2, which reports the regression-adjusted impact of comprehensive teacher induction on math and reading scores for a variety of specifications of the model or changes in the estimation sample.

The top row of table 14.2 shows the impact of comprehensive teacher induction on math scores (first column) and reading scores (second column), with standard errors in parentheses below the estimates. The impact estimates, measured as the percentage of a standard deviation of test scores, are –4.7 for math and –0.5 for reading. Neither is statistically significant, even though the data are sufficient for tightly estimating the parameters. The standard errors—4.2 for math and 3.7 for reading—allow for a policy-relevant, statistically detectable effect as small as eight to nine percentage points.

Table 14.2. Effect of Comprehensive Teacher Induction on Test Score Outcomes

| | Adjusted Impact | | Sample Size | | | |
| | | | Math | | Reading | |
	Math	Reading	T	S	T	S
(1) Benchmark model	−4.72	−0.45	230	3,940	250	4,400
	(4.24)	(3.67)				
(2) Without pretest as	−12.08+	−8.00	230	4,760	250	5,130
control variable	(6.21)	(5.65)				
(3) No student or teacher	−2.50	0.76	230	3,940	250	4,400
covariates	(4.06)	(3.72)				
(4) No teacher covariates	−3.41	0.16	230	3,940	250	4,400
	(3.81)	(3.54)				
(5) ETS districts only	1.38	−0.19	110	1,940	120	2,140
	(4.95)	(5.05)				
(6) NTC districts only	−11.72+	−2.26	120	2,000	130	2,260
	(6.16)	(5.71)				
(7) Without treatment teachers	−3.57	3.31	190	3,410	210	3,710
who received low-intensity	(4.42)	(4.30)				

Notes: Standard errors in parentheses. Sample sizes have been rounded to the nearest ten. T = Teachers; S = Students.
Source: Mathematica analysis of data from 2004–2005 and 2005–2006 provided by participating school districts; Mathematica Teacher Background Survey administered in 2005–2006 to all study teachers.
+ Significant at the 0.10 level, two-tailed test.
None of the differences is significantly different from zero at the 0.05 level, two-tailed test.

The no-impact finding is robust to changes in the sample, covariates, and model specification. One concern may be that the inclusion of a pretest variable in the model limits the sample to students with pretest scores. We therefore checked whether omitting the pretest variable affects the results. By doing so, we included mobile students who could have experienced a different impact of treatment than students with both a posttest and pretest. We also expanded the number of grade three students, some of whom attend districts that did not provide test score data for students in grade two. As shown in row three, the math impact is now estimated at −12.1 (that is, the treatment group performed worse than the control group), with marginal statistical significance. The impact for reading is −8.0, which is statistically insignificant.

Another possible concern is that the specification of the control variables might have an impact on the estimate of the treatment effect; therefore, we tested alternate specifications and found no qualitative change in the results. Because we identify the treatment effect by using a randomized control trial, we included the covariates for precision but note that their inclusion or exclusion from the model does not bias the results. In row three, we report results in models that included district-by-grade fixed effects but dropped all other covariates aside from the pretest. Again, the impact estimates are small and statistically insignificant. As an alternative model, we included student-level control variables but omitted teacher-level controls. Row four shows that the impact estimates differ little from either the preceding row or the benchmark estimates.

When pooling the effects of two comprehensive teacher induction programs, the success of one intervention could be masked by a dysfunctional intervention; we did not, however, find evidence of this. Rows five and six revert to the benchmark model but divide the sample between districts using the ETS program (row five) and those using the NTC program (row six). None of these coefficients is positive and significant. The NTC coefficient in math is, in fact, marginally significantly negative. Because we assigned each participatory district to one of the two providers of comprehensive induction based primarily on district preferences, it is not possible to make direct comparisons of one provider to the other. ETS and NTC worked with different types of districts; therefore, we cannot predict what results NTC would have obtained in the ETS districts or vice versa.

Finally, we address the possibility that weak implementation of the intervention by some districts or mentors could skew the results, but found no evidence of this. We omitted all treatment teachers who reported that they were not assigned a mentor in at least one of the two survey rounds (fall and spring) or who reported that they spent an average of less than an hour a week with their mentor. We retain all control teachers for this analysis. Although this method compromises the purely experimental nature of the findings, it may at least provide an "upper bound" for the effects of comprehensive teacher induction by mimicking the effect of a perfectly implemented intervention. Even use of this most favorable sample, however, shows that the results (row seven) are insignificantly different from zero.

Nonexperimental Analyses

The second research question is whether specific components of teacher induction, regardless of assignment to treatment and control groups, affect student achievement. To answer this, we replace the variable indicating assignment to the treatment or control group with one or more measures of the comprehensiveness or intensity of induction support. We interpret the results with caution because the analyses are correlational and not causal: a high level of induction services might be obtained if an assertive, motivated teacher, who would have otherwise achieved positive outcomes, spends extra time with a mentor by taking the initiative to seek extra help. The estimate of the effect of induction services on outcomes could be spurious because it might confound the true (causal) impact of mentoring with the effect of the teacher's own ability or motivation.

The initial results—shown in columns one (math) and two (reading) of table 14.3—show that some but not all of the induction measures are positively associated with student outcomes. We generated the results by replacing the indicator of assignment to treatment with a measure of induction support. The strongest associations are with content-oriented measures. Estimates for meeting with a literacy or math coach and receiving guidance in math content are positive and significant for math scores; receiving guidance on literacy content is positive and marginally significant for reading scores. Whether the beginning teacher worked with a study group is positively related to math scores with marginal significance, and receiving feedback on teaching is positive and significant for both subjects.

Mere assignment to a mentor is not significantly related to test score outcomes in either subject. Similarly, the amount of time spent in mentoring sessions, the amount of time the mentor spent observing the teacher, or whether the beginning teacher observed others teaching is not significantly related to test score outcomes.

We obtain similar results if we restrict the sample to the treatment group and make use strictly of variation among treatment teachers within tested district-grade combinations (columns three and four). The smaller sample size of the models causes larger standard errors, but the overall pattern of statistical significance does not change much. (In an alternate model using a sample composed only of teachers in control districts, more of the induction measures are statistically significant at the 5 percent level.)

As before, the content-oriented measures—meeting with a subject coach, receiving guidance in math content, and receiving guidance in literacy content—are all positive and significant for at least one subject, although coaching is now significant for reading instead of for math. The estimate for working with a study group is positive, with marginal significance for math but not for reading. Neither measure of time spent in mentoring is significant. The estimates for receiving feedback have shrunk compared to models that include all districts and are only marginally significant for math and not significant for reading. The estimate of whether the beginning teacher observes others teaching is negative and significant.

The most striking result from columns three and four is that assignment to a mentor is negative and marginally significant for math and strongly positive for reading, but these results are driven by a small number of teachers. Given that an average of 95 percent of treatment teachers received assigned mentors, most district-grade combinations consist of a set of teachers in which everyone or no one received an assigned mentor. The estimates rest on a few district-grades in which at least one teacher was not assigned to a mentor and at least one teacher was assigned to a mentor. As a result, the model is sensitive to outliers and to the specification of the control

Table 14.3. Association between Beginning Teaching (BT) Support and Test Scores

| | Induction Measures Entered Individually | | | | | | Induction Measures Entered Jointly | | | |
| | All Districts | | Treatment Districts | | All Districts | | All Districts | | All Districts | |
	(1) Math	(2) Reading	(3) Math	(4) Reading	(5) Math	(6) Reading	(7) Math	(8) Reading	(9) Math	(10) Reading
Types of Teacher Induction										
BT was assigned a mentor	-2.22	4.52	-19.57+	31.65-	-9.97	-1.32	-9.15	-1.15	-10.61	-1.97
	(6.69)	(6.02)	(10.85)	(13.01)	(6.63)	(7.30)	(6.72)	(7.51)	(6.74)	(7.08)
BT met with a literacy or math coach	13.94-	8.69	3.96	19.23-	12.89-	13.02-	12.41-	13.00-	12.27-	11.42+
	(6.17)	(5.62)	(8.62)	(8.94)	(5.23)	(5.78)	(5.26)	(5.76)	(5.15)	(5.91)
BT received guidance in math content	16.96*		22.04*		16.34*		17.62*		13.34*	
	(4.77)		(5.45)		(4.48)		(4.51)		(4.93)	
BT received guidance in literacy content		8.71+		19.59*		9.73+		9.87+		8.35
		(4.62)		(6.72)		(5.25)		(5.36)		(5.32)
BT worked with a study group	8.22+	1.57	14.52+	13.71	6.93	0.01	7.04	0.04	4.63	-2.44
	(4.96)	(5.27)	(7.57)	(8.94)	(4.57)	(4.85)	(4.53)	(4.82)	(4.89)	(5.07)
BT observed others teaching	-6.19	-8.10	-16.81-	-18.50-	-12.35-	-13.41	-11.84-	-13.32-	-13.82*	-14.55-
	(5.44)	(5.39)	(6.59)	(9.14)	(5.18)	(5.57)	(5.23)	(5.53)	(5.14)	(5.64)

Intensity of Teacher Induction

	(1)	(2)	(3)	(4)	(5)	(6)	(7)	(8)	(9)	(10)
Time BT spent in mentoring sessions (hours per week)	0.28 (0.97)	0.45 (0.84)	0.16 (1.55)	0.91 (1.77)	−0.83 (1.09)	−0.16 (0.94)				
Time mentor spent observing the teacher (hours per week)	−4.76 (5.09)	−3.92 (4.62)	−6.15 (7.67)	−9.14 (8.28)						
BT received feedback on teaching (number of times)	2.32* (0.81)	1.64− (0.79)	2.07+ (1.13)	1.33 (1.12)					1.85− (0.83)	1.56+ (0.87)
Sample Size										
Students	3,440	3,770	1,870	2,160	3,340	3,670	3,340	3,670	3,310	3,640
Teachers	200	210	110	120	190	210	190	210	190	210

Notes: Columns one through four show coefficients from individual regression models for each measure of induction support. Each cell in the table in these columns is taken from a different model. Columns five through ten show coefficients from a model in which the measures of induction support are entered jointly. Each column is taken from a different model.

For columns one through four, sample sizes vary across induction variables; modal sample sizes are presented. Sample sizes have been rounded to the nearest ten.

BT = Beginning Teacher.

Standard errors in parentheses.

Source: Mathematica analysis of data from 2004–2005 and 2005–2006 provided by participating school districts; MPR Teacher Background Survey administered in 2005–2006 and First and Second Induction Activities Surveys administered in fall/winter 2005–2006 and spring 2006 to all study teachers.

+Significant at the 10 percent level.

−Significant at the 5 percent level.

*Significant at the 1 percent level.

variables and therefore demands care in interpreting the results, especially in the context of the other columns in table 14.3.

With the coefficient estimates in columns one through four based on regressions that control for measures of induction support one at a time, the coefficients absorb the effect of other induction measures correlated with the measure in the model. For example, if teachers who work with a study group also tend to meet with a subject coach, then the measured effect of working with a study group reflects in part the effect of meeting with a coach. To circumvent this problem, we also estimated models in which the induction measures were entered jointly.

We continued to control for pretest, student demographic characteristics, and teacher characteristics. Columns five through ten of table 14.3 present the results. We used three models, each for math and reading: one model includes the six measures of types of teacher induction (columns five and six), a second model includes these measures plus the time spent in mentoring as an additional control variable measuring the intensity of induction services (columns seven and eight), and a third model replaces time spent in mentoring with the frequency of feedback as a measure of intensity (columns nine and ten).

When the measures of induction comprehensiveness are entered jointly into the model without a separate control for teacher intensity (columns five and six), the results are similar to the results from columns one through four, models in which the measures are entered one at a time. As with the earlier results, content-oriented measures are associated with positive outcomes for students. Meeting with a subject coach and receiving guidance in math content are positively and significantly related to test scores. Receiving guidance in literacy content is positively related to reading test scores with marginal significance. As with other treatment teacher-only results, the estimate for observing others teaching is negative and significant. Working with a study group and the assignment of a mentor are not related to test scores.

The time spent in mentoring sessions is statistically insignificant when included in a model that controls for types of induction (columns seven and eight), paralleling results from columns one through four in which time spent in mentoring sessions was included in models without controls for other induction measures. The specification in columns seven and eight asks whether additional mentoring time is associated with improved outcomes for teachers if they were to receive the same mix of induction services (by controlling statistically for the types of induction support received). The coefficient measures reported in columns seven and eight suggest that additional mentoring time has no effect. The estimates for the types of induction services change little from columns five and six.

The final set of results (columns nine and ten) controls for intensity of teacher induction by using the frequency with which the teacher received feedback rather than time spent in mentoring sessions. In these models, the effect of feedback on teaching is positive and significant for math and positive and marginally significant for reading. The results also illustrate the positive correlations among three induction support measures: meeting with a math or literacy coach, receiving guidance in math or literacy content, and receiving feedback on teaching. The coach and content measures shrink in magnitude with inclusion of the feedback measure.

These nonexperimental results suggest that content-oriented induction measures—meeting with a math or literacy coach, receiving guidance in subject content (especially math), and receiving feedback on teaching—are positively associated with improved student test scores. On the other hand, there is no relationship between student test score outcomes and assignment of a mentor, time spent with that mentor, or time the mentor spent observing the beginning teacher. Group activities such as working with a study group or observing others teaching do not show robustly positive results.

One interpretation of the results is that mentoring programs are not useful in raising student test scores unless a program focuses on content or feedback. However, policy makers must exercise care in applying this or any causal interpretation to the nonexperimental results. An alternative explanation holds that motivated teachers sought out the extra help. On the other hand, a negative selection effect may cause the measure of whether a teacher observed others teaching to be negative and significant in most model specifications. It is possible that struggling teachers are asked to observe other teachers, not that the act of observing other teachers causes teachers to achieve less success.

Focus Group Perspectives

The focus groups provided an opportunity to explore teachers' perceptions of the nature and usefulness of the supports they received, perhaps helping to explain why comprehensive teacher induction did not affect student achievement in the first year. One reason may have been the need for immediate supports to address "survival" needs. Often, teachers sought support from colleagues in neighboring classrooms or in grade-level group meetings rather than from their assigned mentors. At least one treatment teacher in each focus group reported that the study mentors were more difficult to access and unable to respond as quickly to teacher requests as colleagues and mentors who worked in their buildings full time.

Treatment and control teachers also agreed on the importance of a mentor who taught the same grade or subject. At least one treatment teacher in each focus group reported that study mentors were not as familiar with the teacher's subject or grade level as they would have liked. Teachers reported that they worked with mentors who taught the same grade or subject, but among treatment teachers, such mentors were often a second mentor rather than the mentor provided as part of the treatment. The 12:1 ratio of teachers to mentors made it unfeasible to match mentors and teachers by grade and subject for all beginning teachers.

Comprehensive induction services may have provided teachers with more than they were able to absorb in their first year of teaching. Teachers in the treatment group reported that they were overwhelmed by noninstructional school duties and by students who needed extra attention outside instructional time and that such demands cut into the time available for planned discussions. At least one treatment teacher in each focus group said that the time demands of several mentors and various professional development sessions were overwhelming, thereby reducing the amount of preparation time. In many cases, focus group participants reported that the study's professional development sessions were redundant with district in-service sessions and held at inconvenient times and locations.

Finally, the opportunities to effect change during a teacher's first year may be limited. Teachers may not have been able to change practices enough in the course of the first year in ways that would have resulted in statistically significant improvements in student performance. The majority of teachers in the focus groups discussed the challenges of implementing suggested changes to their practices during the first year.

CONCLUSION

A randomized controlled trial of comprehensive teacher induction shows that teachers in treatment schools did not raise student test scores any more than did their counterparts who taught in the same districts and grades in control schools and who received the services typically provided. This result is robust to changes in specification and sample. It is important to remember that the study did not measure the effect of comprehensive support relative to no support. Rather, control teachers received a package of services from a variety of sources that, while quantitatively significantly less than treatment teachers, provided some resources to help them navigate their first year. As summarized in the top panel of table 14.1, although the treatment teachers spent an average of one hour and fifty-two minutes with their mentors, control teachers averaged one hour and twenty-five minutes with their mentors (weighting the results by students in the sample).

Additional, nonexperimental analyses of the available data show that some components of teacher induction are correlated with success in raising student test scores, including meeting with a literacy or math coach and receiving guidance in literacy or math content. Student achievement is not correlated with the total time spent in mentoring sessions, but it is correlated with the frequency with which the teacher received feedback on teaching. Though suggestive of the possibility that mentoring focused on guidance and feedback makes productive use of mentoring time, the results are correlational and not causal; teachers who were more successful with raising student test scores may have been more likely to seek out extra help.

In focus groups, teachers suggested that program mentors who are not in the school building full-time may not be as effective as informal mentors who are on site, that the volume of mentoring and professional development received in the comprehensive induction programs may have been distracting, and that teachers may not have had sufficient time to put to good use the suggestions they received. Consequently, the level of induction services received by the control group may have been sufficient, even though the services were less structured and less intense. Practitioners who design teacher induction programs may wish to consider the results from the nonexperimental analysis and focus groups.

Because the level of teacher supports offered by schools in the study ranged from business-as-usual levels in the control group to a more intense and structured supplemental program of comprehensive teacher induction in the treatment group, our results do not suggest that schools without comprehensive teacher induction programs should decrease the current level of mentoring and professional development provided to new teachers. Our results do, however, caution school districts and state legislatures seeking to improve outcomes for high-poverty schools that investment in an expensive program of comprehensive teacher induction is unlikely to show an impact on student achievement after one year.

For researchers, the study demonstrates the importance of random assignment in creating treatment and control groups. By relying on a purely exogenous source to determine which teachers received treatment, we are able to infer a causal effect of a program of comprehensive teacher induction on student achievement after one year, generating findings that differed from some earlier research. In future work, we will test for delayed impacts of teacher induction by using data from later years of the study to repeat experimental and nonexperimental analyses.

REFERENCES

Bloom, H., J. M. Bos, and S. W. Lee. 1999. Using cluster random assignment to measure program impacts: Statistical implications for the evaluation of education programs. *Evaluation Review* 23(4):445–69.

California Commission on Teacher Credentialing. 1997. *California's standards for the teaching profession*. Sacramento: California Commission on Teacher Credentialing.

Danielson, C. 1996. *Enhancing professional practice: A framework for teaching*. Alexandria, VA: Association for Supervision and Curriculum Development.

Glazerman, S., S. Dolfin, M. Bleeker, A. Johnson, E. Isenberg, J. Lugo-Gil, M. Grider, and E. Britton. 2008. *Impacts of comprehensive teacher induction: Results from the first year of a randomized controlled study* (NCEE 2009-4034). Washington, DC: National Center for Educational Evaluation and Regional Assistance, Institute of Education Sciences, U.S. Department of Education.

Huber, P. J. 1967. The behavior of maximum likelihood estimates under nonstandard conditions. In *Proceedings of the fifth Berkeley symposium on mathematical statistics and probability*, vol. 1, eds. L. M. LeCam and J. Neyman, 221–33. Berkeley: University of California Press.

New Teacher Center. 2002. *Continuum of teacher development*. Santa Cruz, CA: New Teacher Center.

Rockoff, J. 2008. *Does mentoring reduce turnover and improve skills of new employees? Evidence from teachers in New York City*. National Bureau of Economic Research. Retrieved June 3, 2009, from http://www.nber.org/papers/w13868.

Smith, T. M., and R. M. Ingersoll. 2004. What are the effects of induction and mentoring on beginning teacher turnover? *American Educational Research Journal* 41(3):681–714.

Thompson, M., P. Paek, L. Goe, and E. Ponte. 2005. *The impact of new teacher induction on teacher practices and student learning*. Paper presented at the annual meeting of the American Educational Research Association, Montreal.

———. 2004. *Study of the impact of the California formative assessment and support system for teachers: Relationship of BTSA/CFASST engagement and student achievement*. Princeton, NJ: Educational Testing Service.

White, H. 1980. A heteroskedasticity-consistent covariance matrix estimator and a direct test for heteroskedasticity. *Econometrica* 48:817–30.

NOTE

1. Isenberg, Glazerman, Johnson, Dolfin, and Bleeker: Mathematica Policy Research, Inc., P.O. Box 2393, Princeton, NJ 08543-2393. Julieta Lugo-Gil, Mary Grider, Edward Britton, Patricia Nemeth, Linda Mendenko, and Melanie Ali made important contributions to the study.

15

An Investigation of the Achievement Effects of Mentoring

A Step into Uncharted Territory

Leslie Huling, Texas State University System
Virginia Resta, Texas State University–San Marcos

In 2004 the Center for Research, Evaluation and Advancement of Teacher Education (CREATE) launched a large-scale teacher induction study to examine the segment of the staffing pipeline that connects preservice teacher education with school district employers. As teacher induction researchers, we were immediately intrigued with the possibilities when approached by CREATE to serve as principal investigators for this study. It provided ready access to multiple school districts and the opportunity to gather data on both teacher and student performance.

The questions guiding this study were grounded in some of the complexities that have confounded teacher induction research for decades. Attempts to measure the impact of induction programs on novice teachers typically have not accounted for the fact that novice teachers within a program frequently have very different mentoring experiences from one another, depending upon how their individual mentors carried out their mentoring duties (Evans-Andris, Kyle, and Carini, 2006; Wang and Odell, 2003). What was needed were ways to identify the mentoring experiences of each individual novice teacher in substantial detail. In addition, there were no tools available to monitor or track the mentor program infrastructure and its relationship to the actual delivery of mentoring services (Ingersoll and Kralik, 2004; Nielsen, Barry, and Addison, 2007; Wang, Odell, and Schwille, 2008; Wilkins and Clift, 2007; Wong, 2004).

Another factor was the need to examine the combined and interrelated effects of mentor support in combination with, and separate from, the overall workplace ecology. For example, some schools, for a combination of reasons, are considered to be nurturing environments for novice teachers while others are exceptionally challenging environments. Mentor support is one factor that affects novice teacher performance and retention, but school workplace conditions also have a strong impact on novice teacher success and retention (Ingersoll and Kralik, 2004; Ingersoll and Smith, 2003; Wang, Odell, and Schwille, 2008). Workplace ecology, similar to school climate or culture, is the combination of factors that influence how employees feel about their workplace and the ways they do and do not feel that it is an appropriate fit for them. It includes such factors as faculty collegiality, school leadership, building condition and maintenance, parental involvement, and neighborhood safety. In the past induction researchers have not had the tools to look at mentoring support independent from workplace ecology.

Finally, while induction programs have the goal of retaining novice teachers (a relatively straightforward process to track) these programs also aspire to improve the teaching effectiveness (and in turn, the student achievement) of novice teachers. This is a much more difficult link to establish. Policy makers are quick to ask for "proof" that resources invested in induction pay off in terms of student achievement, causing program developers and researchers alike to grapple with the challenge of how such a link may be established in a defensible manner (Ingersoll and Kralik, 2004).

Recognizing the above challenges, we attempted to design tools that could be used to investigate the array of factors discussed above and to allow them to be examined somewhat independently from one another. The larger study, titled *The Relationship of Mentor Support to Novice Teacher Retention and Student Achievement Study*, worked toward the following goals:

1. Clarify and demonstrate, in great detail, what mentor support and mentor program infrastructure entails;
2. Investigate the link between mentor program infrastructure, mentor support, and novice teacher retention;
3. Explore and document workplace ecology as a factor that is highly influential on teacher retention and is separate from, but related to, mentor support;
4. Respond to growing policy maker interests in understanding the effects of mentor support on student achievement and help shape the direction of how such research is approached in the future.

The findings in relation to goals one, two, and three were both compelling and straightforward. A brief summary of these findings is provided in the following section. From the onset, however, the findings in relation to goal four were not easy to interpret. This goal is important in shaping not only how induction researchers approach the effects of mentoring on student achievement but also how teacher performance is defined for the purposes of comparison and, perhaps, compensation. Therefore, goal four is the primary focus of this chapter.

METHODOLOGY

The CREATE study involved four universities and twelve Texas school districts (Huling and Resta, 2007; Huling, Yeargain, and Resta, 2008; Resta and Huling, 2008). We collected data from 451 novice teachers who began their teaching careers in 2005–2006 and from their mentor teachers. We also collected and analyzed teacher retention data and student achievement data.

The interview and survey instruments were developed over a two-year time period beginning in the fall of 2004. Following an examination of readily available instruments used in previous teacher induction studies, we ultimately decided that none were able to address the broad range of research questions in need of exploration and that we needed to develop new instruments.

Through a series of activities involving a panel of researchers, master mentor teachers, and research staff from CREATE, we developed an interview protocol and a survey. The Novice Teacher Interview contained questions on demographics (seventeen items), mentor support (seventeen items), and workplace ecology (twelve items). The Mentor Teacher Survey asked about demographics (eight items) and mentor program infrastructure (twenty items). Instrument development and refinement followed the guidelines as delineated in the Standards for Educational and Psychological Testing published by the American Educational Research Association (AERA), American Psychological Association (APA), and the National Council on Measurement in Education (NCME).

Participants in the Novice Teacher Induction Program (operated by seven universities in the Texas State University System) pilot tested the instruments in spring 2005. The researchers who led the instrument-development team trained interviewers, who then interviewed sixty-five first-year teachers. In addition, thirty-two mentors piloted the first draft of the surveys. Based upon feedback from the interviewers and pilot participants, we made minor revisions in order to improve the clarity of a few items. In addition, we examined the psychometric properties of each instrument for evidence of validity (content and construct) and internal consistency reliability under the direction of a recognized statistical and psychometrics consultant. Results of confirmatory factor analysis provided theoretical support for the underlying factor structure of both scales.

Data Collection

CREATE staff trained teams of interviewers to conduct the novice teacher interview and reached a satisfactory level of interrater reliability (75 percent) in March 2006. In late April and early May (2006), interviews were conducted with 451 first-year teachers from twelve school districts and 140 campuses at their respective schools. The interview sample consisted of 165 elementary teachers, 183 middle school teachers, and 103 high school teachers. Teachers selected for the study met the following conditions: (a) were completing their first year of teaching; (b) were assigned a mentor; (c) had taught in a grade level assessed by the Texas Assessment of Knowledge and Skills (TAKS). Mentors assigned to assist the first-year teachers completed descriptive surveys about the structure of the induction programs in their school and district.

Beginning in summer 2006, classroom mean scale scores and pass rates from the spring 2006 administration of the Texas Assessment of Knowledge and Skills (TAKS) were collected for each participating novice teacher and from every other teacher at the same campus who administered the same TAKS exam. In fall 2006, teacher retention data were collected. Year two achievement data and teacher retention data were collected again in fall 2007.

Data Analysis

Each of the measures for infrastructure, mentor support, and workplace ecology yielded a total score that was the sum of all item scores combined. Retention data were sorted into teachers retained in the same district in which they taught the previous year or teachers not retained in that district. Means on each study measure were compared among various subgroups of participants and correlations were performed to identify significant relationships between and among study measures and district retention. When significant differences were identified, we performed an analysis of variance (ANOVA) to further examine the between-group differences among subgroups such as elementary, middle, and high school teachers, teacher preparation pathways, quartiles for mentor support, etc.

RETENTION, INFRASTRUCTURE, MENTOR
SUPPORT AND WORKPLACE ECOLOGY

Given that the primary focus of this chapter is on the student achievement effects related to mentoring programs, study findings not related to achievement will be only briefly highlighted. A more comprehensive discussion of these particular findings is available in the 2007 CREATE Teacher Induction Study Phase II Report (Huling and Resta, 2007).

Retention

Seventy-seven percent of the novice teachers were retained in the same district and only 4.2 percent of these teachers changed campuses within the district. Elementary novice teachers were retained at a slightly higher rate (79 percent) than those at middle school (76.5 percent) and high school (74.7 percent). Novice teachers who rated their relationship with the mentor as "indifferent" left the district at twice the rate (40 percent) of those who rated their relationship as "close" (20.8 percent). In addition, novice teachers who perceived the administrator's supervision focus to be that of "weeding out" weak novice teachers left the district at three times the rate (51.6 percent) of those who perceived the focus to be on "providing substantial and constructive feedback" (15.79 percent).

Infrastructure and Mentor Support

We found a statistically significant relationship (<0.01) between mentor program infrastructure and the level of mentor support received by novice teachers. We also found a statistically significant relationship (<0.01) between mentor program infrastructure and the district retention of novice teachers. Item analyses indicated that the mentor program infrastructure features that factored most heavily in novice teacher retention related to the mentor stipend, requirements for documentation of mentor/mentee work, and the availability of a common planning period. There was also a statistically significant relationship (<0.05) between mentor support and the retention of novice teachers within the district.

Item analyses reveal that the mentor support components figuring most strongly in novice teacher retention included the frequency of interaction with the mentor, the perceived value of mentor support, and participation in novice teacher meetings beyond orientation. There was also a statistically significant relationship between mentor support and workplace ecology (<0.01). Most novice teachers reported receiving mentor support prior to the opening of school and reported that their mentor helped them with a wide variety of instructional and classroom managerial issues.

Mentors reported a clear understanding of who was coordinating the mentor program, and they perceived principals to have a realistic view of novice teacher development and to be supportive of their role in guiding novice teachers. At the same time, they reported only minimal release time to work with novice teachers and little knowledge about program evaluation results or how results were used for program refinement. Mentors in high schools were less likely than those in elementary and middle schools to have a common planning period for mentors with novices. In addition, elementary novice teachers used more modes of communication with their mentors and reported a slightly closer relationship with their mentors than novice teachers in middle and high schools.

Workplace Ecology

We found a statistically significant relationship between workplace ecology and novice teacher retention within the district (<0.01). Item analyses showed that the focus and supervision of the administrative team, discipline support, and student behavior were the most influential factors. High school teachers reported more support from department chairs than other administrators; elementary teachers reported more support and supervision from building administrators. Overall, novice teachers reported a high degree of faculty collegiality at the schools. They reported receiving a relatively low degree of lesson plan support, but their greatest concerns were related to the prior academic preparation of their students and about the level and type of parental involvement. High school novice teachers reported being less concerned about student discipline issues than teachers in elementary and middle schools.

Study Measures Interactions

The findings related to program infrastructure, mentor support, workplace ecology, and teacher retention were quite dramatic. The more highly structured the induction program, the more mentor support was provided to the novice teacher and the greater the likelihood that the district would retain the novice teacher for a second year of teaching. Stated another way, the data indicate that a district's investment in the induction program pays off in terms of novice teacher retention.

Workplace ecology also had an effect on novice teacher retention. The more positive the novice teacher's perception was of the workplace ecology, the greater likelihood that the novice teacher would be retained. This finding is in no way surprising because many of the aspects of a collegial environment not only contributed to the novice teacher's positive perception of the workplace but also very likely contributed to the support provided to the novice, which in turn contributed to retention. Working with the student achievement data, however, was not nearly as straightforward.

STUDENT ACHIEVEMENT: THE GORILLA IN THE ROOM

Over the past decade policy makers have increasingly asked for evidence that resources invested in teacher induction and mentoring programs translate into increased achievement for the students of novice teachers. Most policy makers suggest that the benchmark for such an investigation be the state standards on the required state standardized achievement tests. This one-dimensional comparison, however, does little to account for a whole host of school and student characteristics that influence student performance, nor does it account for the fact that it is unrealistic to expect the novice teacher to perform like a veteran teacher.

A Hypothetical Example

To make this point, let us consider four approaches to documenting a teacher's impact on students' test scores through a hypothetical example of Ms. Smith, a first-year middle school math teacher, shown in figure 15.1.

We contend that each approach provides additional, important insight about Ms. Smith's performance. In Approach A, one would deduce that Ms. Smith is performing poorly—below the state mean and below the state standard. In Approach B, it appears that Ms. Smith teaches in a district that performs below the state average but meets the state standard. Ms. Smith

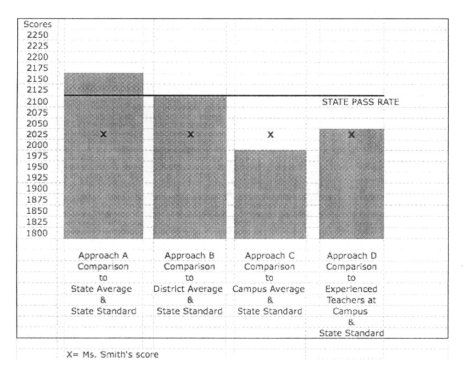

Figure 15.1. Multiple ways of viewing teacher performance: a hypothetical case (Ms. Smith).

performs below the district average. The picture shifts with Approach C, where Ms. Smith is compared to her campus's average test scores. The campus is performing below the district average, but Ms. Smith is performing above the campus average. Of the three approaches, Approach C provides the most information, but still additional information is possible and desirable, especially in terms of researching the student achievement effects of mentoring. Thus we turn to Approach D.

In our hypothetical example, Ms. Smith teaches at a campus that has an unusually large number of first-year teachers, due to a high teacher turnover rate at the campus. This large percentage of first-year teachers, combined with other factors related to the high teacher turnover rate, likely explains why the campus performance is below the district performance. While Ms. Smith is performing better than the campus average, the campus average is skewed because of the large number of inexperienced teachers. In Approach D, we contend that we see the most accurate picture of all. Because the campus has a large number of inexperienced teachers, Ms. Smith performs above the campus average. Her performance is, in fact, comparable to that of the experienced teachers at her campus. We have named this comparison between a novice teacher's performance and that of the experienced teachers at the same campus as "Gap."

THE CONCEPT OF GAP

The premise underlying Gap is that as teachers gain experience, they will become more instructionally effective, and this improvement will translate into increased student achievement. Therefore, it is expected that a Gap would exist between the achievement scores of students taught by experienced teachers when compared with achievement of students taught by novice teachers. To our knowledge, the concept of Gap has not been explored empirically in teacher induction research and the supposition has not been tested prior to this study. We identified and explored the existence of Gap by comparing the test scores of novice teachers with those of experienced colleagues at their same campus, and we also examined factors that might influence Gap. The concept of Gap made it possible to identify "high-performing" novice teachers who, in their first year of teaching, had students who performed as well as or better than those of experienced teachers at the same campus.

Procedures for Measuring Gap

In the CREATE Teacher Induction Study, the student achievement unit of analysis was the classroom and the TAKS, the state-required standardized achievement test. TAKS results yielded both a scale score and a pass rate, based upon the state-established performance standards. We collected classroom scale scores and pass rates for each novice teacher and each experienced teacher who taught the same grade level and subject area at the same campus. The benchmark against which to compare the novice teacher's performance was the average of the scores of all teachers at the same campus with more than one year of experience. The difference between the novice teacher's classroom score and the "benchmark" was the Gap score.

In each TAKS-assessed subject area taught by the novice teacher, the novice teacher had four scores—the actual scale score and pass rate and the scale-score Gap and the pass-rate Gap. Novice teacher Gap scores are generated by subtracting the campus average score from the novice teacher's scores. Using this calculation method, a negative Gap score indicates that the novice teacher scored lower than comparison teachers at the same campus, and a positive Gap score indicates that the novice teacher's students scored higher than those of the comparison teachers at the same campus. The concept of Gap, in a sense, provides a different lens through which to view student achievement, and it can generate new insights about novice teacher performance across campuses.

An Example Using Actual Study Data

For demonstration purposes, let us consider the scores from two actual novice teachers in the CREATE data set who were on two different campuses, each of which had six comparison teachers who were not first-year teachers as shown in table 15.1 below.

When considering only the scale scores and pass rates, it appears then that Teachers 1 and 2 are highly similar (scale scores of 2,147 and 2,144; pass rates of 60 percent and 63 percent). However, when factoring Gap into the picture, the importance of context becomes apparent. Students, as a group, at Campus A have higher student achievement than those at Campus B. By using the "Gap lens," it then becomes evident that the students of Teacher 2, in comparison to the students of the experienced teachers at the campus, are performing better than the students of Teacher 1. To the degree that student achievement is the result of teacher performance, Teacher 2 is presumably performing better than Teacher 1.

Table 15.1. Sample Data of Two Novice Teachers in the CREATE

Teacher	Campus	Grade	#CTs	Campus Avg. SS	Campus Avg. PR	NT SS	NT PR	GAP SS	GAP PR
1	A	4	6	2,266.17	85%	2,147	60%	–119.17	–25%
2	B	4	6	2,199.17	76.67%	2,144	63%	–55.17	–13.67%

FINDINGS RELATED TO GAP

Table 15.2 provides data on the total study sample and shows the average scores of novice teachers and those of comparison teachers at their same campuses.

Table 15.2.   Total Sample Comparisons: Scale Score, Pass Rate, and Gaps

	Comparison Teachers	Novice Teachers	Novice Teacher Gap
English/Lang. Arts			
N	847	240	
Pass Rate Mean	81.29	78.49	−2.8
Pass Rate SD	20.52	15.53	22.38
Scale Score Mean	2,216.77	2,202.98	−13.79
Scale Score SD	71.24	77.54	67.23
Writing			
N	236	78	
Pass Rate Mean	96.8	88.69	−8.14
Pass Rate SD	58.92	9.05	61.04
Scale Score Mean	2,322.42	2,286.55	−35.86
Scale Score SD	78.94	80.08	76.44
Math			
N	723	217	
Pass Rate Mean	75.8	66.5	−9.3
Pass Rate SD	40.41	21.76	40.07
Scale Score Mean	2,207.6	2,174.13	−33.47
Scale Score SD	110.66	100.65	98.63
Social Studies			
N	97	27	
Pass Rate Mean	79.63	69.96	−9.66
Pass Rate SD	12.88	23.99	22.91
Scale Score Mean	2,252.16	2,175.37	−76.79
Scale Score SD	115.04	125.37	144.02
Science			
N	242	67	
Pass Rate Mean	60.29	54.85	−5.44
Pass Rate SD	22.98	23.61	18.43
Scale Score Mean	2,120.85	2,098.45	−22.4
Scale Score SD	98.53	110.27	89.15

It is easier to visualize these Gap phenomena when data are displayed graphically as is shown in figures 15.2 and 15.3. Notice that the shapes of the novice teacher and comparison teacher data in each Gap chart are strikingly similar. Figure 15.3 gives the clearest picture of how novice teacher pass rates typically trail the pass rate of experienced teachers by approximately 5 to 10 percent.

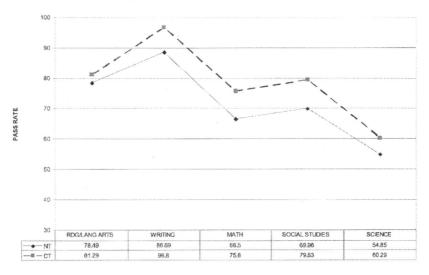

GAP COMPARISONS ALL GRADES BY SUBJECT

	RDG/LANG ARTS	WRITING	MATH	SOCIAL STUDIES	SCIENCE
NT	78.49	86.69	66.5	69.96	54.85
CT	81.29	96.8	75.8	79.53	60.29

NT= Novice Teacher; CT=Comparison Teachers

Figure 15.2. Gap comparisons: percent meeting standard (pass rate), means grades.

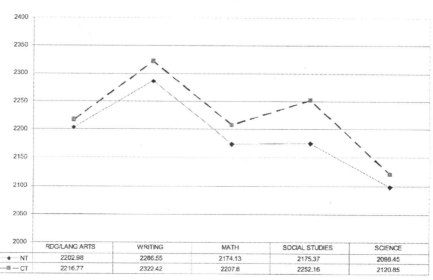

GAP COMPARISONS ALL GRADES

	RDG/LANG ARTS	WRITING	MATH	SOCIAL STUDIES	SCIENCE
NT	2202.98	2286.55	2174.13	2175.37	2098.45
CT	2216.77	2322.42	2207.6	2252.16	2120.85

NT= Novice Teacher; CT=Comparison Teachers

Figure 15.3. Gap comparisons: scale score means, all grades.

Additional insights can be gained by looking at individual subjects with teachers grouped by grade-level bands. This particular type of analysis can be considered using either pass rates or scale scores. For purposes of demonstration, consider the following set of graphs that depict scale scores.

The scale score data reflected in figures 15.4, 15.5, 15.6, and 15.7 naturally reflect many of the same trends shown above, namely that Gap exists across all subject areas and grade levels, suggesting that teacher performance improves with experience. However, a few additional observations are noteworthy. In Reading/Language Arts it should be noted that the Gap is relatively small, possibly indicating the preparation programs are doing well in preparing teachers to teach Language Arts. The Gap in Social Studies is approximately one hundred points in middle school and approximately sixty points in high school. Though the sample sizes are small, this is the largest scale score Gap of any subject and can provide some direction for both preparation programs and mentor support. Also, Science scale scores, and to a slightly lesser degree Math scale scores, in comparison to other subjects are noticeably low.

Factors That Potentially Influence Gap

Because Gap is a new concept, there is no prior research available upon which to predict factors that might influence Gap, which led us to develop and test our own hypotheses. We anticipated that a novice teacher's student achievement would be lower than that of the experienced teachers at the same campus, but we were interested in seeing whether a higher degree of mentor support resulted in a smaller Gap than the situations in which the novice received a lower degree of mentor support, and whether Gap would diminish more between years one and two for teachers who received greater mentor support than those who received less mentor support. We also were interested in whether Gaps were smaller in situations where the novice teacher had a more positive perception of workplace ecology, and whether the type of teacher preparation program (preparation pathway) influenced Gap.

Bearing in mind that the primary contributor to Gap is the lack of teaching experience, it is also interesting to speculate what other factors such as mentor support, workplace ecology, or teacher preparation experiences might also influence Gap. To explore these questions, correlations involving various factors were performed first on "scale score gaps" (the difference between the novice teacher's scale score and the campus average scale score for all non-first-year teachers in the same grade level/subject area) and then on "pass rate gaps" (the difference between the novice teacher's pass rate and the campus average pass rate for all non-first-year teachers in the same grade level/subject area).

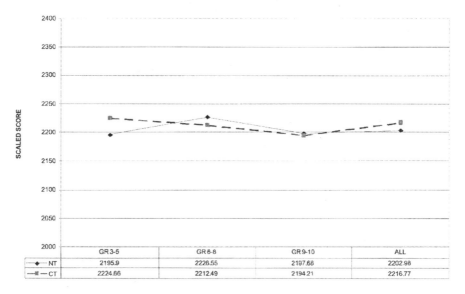

READING/LANG ARTS GAP COMPARISONS

	GR 3-5	GR 6-8	GR 9-10	ALL
NT	2195.9	2226.55	2197.68	2202.98
CT	2224.66	2212.49	2194.21	2216.77

NT= Novice Teacher; CT=Comparison Teachers

Figure 15.4.   Gap comparisons: reading/ELA scale score means.

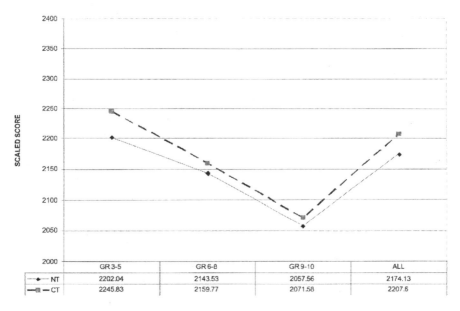

MATH GAP COMPARISONS

	GR 3-5	GR 6-8	GR 9-10	ALL
NT	2202.04	2143.53	2057.56	2174.13
CT	2245.83	2159.77	2071.58	2207.5

NT= Novice Teacher; CT=Comparison Teachers

Figure 15.5.   Gap comparisons: math scale score means.

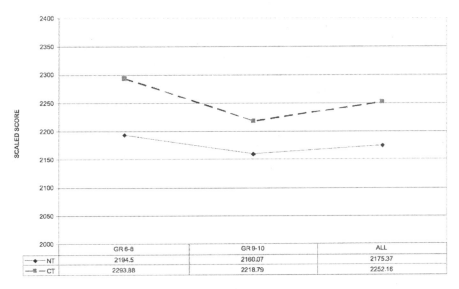

SOCIAL STUDIES GAP COMPARISONS

	GR 6-8	GR 9-10	ALL
NT	2194.5	2160.07	2175.37
CT	2293.88	2218.79	2252.16

NT= Novice Teacher; CT=Comparison Teachers

Figure 15.6.   Gap comparisons: social studies scale score means.

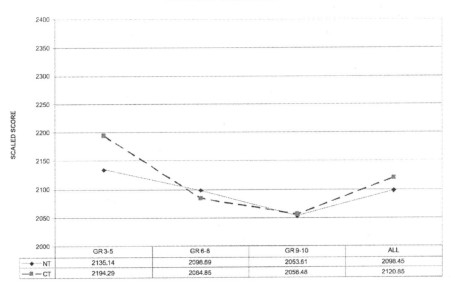

SCIENCE GAP COMPARISONS

	GR 3-5	GR 6-8	GR 9-10	ALL
NT	2135.14	2098.89	2053.61	2098.45
CT	2194.29	2084.85	2056.48	2120.85

NT= Novice Teacher; CT=Comparison Teachers

Figure 15.7.   Gap comparisons: science scale score means.

Table 15.3 indicates that in regard to scale score gaps there were no significant relationships involving mentor support, workplace ecology, or total interview score (the combination of the two dimensions). These findings might indicate that Gap scores are more useful for observing and describing the phenomena of novice teacher performance in relation to experienced teacher performance than for attributing causality to various factors.

High-Performing Novice Teachers

For purposes of this study, any novice teachers who had a Gap score of 0 (indicating that their students performed the same as those of experienced teachers at the campus) or a positive Gap score (indicating that their students outperformed those of the campus teachers) were labeled "high-performing novice teachers." Table 15.4 shows the number and percentage of "high-performing" novice teachers in each subject area at each level.

The preparation pathways of "high-performing" novice teachers were also of interest. Table 15.5 displays the number and percent of novice teachers whose classes performed as well or better than the classes of their more experienced colleagues at the same campuses. Data are displayed by subject area tested by TAKS, by three types of preparation pathway: traditional university prepared via university program; alternative certification programs sponsored by education service centers; and alternative certification programs other than those sponsored by education service centers.

CONCLUSION AND IMPLICATIONS

This study was useful in that it demonstrated and explored the existence of Gap and examined factors that potentially may influence Gap. This new research approach can be useful in considering student achievement in combination with factors such as mentor support, workplace ecology, teacher preparation pathway, and student teaching. The concept of Gap also made it possible to identify "high-performing" novice teachers whose students performed as well as or better than those of experienced teachers at the same campus.

There is a need for a conceptually defensible "peer group" (against which to compare a teacher's performance) that takes into account school and student characteristics and teacher experience, and the concept of Gap offers such a tool. We contend that Gap provides a more in-depth picture of teacher performance than simply using state standards or state, district, or campus averages as a baseline against which to compare an individual teacher's performance.

Table 15.3. Correlation of Novice Teacher Scale Score Mean Gaps with Mentor Support, Workplace Ecology, and Total Interview Scores

Correlations

		support_tot	wecology_tot	TI_scale_total	RDG/ELANT vs EXP TCHR AVE SCALE	WRITING vs EXP TCHR AVE SCALE	MATH NT vs EXP TCHR AVE SCALE	SS NT vs EXP TCHR AVE SCALE	SCIENCE vs EXP TCHR AVE SCALE
support_tot	Pearson correlation	1	0.379ᵃ	0.900ᵃ	-0.064	0.019	-0.024	-0.074	-0.035
	Sig. (2-tailed)		0.000	0.000	0.327	0.868	0.721	0.715	0.776
	N	400	400	400	240	78	217	27	67
wecology_tot	Pearson correlation	0.379ᵃ	1	0.745ᵃ	-0.025	0.137	0.059	0.070	-0.006
	Sig. (2-tailed)	0.000		0.000	0.706	0.231	0.390	0.727	0.961
	N	400	400	400	240	78	217	27	67
TI_scale_total	Pearson correlation	0.900ᵃ	0.745ᵃ	1	-0.057	0.084	0.010	-0.029	-0.027
	Sig. (2-tailed)	0.000	0.000		0.376	0.467	0.895	0.886	0.827
	N	400	400	400	240	78	217	27	67
RDG/ELANT vs EXP TCHR AVE SCALE	Pearson correlation	-0.064	-0.025	-0.057	1	0.587ᵃ	0.630ᵃ	c	0.853ᵃ
	Sig. (2-tailed)	0.327	0.706	0.376		0.000	0.000		0.000
	N	240	240	240	240	77	132	0	20

WRITING vs EXP TCHR AVE SCALE	Pearson correlation	0.019	0.137	0.084	0.587[a]	1	0.306[b]	a	a
	Sig. (2-tailed)	0.868	0.231	0.467	0.000		0.016	0	0
	N	78	78	78	77	78	61		
MATH NT vs EXP TCHR AVE SCALE	Pearson correlation	−0.024	0.059	0.010	0.630	0.306[b]	1	a	0.836[a]
	Sig. (2-tailed)	0.721	0.390	0.885	0.000	0.016		0	0.000
	N	217	217	217	132	61	217		20
SS NT vs EXP TCHR AVE SCALE	Pearson correlation	−0.074	0.070	−0.029	c	c	c	1	c
	Sig. (2-tailed)	0.715	0.727	0.868		c	c		
	N	27	27	27	0	0	0	27	0
SCIENCE vs EXP TCHR AVE SCALE	Pearson correlation	−0.035	−0.006	−0.027	0.853[a]	c	0.863[a]	c	1
	Sig. (2-tailed)	0.776	00.961	0.827	0.000	c	0.000	c	
	N	67	67	67	20	0	20	0	67

[a]Correlation is significant at the 0.01 level (two-tailed).
[b]Correlation is significant at the 0.05 level (two-tailed).
[c]Cannot be computed because at least one of the variables is constant.

Table 15.4.   High–Performing Novice Teachers

Subject Area Grade Level	Novice Teacher (with Scores in This Subject Area)	High-performing Novice Teachers	Percentage of High-performing Novice Teachers
English/Lang. Arts			
3–5	141	46	32.62
6–8	59	30	50.84
9–10	40	18	45.00
Total	240	94	39.16
Writing			
3–5	63	19	30.15
6–8	15	6	40.0
9–10	NA	NA	NA
Total	78	25	32.05
Math			
3–5	136	40	29.41
6–8	65	27	41.53
9–10	16	6	37.5
Total	217	73	33.64
Social Studies			
3–5	NA	NA	NA
6–8	12	2	16.66
9–10	15	4	26.66
Total	27	6	22.22
Science			
3–5	21	4	19.04
6–8	23	9	39.13
9–10	23	13	56.52
Total	67	26	38.80

Future Directions for Additional Research

In the future it will be important that the Gap concept be further tested on additional data sets in order to better test the viability of this data analysis approach. Recall that Gap compares a specific novice teacher's scores with the scores of the experienced teachers at the campus while factoring out the other first-year teachers. Future studies should be conducted to determine what additional insight is gained by using Gap instead of simply comparing the novice teacher's scores to the entire campus average (which will include the scores of all teachers, including the novice and other first-year teachers). Finally, it will be interesting in future studies to investigate to what degree Gap scores yield similar conclusions to the scores produced through more complex and costly statistical approaches used in sophisticated value-added assessment programs.

Table 15.5.   Preparation Pathway of "High-Performing" Novice Teachers

Preparation Pathway	Number	Number of High Performing	Percent of High Performing
English/Language Arts			
Traditional	134	57	42.53
ESC-Sponsored ACP	16	4	25
Non-ESC ACP	71	28	39.43
Total	221	89	
Writing			
Traditional	45	19	42.22
ESC-Sponsored ACP	4	1	25
Non-ESC ACP	25	16	64
Total	74	21	
Math			
Traditional	120	40	33.33
ESC-Sponsored ACP	17	4	23.52
Non-ESC ACP	68	23	33.82
Total	215	67	
Social Studies			
Traditional	8	2	25
ESC-Sponsored ACP	3	0	0
Non-ESC ACP	13	3	23.07
Total	24	5	
Science			
Traditional	31	11	32.35
ESC-Sponsored ACP	7	3	42.85
Non-ESC ACP	28	12	42.85
Total	66	26	

As a research tool, Gap is not as powerful as some of the more labor-intensive and often cost-prohibitive approaches being developed primarily for use in value-added assessment programs tied to teacher compensation packages. It is not being suggested that Gap be used in lieu of these more sophisticated statistical approaches that are possible when multiple years of individual student data are available. Rather, when multiple years of individual student data are not available or when data analysis resources are limited, Gap is a relatively expedient, cost-effective, and straightforward approach that can provide useful insights related to teacher performance and, for the time being, for many researchers it may be the right "tool" for the job at hand.

REFERENCES

Evans-Andris, M., D. W. Kyle, and R. M. Carini. 2006. Is mentoring enough? An examination of the mentoring relationship in the pilot two-year Kentucky Teacher Internship Program. *New Educator* 2(4):289–309.

Huling, L., and V. K. Resta. 2007. *Year 2 final report for CREATE study of the relationship of mentor support to novice teacher retention and student achievement.* Woodlands, TX: Center for Research Evaluation and Advancement of Teacher Education (CREATE).

Huling, L., P. Yeargain, and V. Resta. 2008. A study of the long-term effects of mentoring and novice teacher retention and career progress. *Phi Delta Kappa Research Bulletin* vol. I:11–22.

Ingersoll, R. M., and J. M. Kralik. 2004. The impact of mentoring on teacher retention: What the research says. *ESC Research Review: Teaching Quality,*1–24.

Ingersoll, R. M., and T. M. Smith. 2003. The wrong solution to the teacher shortage. *Educational Leadership* 60(8):30–33.

Nielsen, D. C., A. L. Barry, and A. B. Addison. 2007. A model of a new-teacher induction program and teacher perceptions of beneficial components. *Action in Teacher Education* 28(4):14–24.

Resta, V., and L. Huling. 2008. High performing novice teachers: Implications for preparation and induction from a large-scale study. *Phi Delta Kappa Research Bulletin* vol. II:31–45.

Wang, J., and S. J. Odell. 2003. Learning to teach toward standards-based writing instruction: A critical review. *Review of Educational Research* 72(3):481–546.

Wang, J., S. J. Odell, and S. A. Schwille. 2008. Effects of teacher induction on beginning teachers' teaching: A critical review of the literature. *Journal of Teacher Education* 59(2):132–52.

Wilkins, E. A., and R. T. Clift. 2007. Building a network of support for new teachers. *Action in Teacher Education* 28(4):25–35.

Wong, H. K. 2004. Induction programs that keep new teachers teaching and improving. *NASSP Bulletin* 88(638):41–58.

About the Editors

Dr. Jian Wang is a professor of teacher education in the Department of Curriculum and Instruction at the University of Nevada, Las Vegas. He has published conceptual work, literature reviews, and empirical studies in the areas of teacher learning, mentoring, teacher education, and mathematics learning and teaching from a comparative perspective. He serves as an editor of the *Journal of Teacher Education*.

Sandra Odell is a professor of teacher education and chair of the Department of Curriculum and Instruction at the University of Nevada Las Vegas. She has maintained a career-long research interest in teacher development and learning, teacher induction, and mentoring in the context of collaborative university/school district programs. Dr. Odell is currently editor of the *Journal of Teacher Education*.

Renée Tipton Clift is the associate dean for professional preparation and a professor of teaching, learning, and sociocultural studies at the University of Arizona. Her research investigates factors that affect the process of learning to teach, which includes preservice teachers' learning, educators' continuing professional development, and educational leadership.